ACADEMIC ENCOUNTERS

AMERICAN STUDIES

ACADEMIC ENCOUNTERS

The *Academic Encounters* series uses a sustained content approach to teach students the skills they need to be successful in academic courses. There are two books in the series for each content focus: an *Academic Encounters* title and an *Academic Listening Encounters* title. Please consult your catalog or contact your local sales representative for a current list of available titles.

Titles in the *Academic Encounters* series at publication:

Content Focus and Level	Components	*Academic Encounters*	*Academic Listening Encounters*
HUMAN BEHAVIOR High Intermediate to Low Advanced	Student's Book Teacher's Manual Class Audio Cassettes Class Audio CDs	ISBN 978-0-521-47658-4 ISBN 978-0-521-47660-7	ISBN 978-0-521-60620-2 ISBN 978-0-521-57820-2 ISBN 978-0-521-57819-6 ISBN 978-0-521-78357-6
LIFE IN SOCIETY Intermediate to High Intermediate	Student's Book Teacher's Manual Class Audio Cassettes Class Audio CDs	ISBN 978-0-521-66616-9 ISBN 978-0-521-66613-8	ISBN 978-0-521-75483-5 ISBN 978-0-521-75484-2 ISBN 978-0-521-75485-9 ISBN 978-0-521-75486-6
AMERICAN STUDIES Intermediate	Student's Book Teacher's Manual Class Audio CDs	ISBN 978-0-521-67369-3 ISBN 978-0-521-67370-9	ISBN 978-0-521-68432-3 ISBN 978-0-521-68434-7 ISBN 978-0-521-68433-0

2-Book Sets are available at a discounted price. Each set includes one copy of the Student's Reading Book and one copy of the Student's Listening Book.

Academic Encounters:
Human Behavior 2-Book Set
ISBN 978-0-521-89165-3

Academic Encounters:
Life in Society 2-Book Set
ISBN 978-0-521-54670-6

Academic Encounters:
American Studies 2-Book Set
ISBN 978-0-521-71013-8

ACADEMIC ENCOUNTERS

AMERICAN STUDIES

Reading
Study Skills
Writing

Jessica Williams

Intermediate

CAMBRIDGE UNIVERSITY PRESS
Cambridge, New York, Melbourne, Madrid, Cape Town, Singapore, São Paulo, Delhi

Cambridge University Press
32 Avenue of the Americas, New York, NY 10013–2473, USA

www.cambridge.org
Information on this title: www.cambridge.org/9780521673693

First published 2007
4th printing 2009

Printed in Hong Kong, China, by Golden Cup Printing Company Limited

A catalog record for this book is available from the British Library

Library of Congress Cataloging-in-Publication Data

Williams, Jessica, 1957-
    American studies : reading, study skills, writing / Jessica Williams.
            p. cm. - (Academic encounters)
    "Intermediate."
    Includes bibliographical references and index.
    ISBN 978-0-521-67369-3 (pbk.)
    1. English language—Textbooks for foreign speakers. 2. United
States—Civilization—Problems, exercises, etc. 3. English
language—Rhetoric—Problems, exercises, etc. 4. Study skills—Problems,
exercises, etc. 5. Listening—Problems, exercises, etc. 6. Academic
writing—Problems, exercises, etc. 7. Report writing—Problems, exercises,
etc. I. Title. II. Series.

    PE1128.W7256 2007
    428.0076—dc22

2007008624

ISBN 978-0-521-67369-3 paperback

Cover and book design: Adventure House, NYC
Text composition: Page Designs International

Unit 1 Laws of the Land 1

Chapter 1 | The Foundations of Government

1 From Colonies to United States 4

PREPARING TO READ

Thinking About the Topic Before You Read • Building Vocabulary: Making a Vocabulary Notebook

AFTER YOU READ

Using Headings to Remember Main Ideas • Language Focus: Infinitives • Language Focus: Infinitives of Purpose • Thinking About Symbols

2 A Balance of Power 9

PREPARING TO READ

Examining Graphic Material

AFTER YOU READ

Building Vocabulary: Clues That Signal Definitions • Understanding a Venn Diagram • Language Focus: Showing Contrast • Applying What You Have Read

3 The Bill of Rights 15

PREPARING TO READ

Thinking About the Topic Before You Read

AFTER YOU READ

Applying What You Have Read • Language Focus: Verbs of Permission • Thinking Critically About the Topic

4 Electing the President 20

PREPARING TO READ

Thinking About the Topic Before You Read

AFTER YOU READ

Asking and Answering Questions About a Text • Language Focus: Gerunds • Language Focus: Expressing Numerical Data

Unit 1 Writing Assignment A 26

Chapter 2 | Constitutional Issues Today

1 Freedom of Expression: How Far Does It Go? 28

PREPARING TO READ

Thinking About the Topic Before You Read

AFTER YOU READ

Reading for Main Ideas • Making Generalizations • Building Vocabulary: Words That Can Be Used as Nouns or Verbs • Thinking Critically About the Topic

Chapter 4 | Diversity in Today's United States

Chapter 10 | Global Transformations

Author's Acknowledgments

After so many years in academia, conducting second language acquisition research and teaching in a graduate TESOL program, it has been both refreshing and humbling to finally have the opportunity to put many of the ideas I had been espousing in the classroom into a project that will be seen and used by English language learners. I have learned an enormous amount in the process and I have many people to thank for this opportunity: Robert Romeo and Ellen Zlotnick, for getting me started on the project in the first place, and Jane Mairs and Bernard Seal, for offering me initial encouragement and guidance. I am also grateful to all the hardworking people at Cambridge University Press who have checked my facts and references, sought permissions, researched art, and performed the many tasks necessary in preparing a book for publication: in particular, Cindee Howard, Senior Project Editor; Carlos Rountree and Leslie De Jesus, editorial assistants; and Don Williams, the compositor.

I would like to thank the many teachers who provided reviews during various phases of writing and rewriting: Nancy Braiman, Byron-Bergen High School; Joy Campbell, Michigan State University; Susan Lafond, Guilderland High School; Tim McDaniel, Green River Community College; Juan Gabriel Garduño Moreno, Universidad Autónoma Metropolitana Xochimilco; Anthony James Rosenberg, Centro Universitário Ibero-Americano; Pelly Shaw, American University of Sharjah; Heshim Song, Seokyeong University; and Richmond Stroupe, Soka University.

My deepest appreciation, however, goes to Kathleen O'Reilly, development editor extraordinaire, who should probably get a co-author credit for this volume. Throughout the process, she has been careful, patient and, I am sure, far more diplomatic than I deserved.

Jessica Williams

Introduction

To The Instructor

ABOUT THIS BOOK

Academic Encounters: American Studies is a reading, study skills, and writing text based on content taught in American history and culture courses in high schools, colleges, and universities in the United States.*

New Features

If you are already familiar with the *Academic Encounters* series, you will discover three new features in *Academic Encounters: American Studies*:

- **More emphasis on vocabulary skills**
  More vocabulary tasks are included. Key terms are defined within the context of the readings and students are taught how to recognize these embedded definitions. Students are also instructed in organizing and maintaining a vocabulary notebook.

- **More emphasis on writing skills**
  In addition to tasks in which students answer test questions, complete sentences, and write their own original sentences, a two-page writing section is presented at the end of each chapter. It provides students with an opportunity to develop their academic writing skills in an assignment related to the content of the chapter or unit. Students are guided from the preparing-to-write stage through the actual writing, and are then introduced to post-writing analysis and revision.

- **More emphasis on note-taking skills**
  Students are taught to take notes in several ways. They are also taught how to check the accuracy of their notes and how to use their notes to prepare for tests and writing assignments.

Correlation with Standards

Academic Encounters: American Studies introduces students to many of the topics and skills in the United States secondary school standards for American history and social studies. For more information about the standards, go to www.cambridge.org/us/esl/academicencounters

TOEFL® iBT Skills

Many of the tasks in *Academic Encounters: American Studies* (as well as those in all *Academic Encounters* books) teach academic skills tested on the TOEFL® iBT test. For a complete list of the tasks taught, see the Task Index on page 241.

---

* Although the term *Americas* can be used to refer to all of North and South America, *America* is often used to refer to the United States of America alone. The phrase *American Studies* in this book's title reflects that usage. *American Studies* is an academic discipline with a focus similar to that of this book: United States history and culture.

ABOUT THE ACADEMIC ENCOUNTERS SERIES

This content based series is for students who need to improve their academic skills for further study. The series consists of *Academic Encounters* books that help students improve their reading, study skills, and writing, and *Academic Listening Encounters* books that help students improve their listening, note-taking, and discussion skills. The reading books and listening books are published in pairs, and each pair of books focuses on a subject commonly taught in academic courses. *Academic Encounters: American Studies* and *Academic Listening Encounters: American Studies* focus on topics in American history and culture; *Academic Encounters: Life in Society* and *Academic Listening Encounters: Life in Society* focus on sociology; and *Academic Encounters: Human Behavior* and *Academic Listening Encounters: Human Behavior* focus on psychology and human communications. A reading book and a listening book with the same content focus may be used together to teach a complete four-skills course in English for Academic Purposes.

ACADEMIC ENCOUNTERS READING, STUDY SKILLS, AND WRITING BOOKS

The approach

In the high-intermediate to advanced reading books, students are presented with authentic samples of academic text. The material has been abridged and occasionally reorganized, but on the sentence level, little of the language has been changed. In *Academic Encounters: American Studies*, authentic materials have been used as the basis for texts that use academic content and style in such a way as to be accessible to intermediate students. In all the Reading, Study-Skills, and Writing books, students use the texts to develop their reading and study skills, and the high-interest content of the texts provides stimulus for writing assignments.

The content

The fact that each book in the *Academic Encounters* series has a unified thematic content throughout has several advantages. First, it gives students a realistic sense of studying in an academic course, in which each week's assignments are related to and build on each other. Second, as language and concepts recur, students begin to feel that the readings are getting easier, building their confidence as readers of academic text. Finally, after studying an *Academic Encounters* book, students may feel that they have enough background in the content area to actually take a course in that subject (e.g., American history) to fulfill part of their general education requirements.

The skills

The main goal of the *Academic Encounters* Reading, Study Skills, and Writing books is to give students the skills and the confidence to approach an academic text, read it efficiently and critically, and take notes that extract the main ideas and key details. But the goal of academic reading is not just to retrieve information. It is also important for a student to be able to display that knowledge in a writing assignment or test-taking situation. For this reason, tasks that develop test-preparation and writing skills appear throughout the books. A longer writing assignment is at the end of each chapter.

The format

Each Reading, Study Skills, and Writing book consists of five units on different aspects of the book's content focus. Units are divided into two chapters, with four readings in each chapter. Readings are one to four pages long.

Preparing to read

Each reading is preceded by a one-page section of prereading tasks called "Preparing to read." Prereading is heavily emphasized since it is regarded as a crucial step in the reading process. Some of the prereading activities introduce students to new vocabulary; others teach students how to get an overall idea of the content. Students also learn to skim for main ideas and to survey the text for headings, graphic material, and terms in boldface, all of which provide important content clues. Other tasks have students think about the topic of the reading, predict its content, and recall their prior knowledge and personal experiences in order to help them assimilate the new information they are about to encounter in the reading.

After you read

Each reading is followed by a variety of postreading tasks in a section called "After you read." Some of these tasks ask students to demonstrate their understanding of the text in such ways as answering reading comprehension questions or drawing a graph. Other tasks ask students to reflect on the content to deepen their understanding of it. For example, students may be asked to analyze the structure of the text, looking for main ideas, supporting details, and authorial commentary. Vocabulary tasks require students to learn strategies for comprehending new vocabulary, to demonstrate their understanding of the new vocabulary, to practice using a dictionary, or to update their vocabulary notebooks. In language-focus tasks students look at some of the salient grammatical features of the text. Students also learn how to highlight a text, take notes, and practice test-taking skills. This rich variety of tasks and task types allows students to experiment with different study-skill strategies and to discover their learning-style preferences.

Writing

There are varied opportunities in Reading, Study Skills, and Writing books for students to practice their writing skills. Students write extended definitions, short papers, essays, text summaries, and journal entries, as well as short answers to test questions. At the same time, as students continually read and analyze academic English, they begin to acquire insight into its organization and style, and their own writing develops a more academic tone.

Task pages and text pages

Task pages are clearly differentiated from text pages by a colored vertical bar that runs along the outside edge of the page. The text pages have been designed to look like authentic college textbook pages. The text is in a column that takes up only two-thirds of the page, thus allowing space in the margins for glossed terms and illustrations. Figures, tables, and boxed inserts with additional information related to the topic are also included on text pages, as they are in standard textbooks. This authentic look helps to create a sense for students that they are actually reading from an academic textbook.

Task commentary boxes and task index

When a task type occurs for the first time in the book, it is headed by a colored commentary box that explains what skill is being practiced and why it is important. When the task occurs again later in the book, it may be accompanied by another commentary box, as a reminder or to present new information about the skill. At the back of the book, there is an alphabetized index of all the tasks. Page references in boldface indicate tasks that are headed by commentary boxes.

Opportunities for student interaction

To make the book as lively as possible, student interaction has been built into most activities. Thus, although the books focus on reading, study skills, and writing, speaking activities abound. Students discuss the content of the texts; they work collaboratively to solve task problems; they compare answers in pairs or small groups; and sometimes they perform role plays.

Order of units

In terms of reading topics and vocabulary, the order of units is regarded as optimal. In addition, tasks build upon each other so that, for example, a note-taking task later in the book may draw upon information that has been offered in an earlier unit. Teachers who want to teach the units out of order, however, may do so. They can use the task index at the back of the book to see what types of tasks have been presented in earlier units and build information from those tasks into their lessons.

Course length

Each of the five units of a Reading, Study Skills, and Writing book contains a unit preview section and eight readings, and represents approximately 16–20 hours of classroom material. An *Academic Encounters* book could thus be a suitable course book for a 64- to 80-hour course (when a teacher selects four of the five units) or an 80- to 100-hour course (when all the units are used). The course can, however, be made shorter or longer. To shorten the course, teachers might choose not to do every task in the book and to assign some tasks and texts as homework, rather than do them in class. To lengthen the course, teachers might choose to supplement the book with some content-related material from their own files, to assign Internet research, and to spend more time developing students' writing skills.

To The Student

Welcome to *Academic Encounters: American Studies*. In this book, you are going to read about important ideas and events in American history and culture. The topics in the book have been chosen for their high interest and relevance to American life today.

You will also learn the skills you need to be successful in an academic classroom.

You will learn:

- how to read academic texts
- ways to think critically about what you have read
- strategies for dealing with new vocabulary
- note-taking techniques
- methods of preparing for tests
- how to write in an academic style

As you learn and practice these academic skills, you will have many opportunities to discuss the content of the texts with your classmates.

You will find that by continually reading, studying, discussing, and writing about academic texts your academic reading and writing abilities will improve. After using this book, you may feel that you have enough background information and sufficient academic skills to take an introductory course in American history or another aspect of American culture, to fulfill part of your general education requirements or just for your own interest. Or, perhaps you will have gained the knowledge and confidence to do so at some future date.

We hope that you find *Academic Encounters: American Studies* to be not only useful, but enjoyable. It is important to remember in all your studies that the most successful learning takes place when you enjoy what you are studying and find it interesting.

ACADEMIC ENCOUNTERS

AMERICAN STUDIES

THE 13 ORIGINAL COLONIES

New Hampshire

Massachusetts

New York

Rhode Island

Connecticut

Pennsylvania

New Jersey

Delaware

Maryland

Virginia

North Carolina

South Carolina

Georgia

THE UNITED STATES TODAY

Unit 1

Laws of the Land

"Scene at the Signing of the Constitution of the United States," Howard Chandler Christy

In this unit, we look at important features of the United States government and its laws from their beginnings in the eighteenth century to the present day. In Chapter 1, we see how the United States became a country. We also discuss the documents that are its political and philosophical foundation. In Chapter 2, we focus on how those documents remain important and relevant to today's issues.

Previewing the unit

> Before reading a unit (or chapter) in a textbook, it is a good idea to preview the contents and think about the topics that will be covered. This will help you understand how the unit is organized and what it is going to be about.

Read the contents page for Unit 1, and do the following activities.

Chapter 1: The Foundations of Government

This chapter addresses the origins of the United States and the important documents that are the foundations of its government. It also discusses the process of electing the President.

How much do you know about governments in other countries?
Work in small groups. Choose one or two countries to talk about, and discuss the following questions:

    1 How are leaders elected?
    2 Who writes the laws?

Chapter 2: Constitutional Issues Today

This chapter explores the basic rights and freedoms that are guaranteed by the United States Constitution, especially the part of the Constitution known as the Bill of Rights.

1 Which of the following statements about rights and freedoms in the United States do you think are true? For each statement, put *T* (true) or *F* (false) in the blank.

    _____ **1** Americans are free to say and write whatever they want.
    _____ **2** Most Americans own a gun.
    _____ **3** Americans can criticize their government.
    _____ **4** The national religion of the United States is Christianity.

2 Compare your answers in a small group.

3 With your group, make a list of the three most basic rights and freedoms that you think all individuals should expect.

4 As a class, compare your answers to step 3. Explain why you chose the rights and freedoms you did.

Preparing to read

THINKING ABOUT THE TOPIC BEFORE YOU READ

> Thinking about the topic before you read can make the ideas in a text easier to understand.

Look at this picture. It shows some of the first settlers in America arriving in the winter of 1620. Then, discuss these questions:

1 What do you think the artist is trying to show about the first settlers?

2 How do you think they are feeling? What are they thinking?

BUILDING VOCABULARY: MAKING A VOCABULARY NOTEBOOK

> A vocabulary notebook is a useful tool for learning new words and phrases. It is important to record the context of new vocabulary, that is, the words or sentences surrounding the new word(s), as well as their definitions. The *double entry* method, which uses two columns, is a good way to do this. Here is an example:
>
> **Word in context**
> The **settlers** hoped to have a brighter future.
>
> **Definition**
> people who arrive in a new place and live on the land

Make a notebook or an electronic file for the new vocabulary you will learn in this book.

Now read

Now read the text "From Colonies to United States." When you finish, turn to the tasks on page 7.

The Foundations of Government

We the People *of the United States, in order to form a more perfect union, establish justice, insure domestic tranquility, provide for the common defense, promote the general welfare, and secure the blessings of liberty to ourselves and our posterity, do ordain and establish this Constitution for the United States of America.*

The preamble (introduction) to the U.S. Constitution[1]

1 FROM COLONIES TO UNITED STATES

The first colonists

Many people from Great Britain and other countries in Europe began to settle in Britain's North American **colonies** at the end of the seventeenth century. They came for different reasons. Some came for religious freedom; most came because they wanted a better life. At that time, European society was clearly divided into different classes. If you were born into a lower class, it was difficult to move up in the world. In the American colonies, the settlers hoped to have a brighter future: to buy a farm, to start a small business, to live among equals.

> **1**
>
> **colony**
>
> an area of land controlled by a more powerful country, usually a country that is a long distance from the colony

The road to independence

The colonists wanted to make their own economic and political decisions based on their needs in the "new world." The British king had a different view, however. He wanted the colonists to accept and obey British laws even though the colonists did not have representatives in the British government. The king and the colonists disagreed about many things, especially about money. The king wanted the colonists to pay high taxes on stamps, tea, sugar, and other products. When the colonists protested against the taxes, the king sent his army to force the colonists to obey, and so in 1775, the War for Independence (sometimes called the American Revolution or the Revolutionary War) began. On July 4, 1776, a group of colonial leaders signed the **Declaration of Independence**, which stated the reasons that "the thirteen

> **2**
>
> **Declaration of Independence**
>
> a document written in 1776 that states that the United States is a separate country, independent of Great Britain

1 To see the original document, go to http://www.archives.gov/national-archives-experience/charters/constitution.html

"The Spirit of '76,"
Archibald M. Willard

United States of America" wanted to break away from Great Britain. Finally, in 1783, at the end of the war, the Americans won their independence.

The United States Constitution

Winning the war was only the first step in becoming 3 the United States. The Americans needed to make some decisions: Should each of the old colonies be a separate country? Should they all be states in one big country? Who should govern? Who should make the laws? They did not want a strong central government because of their experiences living under a king. Therefore, for several years they tried a system with strong state governments and a weak central government, but this was a failure.

Then, in 1786, a group of leaders met to discuss how 4 to create a new system. They wanted a republic, that is, a government that is not led by a king. They wanted a democratic government, that is, a system based on the idea that all men are equal and that the government should represent all of the nation's citizens. The result was a **constitution**. The United States Constitution was adopted in 1789. It sets the basic framework for the whole United States government. One of its most important points is the establishment of a federalist system, that is, a system that divides power and responsibility between the states and the federal, or central, government.

George Washington and the Rules of War

George Washington

George Washington was an officer in the American army during the War for Independence. He used some unusual military strategies. At the time, there were traditional rules for war: no fighting during the winter and no fighting at night. Washington decided to change the rules in order to win the war. So, in 1776, when many of the British generals had gone home for the winter, Washington's men crossed the Delaware River on Christmas in the middle of the night and surprised the British troops. The result was the first major American victory at the Battle of Trenton. Washington led the American military for the rest of the war and went on to become the first President of the United States.

After you read

Task 1 USING HEADINGS TO REMEMBER MAIN IDEAS

> Headings in texts give you clues about the ideas and information that
> will follow. You can also use headings to help you remember main ideas.

1 Read the headings below from "From Colonies to United States."

a The first colonists   **c** The United States Constitution
b The road to independence

2 Work with a partner, and decide which heading each statement below belongs to.
Write the letter of the heading (*a, b,* or *c*) in front of the statement.

_____ **1** A group of leaders met to write the Constitution.
_____ **2** People came to North America from many parts of Europe.
_____ **3** The colonists fought for independence because they wanted a voice in
their own government.
_____ **4** They came for many reasons, but most were hoping for a better life.
_____ **5** The Constitution establishes the basic framework for the American
government.
_____ **6** The colonies wanted independence from Great Britain.

3 With your partner, decide which statement in step 2 explains the main idea for
each of the three headings. Circle one statement for each heading.

Task 2 LANGUAGE FOCUS: INFINITIVES

> When two verbs appear together, the second verb is often in the
> infinitive form (*to* + verb).
>
>   The colonists wanted **to make** their own decisions.
>
> **Sometimes this second verb appears after a new subject.**
>
>   first subject   second subject
>   The King wanted the colonists **to obey** English laws.

1 In the text, underline some examples of infinitive verbs.

2 Complete the following sentences based on information in the text.

1 People from Europe began to _____.
2 The settlers hoped to _____.
3 The army forced _____ to _____.
4 The Americans needed to _____.

Task 3 LANGUAGE FOCUS: INFINITIVES OF PURPOSE

> Sometimes the infinitive tells the purpose of an action. It answers the question *Why?*
>
> Why did the King send his army to the colonies?
> He sent it **to punish** the colonists.

1 Find examples in the text of infinitives that answer the question *Why?*

2 Discuss the following questions with a partner. Use the infinitive in your answers.

1 Why did people come to the North American colonies at the end of the seventeenth century?

2 Why did the Americans fight against the British?

3 Why did a group of leaders meet in 1786?

3 Write the answers to the questions in step 2. Use complete sentences.

Task 4 THINKING ABOUT SYMBOLS

1 Look at these pictures, and read the captions underneath them.

The Liberty Bell. Many people believe it rang all day after the Declaration of Independence was signed on July 4, 1776.

The first U.S. flag. It is the original "Star-Spangled Banner," with 13 stars and 13 stripes for the 13 original colonies.

2 The Liberty Bell and the first U.S. flag are symbols that most Americans are familiar with from their childhood history books. A *symbol* is something that reminds you of something else. The Liberty Bell and the first flag remind Americans of their country's fight for independence. As a class, discuss the following questions about symbols:

1 Which national symbols are you familiar with? Which countries are they from? Why are these symbols important to people?

2 Are there any similarities between the symbols you discussed in question 1 and the American symbols in the pictures above? What are they?

Preparing to read

EXAMINING GRAPHIC MATERIAL

Before reading a text, it is helpful to look at any graphs, charts (sometimes called tables), or diagrams. This will give you an idea of the content of the text.

1 In the United States, power and responsibilities are divided among three branches of government: the executive branch, headed by the President; the legislative branch, or the Congress (senators and representatives); and the judicial branch, which includes the Supreme Court, the highest court in the nation.

With a partner, look at Figure 1.1 on page 11. This flowchart shows the responsibilities that belong to the President, Congress, and the Supreme Court. Based on the information in the chart, put the appropriate letter in front of each responsibility listed below.

P = a responsibility of the President
C = a responsibility of Congress
SC = a responsibility of the Supreme Court

_____ **1** declares war on other countries
_____ **2** makes laws
_____ **3** leads the military
_____ **4** decides if laws support the Constitution
_____ **5** makes decisions about government spending
_____ **6** appoints judges
_____ **7** makes decisions about taxes
_____ **8** makes agreements with other countries

2 Compare your answers with a partner or in a small group.

Now read

Now read the text "A Balance of Power." When you finish, turn to the tasks on page 12.

2 A BALANCE OF POWER

The men who met to write the United States Constitution had a difficult task. Although they wanted a strong leader, they also wanted a representative government. They wanted judges who would be independent of politicians. They did not want any part of the government to have too much power. Therefore, they divided power among three branches: legislative, executive, and judicial.

Congress

The three branches of government

Although people often think that the President is the center of government, the Constitution lists the legislative branch first. The legislative branch is called Congress. It is made up of two parts: the Senate and the House of Representatives. The Senate has 100 members – two from each of America's 50 states. The House of Representatives has more – 435. The number of members each state has in the House depends on the state's population. The Constitution names two people in the executive branch – the President and the Vice President. In the judicial branch, the Constitution establishes a Supreme Court, which is the highest court, and gives Congress the power to create other courts.

The White House: the President's official residence

Checks and balances

The Constitution gives each branch ways to limit the power of the other two. This system is called *checks and balances*. For example, the President can veto, or block, laws passed by the legislative branch (Congress). However, if Congress can gather enough votes, it can override, that is, reject, the President's veto. Congress can even vote to remove the President from office if the President has done something illegal. Finally, the Supreme Court can reject both the laws passed by Congress and the actions of the President, if it thinks

The Supreme Court

that the laws and actions are **unconstitutional**. Figure 1.1 shows some of the most important checks and balances.

unconstitutional
| not permitted by the
| constitution

A federalist system

The U.S. Constitution also provides for a government based on federalism, that is, a balance of power between the federal, or central, government and the state governments. The federal government is responsible for things that affect American citizens as a nation. The state governments, on the other hand, are responsible for issues that relate to the states. However, both governments share certain powers.

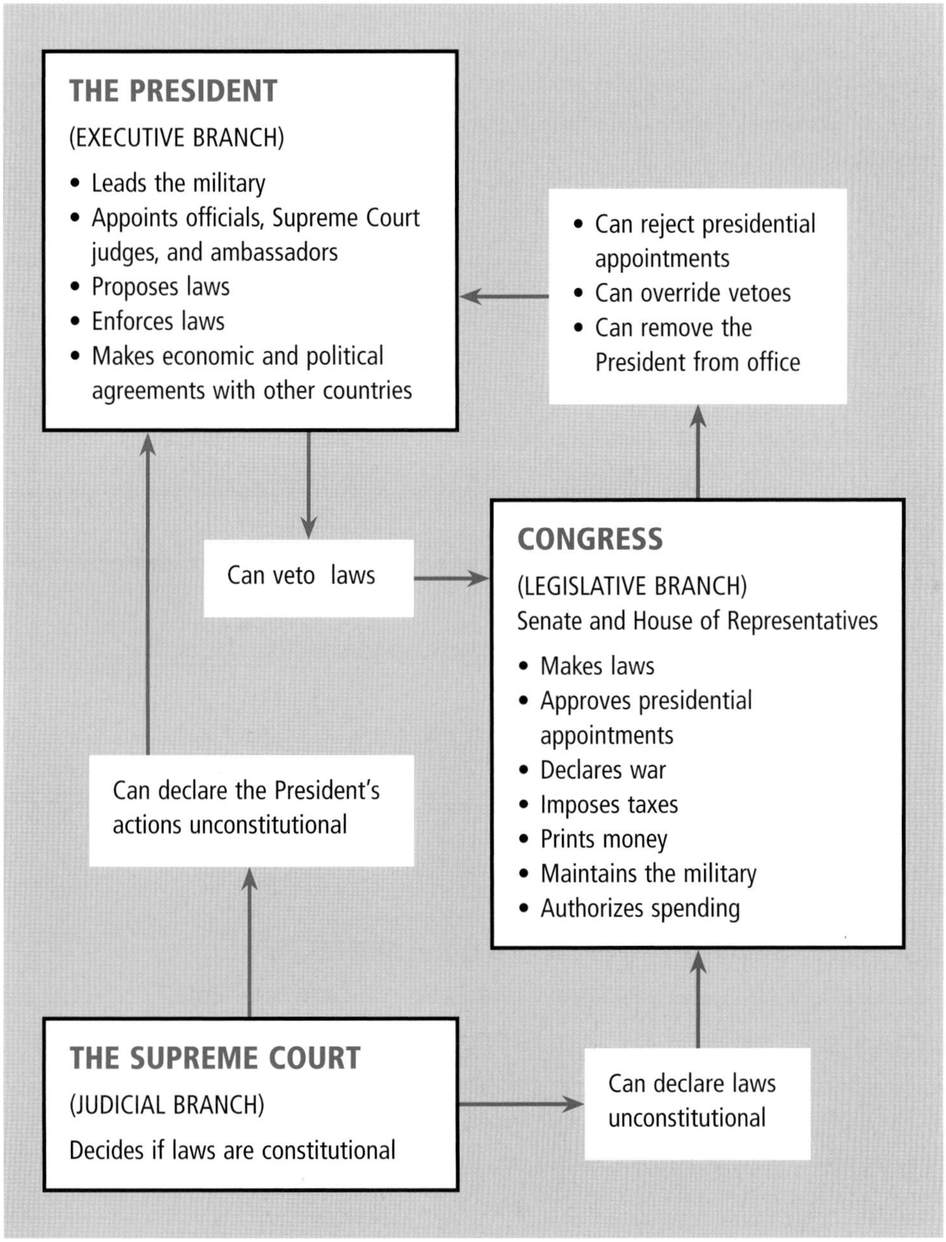

4

Figure 1.1 Examples of checks and balances among the three branches of government.

THE PRESIDENT

(EXECUTIVE BRANCH)

- Leads the military
- Appoints officials, Supreme Court judges, and ambassadors
- Proposes laws
- Enforces laws
- Makes economic and political agreements with other countries

- Can reject presidential appointments
- Can override vetoes
- Can remove the President from office

Can veto laws

CONGRESS

(LEGISLATIVE BRANCH)
Senate and House of Representatives

- Makes laws
- Approves presidential appointments
- Declares war
- Imposes taxes
- Prints money
- Maintains the military
- Authorizes spending

Can declare the President's actions unconstitutional

THE SUPREME COURT

(JUDICIAL BRANCH)

Decides if laws are constitutional

Can declare laws unconstitutional

After you read

Task 1 BUILDING VOCABULARY: CLUES THAT SIGNAL DEFINITIONS

> As you read more difficult texts, it is important to try to understand them without stopping to look up every new word. Often the definition of a new word is right there in the text.

1 Look at the excerpts from the text below. They contain terms that may be new to you: *veto, the legislative branch,* and *override.* These are technical terms about political institutions and processes.

- For example, the President can **veto**, or block, laws passed by **the legislative branch** (Congress).
- However, if Congress can gather enough votes, it can **override**, that is, reject, the President's veto.

2 Each of the terms in bold in the sentences above is defined within the sentence. Below are the three ways that these definitions are presented. In the blank before each one, write the term that is defined in this way. After each one, write the definition.

the legislative branch   **1** (definition)   *Congress*
_____   **2** , or <u>definition</u>,   _____
_____   **3** , that is, <u>definition</u>,   _____

3 Fill in the blanks below with the appropriate word or phrase from the excerpts in step 1.

1 Sometimes _____ is called the legislative branch.

2 If the President vetoes a law, he _____ it.

3 If the members of Congress override his veto, they _____ it.

4 Complete the definitions of the words in bold, using information from the text.

1 The Constitution establishes **the Supreme Court**, that is,

_____.

2 A federalist system divides power between the **federal**, or

_____, government and the state governments.

3 The Supreme Court decides if laws **support the Constitution**, that is, if they

are _____.

5 Now choose your own words to define. Write three sentences with short definitions. Use parentheses, *that is,* or *or.* Be sure to use correct punctuation.

Task 2 UNDERSTANDING A VENN DIAGRAM

Venn diagrams use overlapping circles to show relationships. They can show information that is true only for "A" (one circle), other information that is true only for "B" (the other circle), and information that is true for "A + B" (both circles).

1 Study this Venn diagram of examples of the division of power between the federal and state governments.

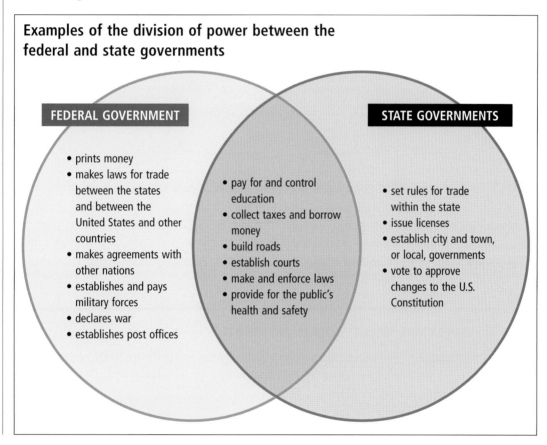

Examples of the division of power between the federal and state governments

FEDERAL GOVERNMENT
- prints money
- makes laws for trade between the states and between the United States and other countries
- makes agreements with other nations
- establishes and pays military forces
- declares war
- establishes post offices

- pay for and control education
- collect taxes and borrow money
- build roads
- establish courts
- make and enforce laws
- provide for the public's health and safety

STATE GOVERNMENTS
- set rules for trade within the state
- issue licenses
- establish city and town, or local, governments
- vote to approve changes to the U.S. Constitution

2 Based on the information in the Venn diagram, decide if the following statements are true (*T*) or false (*F*).

_____ **1** State governments can print their own money.

_____ **2** Only the federal government can have an army.

_____ **3** Federal and state governments pay for public education.

_____ **4** There are courts at both the federal and state level.

_____ **5** A state, such as New Jersey, can declare war against another country.

_____ **6** Only the federal government can ask citizens to pay taxes.

_____ **7** There is no federal driver's license; only the states offer driver's licenses.

Task 3 LANGUAGE FOCUS: SHOWING CONTRAST

> Writers can contrast ideas, that is, show the difference between them, by using words such as *however* and *although*.
>
> *However* is always separated from the sentence by a comma.
>
> comma
>
> • Congress makes laws. **However**, the President can veto them.
>
> comma
>
> • Congress makes laws. The President can veto them, **however**.
>
> *Although* always introduces a clause. When the clause introduced by *although* is at the beginning of a sentence, there is always a comma at the end of the clause.
>
> clause introduced by *although*   comma   clause
>
> **Although** Congress has the power to make laws, the President can veto them.

1 Find and underline the words *however* and *although* in the text.

2 Use information from the text and Figure 1.1 on page 11, and explain two things about the balance of power in the U.S. political system. Write your answers, using *however* and *although*. Be sure you use correct punctuation.

3 Work with a partner and check each other's sentences. Make sure they are true and that they have correct punctuation.

Task 4 APPLYING WHAT YOU HAVE READ

> Finding ways to apply new knowledge helps you to see how well you understand new subject matter.

With a partner or small group, compare what you have learned about the U.S. system of government to the government of another country that you are familiar with. Use the questions below to help your discussion:

1 Is the government based on a federalist system?

2 Are there checks and balances on power?

3 How are the people represented in government?

4 Is the system similar to or very different from the U.S. system?

Preparing to read

THINKING ABOUT THE TOPIC BEFORE YOU READ

1 With a partner, read the situations listed below. Decide which ones you think are *legal*, or allowed by law, in the United States and which ones you think are *illegal*, that is, against the law. Put a check (✔) next to each situation that you think is legal.

_____ **1** Ms. Taylor is having a party. The police drive by and see the party. They think that some of Ms. Taylor's guests may be selling illegal drugs. They enter the house and search it.

_____ **2** Mr. Jones gives a speech and says that a specific group of people (for example, a racial or religious group) is the cause of many problems and should be forced to leave the United States.

_____ **3** Mr. Jones gives another speech and says that the same racial or religious group of people is the cause of many problems and should be killed.

_____ **4** Ms. Johnson, a public school teacher, reads a religious prayer to her class at the beginning of the school day.

_____ **5** Mr. Stevens tells lies about his neighbor, Mr. Elliot, on an Internet site. He writes that Mr. Elliot is a terrorist. As a result, Mr. Elliot loses his job. Mr. Stevens claims he is free to express his opinions.

_____ **6** Mr. Stone keeps a gun next to his bed at home.

_____ **7** Ms. Wilson is arrested at her home in California. She is kept in prison for six months. The police do not tell her what her crime is.

_____ **8** Ms. Evans shouts at the President as he passes through a crowd. She says he is hurting the country.

2 Explain your answers to the class. Use phrases such as these:

We think it's against the law to _____ because . . .
I think it's illegal to _____ because . . .

Now read

Now read the text "The Bill of Rights." Then check your answers to step 1 of the task above. When you finish, turn to the tasks on page 18.

3 THE BILL OF RIGHTS

In 1788, the U.S. Constitution established most of the systems and rules
to form a new government. However, many leaders thought that something was missing. They wanted to include a new idea: the guarantee
of individual rights and freedoms and the protection of citizens *against*
the government. As a result, three years later, the Bill of Rights, in the
form of 10 amendments, or changes, to the Constitution, was passed.

The Bill of Rights is one of the most important documents in
United States history; its ideas are an essential part of American culture. Although it is only 462 words long (about the length of this text),
it provides for many rights and freedoms. When people say, "the United
States is a free country," they are thinking of the Bill of Rights.

The Bill of Rights consists of 10 amendments, most of which can be
divided into three basic categories. Some amendments guarantee individual freedoms. Other amendments protect citizens against the misuse
of power by the government. Others protect the rights of criminal suspects, that is, people who are accused of crimes. The last amendment
states that any power that the Constitution does not specifically give
to the federal government is a power belonging to "the states . . . or to
the people."[2]

Guarantee of individual rights

The First Amendment guarantees freedom of religion, freedom of
speech, and freedom of the press. This means that every U.S. citizen
is free to practice any religion or none at all. The government may
not establish or support any religion. The amendment also guarantees
all citizens the freedom to say or publish what they believe, even if it
is unpopular or critical of the government. There are limits, however.
The First Amendment does not allow anyone to say or write lies about
someone that could cause harm to that person; no one may say or write
anything that could be dangerous to others. For example, it does not
allow speech that encourages people to burn down a building or kill
people. Finally, the First Amendment allows people to protest against
the government if they think it is doing something wrong. It permits
them to criticize the government in speech or in writing.

Protection against misuse of government power

The Second and Fourth Amendments help protect all citizens against
misuse of power by the government and especially the police. The Second Amendment permits people to form a militia, or army of citizens,
and to keep guns. The Fourth Amendment forbids police searches without permission from a judge. To get a judge's permission to search a

---

2 To read the complete Bill of Rights, go to
  http://usinfo.state.gov/usa/infousa/facts/funddocs/billeng.htm

person's home or possessions, the police must give a very good reason based on existing laws.

Protection of the rights of criminal suspects

The Fifth, Sixth, Seventh, and Eighth Amendments provide protection for people who are accused of crimes. The police may not arrest them and put them in prison without an explanation of the crime they are accused of committing. They have the right to "a **speedy** and public **trial**" and to the assistance of a lawyer. They also have the right to a trial that is decided by a **jury** of 12 ordinary people and not by only a single judge.

6

speedy trial
a trial that takes place soon after a suspect has been accused

jury
a group of people that decides the outcome of a trial

The Eighteenth Amendment: Prohibition

Since the Bill of Rights, there have been 17 more amendments to the Constitution. Only one of them – the Eighteenth Amendment – has ever been repealed, that is, reversed. The Eighteenth Amendment, passed in 1919, prohibited the manufacture and sale of alcohol. However, during the period of the Eighteenth Amendment, known as Prohibition (1919–1933), Americans did not stop drinking. Instead they bought illegal alcohol. Most of the illegal alcohol business was controlled by gangs, such as the one led by Al Capone in Chicago. Prohibition ended in 1933 when the Twenty-First Amendment was passed to repeal (cancel) the Eighteenth Amendment.

Al Capone

After you read

Task 1 APPLYING WHAT YOU HAVE READ

1 Review the text. According to the text, which of the three headings listed below does each statement belong to? Then, without looking back at the text, work with a partner and write *a, b,* or *c* in each blank.

a Guarantee of individual rights
b Protection against misuse of government power
c Protection of the rights of criminal suspects

_____ **1** Anyone can criticize the government.
_____ **2** Citizens may buy guns.
_____ **3** A person who is accused of a crime may get assistance from a lawyer.
_____ **4** Free speech does not include speech that encourages violence.
_____ **5** No one can publish lies that are harmful to others.
_____ **6** People are free to practice their religion.
_____ **7** Police may not search a person's home or possessions without a good reason based on the law.
_____ **8** The government is not permitted to support any specific religion.
_____ **9** The police must tell a criminal suspect why he or she is in prison.

2 With your partner, look back at the eight situations in "Preparing to read" on page 15. Decide which part of the Bill of Rights listed in step 1 (*a, b,* or *c*) would help to determine whether the action in each situation is constitutional.

_____ **1**   _____ **3**   _____ **5**   _____ **7**
_____ **2**   _____ **4**   _____ **6**   _____ **8**

3 Compare your answers to steps 1 and 2 in a small group.

Task 2 LANGUAGE FOCUS: VERBS OF PERMISSION

1 Verbs of permission express what you may or may not do. Reread "The Bill of Rights" (including the boxed text), and highlight each use of the following verbs of permission: *allow, forbid, permit, prohibit.*

2 Think about whether the verbs of permission in step 1 express something you may do or something you may not do. Circle the correct meaning.

1 *Allow*   refers to actions you MAY/MAY NOT do.
2 *Forbid*   refers to actions you MAY/MAY NOT do.
3 *Permit*   refers to actions you MAY/MAY NOT do.
4 *Prohibit*   refers to actions you MAY/MAY NOT do.

3 Write a sentence for each of the actions listed below, using one of the four verbs of permission in step 2. Make sure you choose a verb that makes the sentence true according to the text. You may need to use the negative form of the verb. Begin each sentence like this: *The Bill of Rights . . .*

1 religious freedom
The Bill of Rights permits religious freedom.
2 criticism of the government
3 speech or writing that is dangerous to others
4 police searches without permission from a judge
5 freedom of expression
6 publication of lies that will hurt people

4 Look at the grammatical pattern of the sentences in step 3.

The verbs *permit, allow,* and *forbid* can also appear in a different pattern.

5 Work with a partner. For each verb, write a sentence that describes what the Constitution allows/permits/forbids someone to do.

1 The Bill of Rights forbids *(the government/citizens/the police)* to . . .
2 The Bill of Rights permits _____ to . . .
3 The Bill of Rights allows _____ to . . .

Task 3 THINKING CRITICALLY ABOUT THE TOPIC

> You will not always agree with what you read. Think about the ideas in a text and compare them to your own knowledge and experiences.

The Bill of Rights provides broad protection to the people of the United States. With a partner or small group, discuss what you think might be any negative effects of the Bill of Rights. The questions below will help you get started:

1 Can you think of any cases in which freedom of expression could be a bad idea?
2 Is it possible to provide too much protection or too much freedom?

Preparing to read

THINKING ABOUT THE TOPIC BEFORE YOU READ

Voting is one of the most important rights of an American citizen. However, voting has not always been easy. You may be surprised to know that the right to vote was not guaranteed by the Constitution.

1 | Find out who has been prevented from voting since the United States became a nation by taking the quiz below.

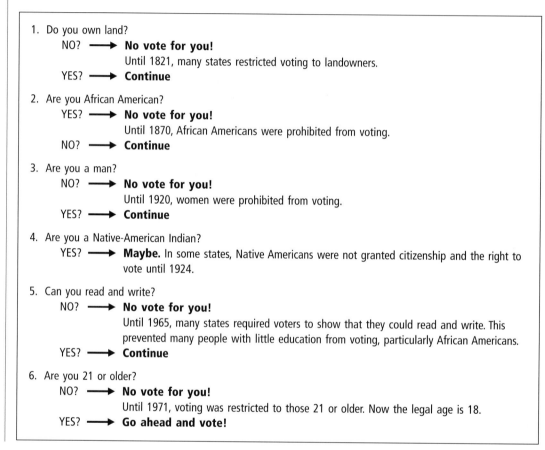

1. Do you own land?
   NO? ⟶ **No vote for you!**
   Until 1821, many states restricted voting to landowners.
   YES? ⟶ **Continue**

2. Are you African American?
   YES? ⟶ **No vote for you!**
   Until 1870, African Americans were prohibited from voting.
   NO? ⟶ **Continue**

3. Are you a man?
   NO? ⟶ **No vote for you!**
   Until 1920, women were prohibited from voting.
   YES? ⟶ **Continue**

4. Are you a Native-American Indian?
   YES? ⟶ **Maybe.** In some states, Native Americans were not granted citizenship and the right to vote until 1924.

5. Can you read and write?
   NO? ⟶ **No vote for you!**
   Until 1965, many states required voters to show that they could read and write. This prevented many people with little education from voting, particularly African Americans.
   YES? ⟶ **Continue**

6. Are you 21 or older?
   NO? ⟶ **No vote for you!**
   Until 1971, voting was restricted to those 21 or older. Now the legal age is 18.
   YES? ⟶ **Go ahead and vote!**

2 | As a class, make a list of which classmates would not have been allowed to vote in the United States in 1820. Explain why.

Now read

Now read the text "Electing the President." When you finish, turn to the tasks on page 24.

Republican National Convention, 2004

Democratic National Convention, 2004

4 ELECTING THE PRESIDENT

The process of electing a President is complex. Even many Americans find it confusing. Only a small part of the process is described in the U.S. Constitution; other details of the process have developed over the past 200 years.

The Constitution specifies that the President must be at least 35 years old and must be born in the United States. It also states that the President serves a four-year term and then can run for reelection. At the time the Constitution was written, there was no limit on the number of terms that a President could serve. In 1951, the Twenty-Second Amendment was passed. It limited a President to two terms.

The primary election

There are two major **political parties** in the United States: the Republicans and the Democrats. Each party has a primary election, that is, an election in which citizens choose their party's nominee, or candidate, for President. Then the Republicans and the Democrats each hold a convention and officially announce their candidates for President and Vice President.

political party
a group of people with similar political views that competes in elections

The presidential campaign

During the campaign, the presidential candidates from each party compete against each other by advertising on television and talking to people about their plans for the country's future. They also participate in televised debates. In these debates, the candidates explain their points of view and argue about the best way to solve the country's problems. Each candidate tries to convince viewers that he or she has the best ideas and is the best choice for President.

Source: Federal Election Commission, 2006.

Figure 1.2 Distribution of electoral votes by state, 1991–2000.

The popular vote and the electoral vote

On Election Day, citizens vote for the candidate of their choice. This is called the *popular vote,* or people's vote. Many Americans think that when they vote, they are voting directly for their candidate. This is not the case; instead, they are voting for electors who then vote for one of the candidates. This second vote is called the *electoral vote.*

The number of electors in each state is equal to the number of its legislators (senators + representatives). Since states with larger populations have more representatives, these states have more electoral votes than smaller states. (See Figure 1.2.)

In most states, all of the electoral votes for a state go to the candidate who wins the most votes in that state. This "winner takes all" system can produce strange results. It is possible for one candidate to get the largest number of popular votes and the other candidate to get the largest number of electoral votes. This is exactly what happened in the presidential election of 2000. The vote was very close. Although Al Gore won a half million more popular votes than George W. Bush, Bush won 10 more electoral votes than Gore. Therefore, Bush became President.

Why don't citizens vote directly for the President? Some of the writers of the Constitution wanted Congress to elect the President; others wanted the President to be elected directly by the citizens. The system of electoral votes was a compromise between these ideas.

How many people vote?

Although voting is an important responsibility for citizens of any country, Americans do not always vote. Voter turnout, or the percentage of possible voters who actually vote, varies a great deal from one country to another. The chart below shows voter turnout, that is, the number of people who vote in national elections, in 10 countries, including the United States.

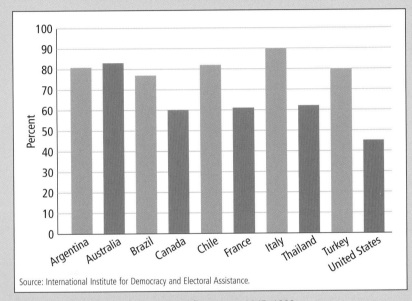

Source: International Institute for Democracy and Electoral Assistance.

Figure 1.3 Percentage of voter turnout by country, 1945–1998.

After you read

Task 1 ASKING AND ANSWERING QUESTIONS ABOUT A TEXT

> Asking and answering questions about a text is a good way to make
> sure you understood what you have read. You can do it alone or with
> a partner.

Reread "The Presidential Election." Stop after each paragraph, and practice asking
and answering questions about what you read with a partner. Here are some questions
you can use:

1 What is the primary election?
2 What is the purpose of the presidential campaign?
3 How can the electoral vote produce strange results?
4 What is the historical reason for the electoral vote?

Task 2 LANGUAGE FOCUS: GERUNDS

> A *gerund* is a verb in its *-ing* form that is used as a noun. A gerund is
> used when the meaning requires an action but the grammar requires a
> noun.
>
> Congress has many important responsibilities, such as **making** laws,
> **imposing** taxes, **declaring** war, and **printing** money.
>
> Because gerunds are nouns, they can follow prepositions, such as *for,*
> *from,* and *of.*

1 | Reread the section of the text headed "The presidential campaign." Complete the
sentence below by listing some of the candidates' activities during the campaign.
Use the gerund form in your answers.

The candidates' activities during the campaign include (1) _explaining their_
points of view to voters , (2) _____ ,
(3) _____ , and (4) _____ .

2 Complete the following sentences using the gerund form in your answers. Use information from the texts in this chapter. You will need more than one word to complete some of the sentences.

1 The quiz in "Preparing to read," on page 20, is about the history **of**
_____ in the United States.

2 The Sixth Amendment prohibits the police **from** _____.

3 The federal government is responsible **for** _____.

4 Until 1965, many state laws prevented African Americans **from**

_____ .

Task 3 LANGUAGE FOCUS: EXPRESSING NUMERICAL DATA

Learning ways to express numerical data is an important skill that you will need for academic writing assignments.

1 Look at this chart of words and expressions that you can use to express the numerical data shown in Figure 1.3 on page 23.

more than less than (just) over (just) under nearly almost about approximately	half a quarter a third 50% 80%	of the voting age population . . .

2 Write three sentences that describe voter turnout as shown in Figure 1.3. Here is an example:

Less than half of the voting age population of the United States votes in national elections.

3 As a class, discuss this question: Did any of the information in the graph surprise you? Why or why not?

UNIT 1 WRITING ASSIGNMENT A

This assignment refers to information you learned in Chapter 1. You will begin by writing simple one-sentence definitions of terms. Then you will write an expanded one-paragraph definition of one term, *the Bill of Rights*.

Preparing to write

1 Look at these two common formats for one-sentence definitions of terms:

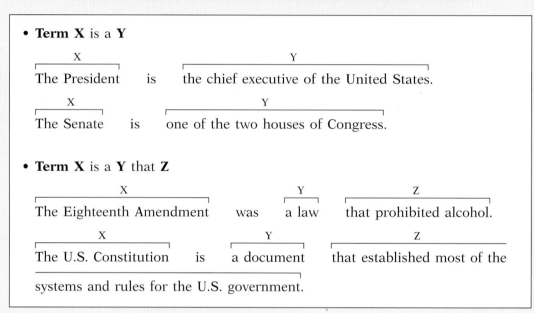

- **Term X is a Y**

  $\overbrace{\text{The President}}^{X}$ is $\overbrace{\text{the chief executive of the United States.}}^{Y}$

  $\overbrace{\text{The Senate}}^{X}$ is $\overbrace{\text{one of the two houses of Congress.}}^{Y}$

- **Term X is a Y that Z**

  $\overbrace{\text{The Eighteenth Amendment}}^{X}$ was $\overbrace{\text{a law}}^{Y}$ $\overbrace{\text{that prohibited alcohol.}}^{Z}$

  $\overbrace{\text{The U.S. Constitution}}^{X}$ is $\overbrace{\text{a document}}^{Y}$ $\overbrace{\text{that established most of the}}^{Z}$ systems and rules for the U.S. government.

2 With a partner, write one-sentence definitions for the terms below. Begin by deciding which format is best for the definition: XY or XYZ. Write at least two definitions using the XYZ format.

   1 July 4, 1776, . . .
   2 The Liberty Bell . . .
   3 The Bill of Rights . . .
   4 Federalism . . .
   5 Voter turnout . . .
   6 The Democratic Party . . .

3 Look at the paragraph below, which is an expanded definition of the term the *U.S. Constitution*. An expanded definition explains the meaning of a term and also gives one or two examples. Notice that this expanded definition begins with the XYZ definition from step 1.

> The U.S. Constitution is a document that established most of the systems and rules for the U.S. government. It established the three branches of government: the legislative, the executive, and the judicial branches. It described the responsibilities of each branch and the checks and balances among the branches. The Constitution also established a federalist system of government.

4 You are going to write a short paragraph that is an expanded definition of the term *the Bill of Rights*. Decide if you are satisfied with the one-sentence definition of the Bill of Rights that you wrote in step 2. Revise it if you wish.

5 With your partner, discuss what important information you might include in your paragraph about the Bill of Rights. You shouldn't include everything. Use the headings in the text "The Bill of Rights" on page 16 to help you organize your ideas.

6 Make notes about what you might include. Do not look at the text while you are making notes. This will help you to write in your own words instead of simply copying the words in the text. Copying more than a few key words or phrases from someone else's writing without giving them credit is called *plagiarism*. Plagiarism is considered a form of dishonesty in American academic institutions, and it has serious consequences.

Now write

Now write your paragraph. Begin the paragraph with your XYZ sentence. Complete it with the information from your notes.

After you write

Compare and discuss your paragraphs in small groups.

Preparing to read

THINKING ABOUT THE TOPIC BEFORE YOU READ

1 Look at these photographs and read the captions.

These people are marching and carrying signs to protest the policies of the U.S. President and government.

Burning a cross has been used by political groups as a symbol of hatred against nonwhites and non-Christians.

2 Discuss the questions below with your classmates:

1 Do you think the activities in these photographs are legal in the United States?

2 Would these kinds of activities be acceptable in other countries that you know about?

3 What is your opinion of these activities? Do you think they are acceptable?

You can use phrases such as these in your discussion:

- I think it is illegal for people to _____ because . . .
- In my opinion, it is (not) acceptable to _____ because . . .

Now read

Now read the text "Freedom of Expression: How Far Does It Go?" When you finish, turn to the tasks on page 31.

Constitutional Issues Today

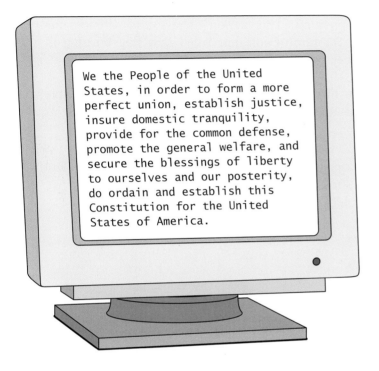

We the People of the United States, in order to form a more perfect union, establish justice, insure domestic tranquility, provide for the common defense, promote the general welfare, and secure the blessings of liberty to ourselves and our posterity, do ordain and establish this Constitution for the United States of America.

1 FREEDOM OF EXPRESSION: HOW FAR DOES IT GO?

Since the First Amendment was written, the term *freedom of speech* has gained a broader interpretation, or meaning. It includes not just what people say, but other forms of expression, such as what they write and do. Most people support the free expression of ideas that they agree with. However, the First Amendment protects even the expression of opinions that many people do not like.

In 1977, the American Nazi Party decided to march in a town in Illinois. More than half of the people in this town were Jewish; many had escaped death during World War II when most of Europe was under Nazi control. The town's government did not like the idea of Nazis marching in their town, and they tried to stop it. The case went to court. The court decided that the effort to stop the march was unconstitutional because it would limit the Nazis' freedom of speech.

In 1998, several men in Virginia were convicted, that is, found guilty, of burning crosses near the homes of African-American families.

They burned the crosses to show their hatred of African Americans. At that time, Virginia had a law that prohibited cross burning. However, the Virginia Supreme Court decided that the law was unconstitutional because the First Amendment protects people's right to use symbols, even burning crosses, to express their ideas.

Perhaps the most controversial example of free speech in recent times has been the burning of the American flag. People who want to protest against the American government sometimes burn the flag to express their opposition. This action angers and offends many Americans. Yet, the Supreme Court has ruled that flag burning is a legal form of political protest; therefore, any law that prohibits it is unconstitutional. 4

Even though the First Amendment guarantees freedom of expression, there are some forms of expression that are not permitted. You are prohibited from: 5

- destroying someone else's property as a form of expression.
- encouraging other people to commit a crime or to become violent.
- telling lies about someone that will hurt them.
- promoting the violent destruction of the government.

Oliver Wendell Holmes was a judge on the Supreme Court from 1902 to 1932. He once described freedom of expression as "the principle of free thought – not free thought for those who agree with us but freedom for the thought we hate." (*U.S. versus Schwimmer*, 1929)

Oliver Wendell Holmes

After you read

Task 1 READING FOR MAIN IDEAS

Understanding how to identify main ideas is an essential skill when
reading an academic text. You must be able to quickly identify the main
topic of a paragraph. You must also be able to identify the main idea of
the whole text – the point that the writer is trying to make.

1 Look back at the text quickly, and write the number of the paragraph that deals
with each of the following topics:

   1 the use of symbols as a form of free speech   par. _____

   2 a controversial form of protest against the government   par. _____

   3 what free speech means   par. _____

   4 the right of free speech for an unpopular group   par. _____

2 Decide which of the statements below expresses the main idea of the whole text:

   1 Free speech does not include speech that encourages violence.

   2 Freedom of speech is broad enough to protect unpopular and offensive ideas.

   3 Freedom of speech has always been the law in the United States.

   4 Freedom of speech includes protests.

3 Compare your answers with a partner. Then highlight the sentence in the text that
states the main idea you chose in step 2.

Task 2 MAKING GENERALIZATIONS

Authors do not always state an idea directly. Sometimes they give
examples, and you have to figure out the general meaning, or
generalization, that the examples illustrate.

1 Reread the examples of practices that are *not* permitted by the First Amendment
in paragraph 5.

2 With a partner, decide what the examples in paragraph 5 have in common.

3 Write a sentence that makes a generalization about these examples. Here are two
possible ways you can organize your sentence:

   • The First Amendment prohibits people from _____.

   • _____ is not allowed by the First Amendment.

Task 3 BUILDING VOCABULARY: WORDS THAT CAN BE USED AS NOUNS OR VERBS

> English has many words that can be used as either nouns or verbs.
> Learning both uses of these words will help you increase your vocabulary.

1 Read these sentences based on the text. These sentences show how the words in bold, *march* and *limit,* can be used as either nouns or verbs:

- The American Nazi Party planned a **march** in a town in Illinois.
  The American Nazi Party decided to **march** in a town in Illinois.

- The court did not put a **limit** on the Nazis' freedom of speech.
  The court did not **limit** the Nazis' freedom of speech.

2 In the sentences below, the words in bold are nouns, but they can also be used as verbs. Rewrite each sentence using the word in bold as a verb.

1 The first settlers had **hopes** for a better future.

_____

2 The presidential candidates have **debates** about their ideas.

_____

3 Choose two words from the list below. Look back at the text to see how the words you chose are used. You can also look them up in a dictionary. For each word, write two sentences. In one sentence, use the word as a noun; in the other sentence, use the word as a verb.

control   guarantee   protest   support

Task 4 THINKING CRITICALLY ABOUT THE TOPIC

In a small group, discuss the following questions:

1 Do you think citizens should be able to do these things? Why or why not?

  a Join an Internet discussion group that favors the violent defeat of the government

  b Hang a sign that expresses racial hatred

  c Publish pictures of people in private situations

  d Insult government officials in public

  e Publish private (but true) information about government officials that would make them feel uncomfortable

  f Publish instructions for building a bomb on the Internet

  g Publish government secrets

2 What do you think the limits of freedom of expression should be?

Preparing to read

EXAMINING GRAPHIC MATERIAL

Look at the two graphs below that concern religion in the United States and other countries. Then discuss the questions next to the graphs with a partner or small group.

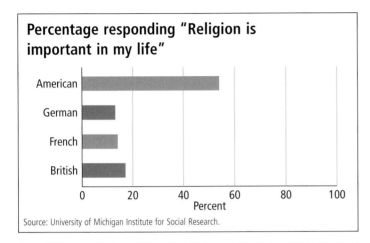

Percentage responding "Religion is important in my life"

Source: University of Michigan Institute for Social Research.

1 What do the graphs tell you about the importance of religion in the United States?

2 The research institute that collected this information concluded that the United States has higher attendance at religious services than any country at a similar level of development. Does this conclusion surprise you? Why or why not?

3 How does the information in these graphs compare with other countries that you know?

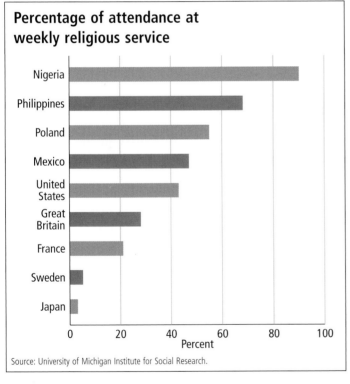

Percentage of attendance at weekly religious service

Source: University of Michigan Institute for Social Research.

Now read

Now read the text "Separating Religion and Government." When you finish, turn to the tasks on page 35.

2 SEPARATING RELIGION AND GOVERNMENT

The men who wrote the U.S. Constitution wanted to prevent conflicts among religious groups, which were common in many countries in Europe at that time. They decided that a complete separation between religion and government was the best way to avoid these problems. This principle is often referred to as the **separation of church and state**. 1

The First Amendment to the Constitution supports the idea that religious beliefs are a personal matter. It states that the government may not interfere with people's private religious beliefs. The government may not establish a church or force people to practice a particular religion or any religion at all. It may not favor or support one religion more than another. This means that in general, religious practices and symbols are not permitted on government property, such as courts and public (government-supported) schools. For example, teachers in public schools may not say prayers in class. The reason is that students who choose not to participate in this activity may feel uncomfortable because everyone else is praying. The guarantee of religious freedom in the First Amendment also means that individuals may not impose their religious beliefs on others; in other words, they cannot force other people to believe what they do. 2

These guidelines sound simple, but sometimes the First Amendment conflicts with religious practices. The situations below are examples of possible conflicts between religious practices and the First Amendment that have led to legal cases. 3

1. In a public courtroom, a judge displays the Ten Commandments, a religious document that is important in Christian and Jewish faiths.
2. A Christian prayer is said before a football game at a public school.
3. A Muslim woman covers her head and face in her driver's license photograph. It is hard to identify her in the photograph.
4. A man's religion allows him to have more than one wife, a practice that is against the law.
5. Parents from a religious group that prohibits certain medical treatments will not allow surgery for their child even though it could save the child's life.
6. A Native-American religious ceremony requires participants to eat a local plant, which contains an illegal drug.
7. A public school provides a separate room and time for Muslim students to pray during the holy month of Ramadan.
8. Some religious groups prohibit their members from fighting in wars. Their members refuse to serve in the military.

After you read

Task 1 READING TO FIND SUPPORT FOR MAIN IDEAS

> Academic texts usually include evidence, such as examples, quotations, and statistics, to support the main ideas. You will often be expected to present this supporting evidence in class discussions or on tests.

1 | Read the sentence below, which expresses the main idea of the text "Separating Religion and Government."

> The First Amendment to the Constitution supports the idea that religious beliefs are a personal matter.

2 | Highlight three examples in the text that support the main idea in step 1.

3 | Look back at "Reading for Main Ideas" on page 31 to remind yourself of the main idea of the text "Freedom of Expression: How Far Does It Go?" Then find and highlight three examples in that text that support its main idea.

4 | Compare your answers to steps 2 and 3 in a small group.

Task 2 APPLYING WHAT YOU HAVE READ

1 | Reread the examples of conflicts between religious beliefs and the First Amendment at the end of "Separating Religion and Government." They are all actual cases that have occurred in the United States. Some cases have already been decided in court; others have not.

2 | Take turns with a partner explaining how each situation might violate (act against) the principle of separation of church and state.

3 | Choose two conflicts that you think have a solution. Explain to your partner how you think each conflict could be resolved. Here is an example:

SITUATION 8: "Some religious groups prohibit their members from fighting in wars. Their members refuse to serve in the military."

Conflict: The First Amendment protects people's rights to follow their own religious beliefs. Sometimes military duty conflicts with those beliefs.

Resolution: Their refusal to fight is because of a religious belief; therefore, these people should not have to fight in wars. However, they could serve the country in other ways: in hospitals, parks, and building projects.

4 | Share your resolution to one of the situations you discussed in step 3 with the class.

Task 3 BUILDING VOCABULARY: LEARNING VERBS WITH THEIR PREPOSITIONS

> Some verbs frequently occur with specific prepositions. When you learn a new verb, see if a preposition follows. Try to learn them together as one unit.

1 The verbs in bold are frequently followed by a specific preposition. The number in parentheses shows the paragraph in the text where the verb and preposition can be found. Fill in the missing preposition.

1 It states that the government may not **interfere** _____ people's private religious beliefs. (par. 2)

2 Some students may not wish to **participate** _____ this activity. (par. 2)

3 Individuals may not **impose** their religious beliefs _____ others. (par. 2)

4 Sometimes the First Amendment **conflicts** _____ religious practices. (par. 3)

2 Complete the sentences below. First, add the correct preposition for the verb in bold. Then select an appropriate ending from the choices listed.

poor people
athletic activities after school
the private lives of its citizens
the quiet and relaxing atmosphere

1 Many school children **participate** _____.

2 The new taxes **impose** a heavy burden _____.

3 The loud music **conflicts** _____.

4 The government sometimes **interferes** _____.

3 Complete the sentences below with something that is true for you.

1 I never participate _____
_____.

2 I think _____ conflicts _____
_____.

3 People should not interfere _____
_____.

Task 4 LANGUAGE FOCUS: GIVING REASONS

Academic writing often includes reasons *why* a situation or an event occurred or existed. Reasons are signaled with connecting words that show cause, for example: *because, since, therefore, as a result.*

A reason may be provided before or after the event or situation it explains. The order affects the choice of connector as well as the punctuation. In the following examples, notice the placement of the connecting words and the punctuation:

- The authors of the Constitution established a system of checks and balances *because* they were worried about abuse of power.

  event/situation ➔ *because/since* ➔ reason

- *Because* they were worried about abuse of power, the authors of the Constitution established a system of checks and balances.

  Because/Since ➔ reason, ➔ event/situation

- The authors of the Constitution were worried about abuse of power; *therefore,* they established a system of checks and balances.

  reason ➔ ; *therefore/as a result,* ➔ event/situation

1 Read the following sentences. Underline the reason. Circle the situation or event that it explains.

   1 The authors of the Constitution included religious freedom in the First Amendment because they wanted to avoid religious conflicts.

   2 The Constitution establishes a policy of "separation of church and state"; therefore, there is no national religion.

   3 Because the Constitution establishes a policy of "separation of church and state," there is no national religion.

   4 Since the Supreme Court has ruled that flag burning is a legal form of political protest, any law that prohibits it is unconstitutional.

2 Read the events or situations below. For each one, write a sentence that gives a reason. Use connecting words from the box above, and be sure to use correct punctuation.

   1 Religious practices and symbols are not permitted on government property, such as courts and public schools.

   2 Many people left Europe for the American colonies.

   3 The police cannot enter a house without permission from a judge.

Preparing to read

THINKING ABOUT THE TOPIC BEFORE YOU READ

1 The title of the text you are going to read is "Guns in America: The Right to Bear Arms."

The right to bear arms is another way of saying *the right to have firearms,* or guns. You have been reading about the rights guaranteed by the Bill of Rights. What kind of information do you think this text will include?

2 Look at these pictures of people with guns. Then discuss the questions below in a small group.

1 Do you think it is easy to buy a gun in the United States?
2 Do you think many Americans own guns?
3 Is gun ownership common in other countries that you know?
4 Do you think of the United States as a violent country where people often shoot one another? Explain.
5 Do you think it is a good idea to allow people to own guns? Explain.

Now read

Now read the text "Guns in America: The Right to Bear Arms." When you finish, turn to the tasks on page 40.

3 GUNS IN AMERICA: THE RIGHT TO BEAR ARMS

The Second Amendment may be the most controversial amendment in the Bill of Rights. To understand it, we must go back in history.   1

The early Americans settlers had more difficult and dangerous lives   2
than most of us have today. They had to hunt for food and protect themselves against wild animals. There were no police to protect them, so they needed guns for their own defense.

There were also conflicts between the settlers and the British army.   3
Because of these dangers, each colony maintained its own army of citizens, called a *militia,* to protect the residents. The men who wrote the Constitution wanted to be sure that Americans would always be able to protect themselves, so they included the Second Amendment in the Constitution.

Unfortunately, the wording of the amendment is not clear, and different people interpret it in different ways. This is a paraphrase of what   4
it says:

The government should not interfere with the people's right to keep and carry guns because a militia is important for security.

Because the wording is not clear, there are two very different interpretations. The first one is narrow; the second one is broad:

1. Communities should be permitted to have militias, and these militias should carry guns. (Today, *militias* would be the police or the military.)
2. Anyone should be permitted to own and carry a gun. The government must not interfere with this right.

The majority of the American population believes that the second interpretation is correct. Approximately 65 million Americans own at least one gun. This is more than 20 percent of the population. There are more than 250 million firearms in American homes.

Gun ownership is an emotional issue for Americans: Some people   5
believe that owning a gun is a fundamental right; others believe that people should not be allowed to own guns.

These are some of the arguments for and against owning guns.   6

For gun ownership
- Banning guns will not prevent criminals from getting guns.
- Citizens should be allowed to own guns for their own protection.
- Gun use can save lives and prevent crimes.
- Guns are used for hunting.
- Gun ownership is guaranteed by the Constitution.

Against gun ownership
- Guns are a major cause of violence and death. There is a clear relationship between widespread gun ownership and gun deaths.
- Guns are used by criminals.
- Guns are often involved in accidents.
- Guns can be used against their owners.

After you read

Task 1 SCANNING

You will often need to scan when studying for a test or preparing to
write an assignment. Scanning a text means reading quickly to find
specific information. When you scan, you do not read every word. Your
eyes pass over the text, stopping only when you find the information
you are looking for.

Scan the text to find the following information:

1 What were two dangers that faced early settlers in America?
2 What is the definition of *militia*?
3 Do most Americans believe the narrow or broad interpretation of the Second
   Amendment?
4 What percentage of Americans own guns?

Task 2 APPLYING WHAT YOU HAVE READ

1 Read the short newspaper article below. It tells the story of how one man shot
another man in self-defense, that is, to protect himself.

HAMPTON, VIRGINIA – A 22-year-old man shot at two attackers early
Sunday, killing one of them, a police spokesperson said.

Based on police interviews with witnesses, it appears that the young
man was acting in self-defense. He was attending a party at a friend's
house. Someone told him that there were people outside who wanted
to talk to him. A witness said that when the young man went outside,
two men approached him and started arguing with him.

The two men then jumped on him, knocked him to the ground, and
began beating him. The 22-year-old pulled out a gun and fired. A shot hit
one of the attackers. The injured man died a few hours later.

2 With a partner or small group, discuss how you think this incident might have
ended if the young man did not have a gun.

3 Review the arguments for and against gun ownership at the end of the text. With
your partner or small group, discuss which arguments are relevant to this article.

4 Explain whether the incident described in the article makes a good argument for
the narrow or the broad interpretation of the Second Amendment.

Task 3 UNDERSTANDING THE FUNCTION OF TOPIC SENTENCES

> The topic sentence of a paragraph is a general statement that tells the reader what to expect in the rest of the paragraph. It gives the topic and the main point of the paragraph.

1 Decide which one of the statements below would be the best topic sentence for a paragraph that gives reasons *for* gun ownership. Put an *F* (for) next to the appropriate statement. Remember that you want to choose a *general* statement. Some of the statements below are too specific or too emotional.

_____ **1** Gun-related deaths are higher in the United States than in any other country.

_____ **2** Americans have strong opinions about gun ownership.

_____ **3** There are several important reasons why many Americans favor gun ownership.

_____ **4** Citizens should be allowed to carry guns for protection against criminals.

_____ **5** Many Americans oppose gun ownership.

_____ **6** There is a clear relationship between gun ownership and gun-related deaths.

_____ **7** Gun ownership is guaranteed by the Second Amendment, and no one should take this right away.

_____ **8** Americans have always loved guns.

2 Now decide which one of the statements in step 1 would be the best topic sentence for a paragraph that gives reasons *against* gun ownership. Put an *A* (against) next to the appropriate statement.

3 Compare your answers to steps 1 and 2 as a class or in small groups. Explain why the sentences you did not choose are not appropriate for a topic sentence.

4 Using the information for and against gun ownership at the end of the text, choose three reasons that would support each of the topic sentences you have chosen.

Task 4 THINKING CRITICALLY ABOUT THE TOPIC

With a partner or in a small group, discuss which evidence in the text is most convincing: the evidence for gun ownership or the evidence against gun ownership. Explain the reasons for your choice.

Preparing to read

REVIEWING WHAT YOU HAVE ALREADY READ

When you are reading several texts about the same or similar topics, it is useful to pause from time to time and review what you have already read. This will help you remember main ideas and understand how the texts are related.

1 Review the first three texts in this chapter and the text on the Bill of Rights in Chapter 1. Based on the information in the texts, make a list of the rights and freedoms the U.S. Constitution guarantees its citizens.

2 Put a check (✔) next to the rights and freedoms in your list that you think are the most important.

3 Discuss the reasons for your answers to step 2 with a partner or in a small group.

BUILDING VOCABULARY: PREVIEWING KEY TERMS

Learning the meaning of key terms before you read will introduce you to important concepts in a text and make it easier to understand.

1 Look up the following key terms from the text in a dictionary:

security
civil liberty
versus

2 The title of the text you are going to read is "Security Versus Civil Liberty." Discuss what you think this title means with your partner or group.

3 Compare your answers to step 2 as a class.

Now read

Now read the text "Security Versus Civil Liberty." When you finish, turn to the tasks on page 44.

4 SECURITY VERSUS CIVIL LIBERTY

The United States has always struggled to balance security with individual freedom. Several times in the nation's history, especially during times of war, the U.S. government has restricted civil liberties in an effort to protect citizens. Since the September 11, 2001, terrorist attacks, the American government has been watching what people say and do much more carefully. 1

A set of recent laws, known as the Patriot Act, allows government officials and police to listen to private conversations and track computer use even if there is no evidence of a crime. The Patriot Act permits the police to put suspects in prison without charging them with a crime and without allowing them to see their lawyers. Internet service providers and businesses are required to give customers' records to the government in terrorism investigations. The government can check private records of individuals, even when they are not suspects in any crime. The new laws are so powerful that the government can even check library records. 2

Following September 11, the United States government held more than 1,200 people in prison as terrorist suspects. The prisoners could not contact their families or lawyers. The President ordered secret trials to decide if the suspects should be charged with a crime. Journalists were not allowed to attend them; as a result, the public does not know what happened at these trials. 3

Many Americans have been happy to see these developments; they see them as an important part of the war on terrorism. But some citizens are protesting the government's actions. They are asking how much restriction of civil liberties is necessary in order to prevent terrorism. People who are concerned about civil liberties say that the restrictions take away basic freedoms, such as the right to know why you are in prison, the right to a lawyer, and the right to a public trial. They believe that many parts of the Patriot Act may be unconstitutional. 4

The public is divided on this topic. As long as Americans feel they are in danger, there will probably be disagreement about the best way to balance security and the protection of civil liberties. 5

After you read

Task 1 INFERRING THE AUTHOR'S OPINION

Some academic texts provide information in a neutral manner. Often, however, authors insert their own opinions into their writing in ways that may not be obvious. When you read, it is important to be able to figure out, that is, to *infer*, an author's opinions even if these opinions are not stated directly.

1 The left column below contains excerpts from the text. The right column contains the author's opinions that might be inferred from these excerpts. Match each excerpt to the opinion that might be inferred. You may use some excerpts more than once, and some opinions may match more than one excerpt.

Excerpts from the text

a The Patriot Act allows [them] to listen to private conversations and track computer use even if there is no evidence of a crime.

b The Patriot Act permits the police to put suspects in prison without charging them with a crime and without allowing them to see their lawyers.

c The President ordered secret trials . . . , as a result, the public does not know what happened at these trials.

d Internet service providers and businesses are required to give customers' records to the government.

e The cartoon that accompanies the article

Author's opinions

_____ **1** This law may be unconstitutional because the Sixth Amendment guarantees a suspect's right to legal advice.

_____ **2** The government is going too far in pursuing terrorists. Sometimes the result is silly.

_____ **3** This law may be unconstitutional because the Fourth Amendment protects citizens against unreasonable searches.

_____ **4** This law may violate the Sixth Amendment, which states that a suspect must be told why he or she has been arrested.

_____ **5** This law may be unconstitutional because the Sixth Amendment guarantees a public trial.

2 Compare your answers to step 1 in a small group.

3 In your group, discuss the following questions:

1 What do you think the author's opinion of the Patriot Act is? Explain the reasons for your answer.

2 Do you think it is acceptable for authors to express their opinions directly in newspaper articles? Is it acceptable for them to insert their opinions in ways that may not be obvious? Explain.

Task 2 TEST TAKING: UNDERSTANDING DIFFERENT TYPES OF TEST QUESTIONS

When taking a test, it is important for you to understand what kind of information you are expected to give in response to a question. Here are three common types of questions:

- Type 1: Simple questions that ask you to identify terms (They usually ask you to describe *who, what, when,* or *where.*)
- Type 2: Questions that ask you to explain relationships among ideas and information in the text
- Type 3: Questions that ask you to evaluate ideas and information in the text

1 With a partner, decide whether each question below is Type 1, 2, or 3. Put the appropriate number in the blank.

_____ **a** What kinds of checks does the judicial branch have on the legislative branch?

_____ **b** Is the Patriot Act constitutional?

_____ **c** What is a militia?

_____ **d** What is the difference between the popular vote and the electoral vote?

_____ **e** How does the importance of religion in the United States compare with its importance in Europe?

_____ **f** Should burning the flag be against the law? Why or why not?

2 Look at the sample answers below. What type of question does each one answer: 1, 2, or 3? Put the appropriate number in the blank.

_____ **a**
> Religion is important in the lives of many Americans, more important than in the lives of most Europeans. Almost half of all Americans report that they attend weekly religious services. In contrast, just over 20 percent of all French people attend church weekly. An even greater number of Americans report that their religious beliefs are important in their lives. Again, the French report a much lower figure.

_____ **b**
> The Patriot Act makes it very easy for the government to put innocent people in prison. This may be a violation of their civil rights. Because the government's actions are secret, the public usually never finds out about them. Even Congress often does not know. One example occurred after the terrorist bombings in Madrid in 2004. A lawyer in Oregon was arrested because the government had collected evidence that suggested he might be involved with the Madrid bombings. He was found to be innocent, but the collection of evidence against him was only possible because of the Patriot Act.

_____ **c**
> The United States Constitution was adopted in 1789.

3 Using any of the information in this unit, write one question of each type.

4 Exchange your questions with a partner, and try to answer his or her questions.

Task 3 BUILDING VOCABULARY: ORGANIZING A VOCABULARY NOTEBOOK

Two common ways to organize a vocabulary notebook are:

- by topic or subject
     Examples: government   rights and freedoms   elections
- by part of speech
     Examples: nouns   verbs   adjectives   adverbs

The important thing is to organize your notebook in a way that is easy for you to use.

Review your vocabulary notebook. Have you organized it in a way that is easy for you to use? If not, change its organization now. You might want to use one of the ways described in the box above.

Task 4 BUILDING VOCABULARY: REMEMBERING NEW WORDS AND PHRASES

Learning the meaning of new words and phrases is just the first step in building your vocabulary. The most important factor in learning new vocabulary is the number of times you think about, read, hear, or use the word or phrase. Here are some ways you can do this:

- Say the word or phrase out loud to yourself. Then say the definition.
- Say the word or phrase in the context that you wrote in your notebook.
- Make up a new sentence with the word or phrase.

1 Make sure you have entered the words and phrases you have learned in this unit in your vocabulary notebook.

2 Try two of the strategies described in the box above to help you remember the words and phrases that you have learned in this unit.

UNIT 1   WRITING ASSIGNMENT B

This assignment refers to information you learned in Chapters 1 and 2. In these chapters, you have read about the rights and freedoms that Americans value so highly. Your assignment is to choose one of the rights or freedoms you think is important and to write a paragraph in which you explain why.

Preparing to write

1   Study the example paragraph below. It explains why the protection against unreasonable searches by the police is an important right. The paragraph includes these features:

- A topic sentence that tells what the paragraph will be about
- One reason for this choice
- Two examples that support the reason
  Examples include:
    (1) the benefits of this right
    (2) what might happen if this right did not exist

Notice that although this topic sentence states the author's opinion, it does not include phrases like *I think* or *I believe*. In academic writing, you don't need to use such phrases. It will be clear that you are expressing your opinion.

Topic sentence ——————→	[The protection against unreasonable searches by the police is one of the most important rights guaranteed by the Bill of Rights.] This right is part of the Fourth Amendment.
A reason that supports the claim in the topic sentence. ——→	[It protects citizens against the police.] The police work very hard to find criminals, so they may sometimes forget about individual rights.
First example. It shows a benefit of the protection against unreasonable searches. ——→	[The police cannot come into your house without a judge's permission and look for some evidence against you.]
Second example. It shows what might happen if this protection was not included in the Fourth Amendment. ——→	[Without the Fourth Amendment, they could come to your door whenever they wanted to and search through your house. That could be very frightening.]

2 Read the rights and freedoms listed below. Choose one that you think is important.

- the freedom to express your ideas and opinions
- the freedom to practice your religion
- the right to keep guns
- the right to talk to a lawyer; to have a fair trial, that is, a speedy and public trial; and to know the charges against you

3 In a small group, explain the reasons why you think your choice from step 2 is important. Hearing the choices and reasons of other group members will help you get ideas for your paragraph.

4 Make notes about one of the reasons for your choice. Also make notes about at least two examples you could give that support your reason. You can include two types of examples: (a) the benefits of the right and/or (b) what might happen if the right did not exist.

Now write

Now write your paragraph. Make sure it includes the three features listed in step 1 of "Preparing to Write."

After you write

1 Exchange paragraphs with a partner. Discuss the following questions about your paragraphs:

1 What right has your partner chosen?
2 Has your partner written a good topic sentence?
3 Has your partner explained the right clearly?
4 Has your partner explained his or her reason clearly?
5 Do the examples support your partner's choice? Are they clear?

2 Discuss any suggestions you have for how your partner could improve his or her paragraph.

A Diverse Nation

In this unit, we look at issues of ethnic diversity in the United States. The term *ethnic diversity* refers to people of different races, cultures, and places of birth. In Chapter 3, we focus on the historical background of ethnic diversity in the United States. We also examine the challenges and hardships that native people, slaves, and immigrants have encountered. In Chapter 4, we look at diversity today, including the reasons for the continuing arrival of immigrants, both legal and illegal.

Previewing the unit

Read the contents page for Unit 2, and do the following activities.

Chapter 3: The Origins of Diversity

Discuss the following questions with a partner or small group:

1 We often think of North America as almost empty when the Europeans arrived. What do you think the size of the native population was, compared to the number of European settlers?
2 Before the middle of the twentieth century, which countries do you think the largest number of immigrants to the United States came from?
3 Read the quotation below. What do you think it means?

> Every American has the soul of an immigrant.
>
> – Jim Sheridan, Irish film director

Chapter 4: Diversity in Today's United States

Examine the pictures on page 49. Then discuss these questions with your partner or group:

1 Which countries do you think people are immigrating to the United States from today? Explain the reasons for your answer.
2 What challenges do you think today's immigrants have when they arrive?
3 What special problems do you think minorities face, that is, people who are not from a white European background?
4 Immigrants can become American citizens, but do you think they all become "American"?

Unit Contents 2

Preparing to read

THINKING ABOUT THE TOPIC BEFORE YOU READ

1 | Many people, both from the United States and other countries, get their information about the first people of America, often called *Native Americans* or *Indians*, from movies. With a partner or small group, discuss the following question: What have you learned about Native Americans from movies?

2 | With your partner or group, look at the maps below and discuss this question: What do you think the text "America's First People" will be about?

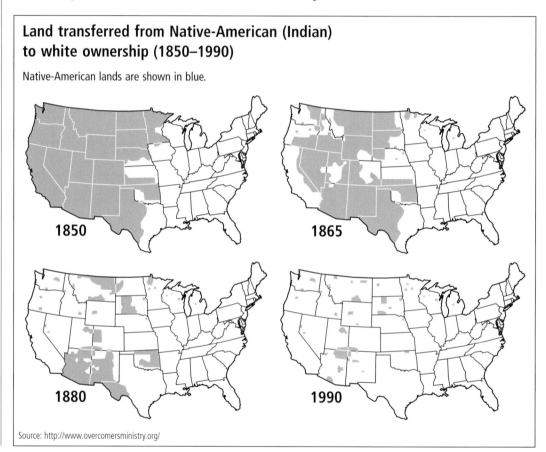

Land transferred from Native-American (Indian) to white ownership (1850–1990)

Native-American lands are shown in blue.

1850

1865

1880

1990

Source: http://www.overcomersministry.org/

Now read

Now read the text "America's First People." When you finish, turn to the tasks on page 55.

The Origins of Diversity

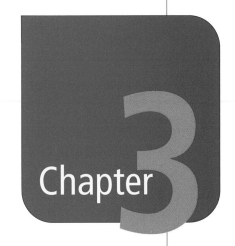

Chapter 3

1 AMERICA'S FIRST PEOPLE

When European settlers arrived in North America at the end of the fifteenth century, there were approximately 10 million Native Americans who spoke over 300 different native languages. The first Europeans believed they had landed in India, so they called the native people *Indians*. The Native-American and European cultures were very different, and the two groups often had problems understanding each other. Indian communities stretched from one end of North America to the other, and they all had their own characteristics. However, all the native communities shared a deep respect for the natural world. They believed that if they took care of the land, they could use it to live on, hunt, and grow crops. In contrast, Europeans believed that individuals could own land.

Relations between Indians and Europeans ranged from cooperation to violent conflict. At first, the European settlers often depended on native people for assistance and trade. As the number of settlers increased, however, they began to move into **Indian territory**, and conflicts became more frequent and more violent. There was death and destruction on both sides, but native people were frequently the losers in these struggles for control of the land.

Many Native-American communities were almost destroyed by the actions of the settlers and the policies of the American government. When the Europeans first arrived, they brought new diseases, such as measles and smallpox, which killed huge numbers of Indians. As more

Indian territory
the part of the country where many Native Americans lived

1

2

3

tribe

a group of people, often of related families, who live in the same area and share the same language, culture, and history

reservation

an area of land set aside by the U.S. government for native people

"The Trail of Tears,"
Robert Lindneux

assimilation

the process of becoming similar to a larger community or environment

census

the official count of the population size

settlers came and wanted the rich farmland that the **tribes** lived on, there were battles between the American military and various Native-American tribes for this land.

Starting in 1778, the United States government made hundreds of treaties, or written agreements, with native tribes in order to provide more space for the settlers. The Indians gave up their rights to their territory in exchange for food, money, and, perhaps most importantly, the government's promise to leave them in peace. Sometimes a tribe was allowed to stay on a small part of its original land. This small area was called a **reservation**. In other cases, the tribe simply moved west. This was the beginning of the loss of Indian land.

Most European Americans in the eighteenth and nineteenth centuries believed that whites were superior to Native Americans. President Andrew Jackson described native people as children who needed his guidance and protection. He, as well as many other Americans, believed the treaties were good for the Indians because they allowed native people to live in peace, separate from whites. Unfortunately, the promises in the treaties were often broken. As the country continued to grow, settlers needed still more land, even the land that the government had given to the native tribes in treaties. The government began a policy of removal, that is, pushing more and more native people farther west or onto reservations.

In 1830, Congress passed the Removal Act. This law required Native-American tribes to leave their land and settle in Indian Territory, west of the Mississippi River. Some Indians refused to go, particularly the Cherokee. So in 1838, thousands of soldiers and volunteers forced the Cherokee Indians to leave their homes. Hundreds of Cherokee were beaten, imprisoned, or murdered. The Cherokee who survived were forced to travel 1,000 miles to the Indian Territory, with little food, water, or protection. Approximately 4,000 Cherokee died on this journey, which has been called the *Trail of Tears*.

Another factor that contributed to the destruction of Native-American culture was education policy. The federal government's goal for Indian education from the 1880s through the 1920s was the **assimilation** of native children into European American culture. Many native children were required to leave their families and attend government boarding schools. At these schools, traditional Indian ways were replaced by the customs and behavior of white Americans. The government hoped that young Native Americans would learn the values and culture of white American society and give up their own traditions.

By 1900, the Native American population had dropped to about 250,000. Today, however, the population is growing again; on the 2000 **census**, 4.3 million people reported that they were Native American. Nevertheless, some believe that Native-American culture remains in danger. It is estimated that more than two-thirds of the original 300 native languages are dead or dying. Only a few have more than 5,000 speakers.

After you read

Task 1 THINKING ABOUT THE TOPIC

1 | Find and highlight three pieces of evidence in the text that show the attitudes of whites toward native people.

2 | Discuss the following questions with a partner or in a small group:

   1 What was the main reason for the conflict between the settlers and the Native Americans?
   2 Look at the photographs below. What do you think happened in Tom Torlino's life between 1882 and 1885?
   3 What do the photographs below and the maps on page 52 have in common?

Tom Torlino in 1882.

Tom Torlino in 1885.

Task 2 APPLYING WHAT YOU HAVE READ

Discuss the following questions as a class:

   1 The United States was not the only place where native people were treated badly by settlers from other countries. Describe any other cases you know.
   2 Do you know of any examples of relationships between settlers and native people that were more successful? Explain.

Task 3 LANGUAGE FOCUS: RECOGNIZING THE PASSIVE

> The passive form of the verb (*be* + past participle) is common in academic writing, so it is important to be able to recognize this form and understand its use.
>
> The passive is a good choice if any of these are true:
>
> • the writer wants to focus on the person or thing being acted upon
> • the performer of the action is unknown
> • the performer of the action is unimportant
>
> Sometimes a writer may use the passive for more than one of the reasons listed above.
>
> Here are some examples of the passive:
>
> • The Constitution **was adopted** in 1789.
> • Guns **are used** by criminals against innocent people.
> • Religious freedom **is guaranteed** by the First Amendment.

1 Underline the passive verb form in each sentence from the text below:

   1 Sometimes a tribe was allowed to stay on a small part of its original land.
   2 Many Native-American communities were almost destroyed by the actions of the settlers and the policies of the American government.
   3 The Cherokee who survived were forced to march 1,000 miles.
   4 Traditional Indian ways were replaced by the customs and behavior of white Americans.

2 With a partner, discuss the reason you think the author chose the passive for each of the sentences in step 1.

3 With your partner, complete each sentence below by choosing either the active or passive form of the verb. Circle your choices and discuss your reasons for them.

   1 The long journey of the Cherokee called/is called the *Trail of Tears*.
   2 Many Cherokee imprisoned or killed/were imprisoned or killed when they would not leave their land.
   3 The United States government broke/was broken many of its treaties with Native-American tribes.
   4 Native Americans forced/were forced to move west of the Mississippi River.
   5 Competition for land created/was created conflict between the Europeans and Native Americans.

Preparing to read

BUILDING BACKGROUND KNOWLEDGE OF THE TOPIC

Getting information about important ideas and facts about a topic before you read a text on the topic helps you to build your background knowledge. This will help you to read more effectively.

With a partner, look at these illustrations from the eighteenth century.

1 The illustration on the left is of a slave ship. If you don't know the word *slave,* look it up in a dictionary. Then discuss what you think a *slave ship* is.

2 To understand the illustration on the right, look up the words *auction* and *Negro* in a dictionary. Then discuss what you think "Auction Sale of Negros" means.

Now read

Now read the text "Slavery: The Early History of African Americans." When you finish, turn to the tasks on page 60.

2 SLAVERY: THE EARLY HISTORY OF AFRICAN AMERICANS

The economics of slavery

The work of slaves was essential to the economy of the southern United States, especially for growing cotton. Growing cotton required a large number of workers. For cotton farmers, slave labor was an answer to this problem. However, the business of slavery went beyond the cotton growers in the South; there were many other participants in the business. Africans, who had been taken from their villages, were loaded onto ships that were owned by businessmen from all over the United States and Europe. The ships sailed to ports in the Caribbean islands and the southern United States, where the Africans were sold as slaves. In the Caribbean ports, the ships picked up molasses, a raw syrup made from Caribbean sugar, and brought it to northern cities such as Boston and New York. The molasses was then made into rum, an alcoholic drink, and shipped to Africa. In Africa, the rum was sold in exchange for slaves. The slaves were then shipped to the Caribbean, and the cycle began again. This process was called *Triangular Trade* because the path formed a large triangle that stretched across the Atlantic Ocean. The cotton that the slaves picked was shipped to factories in the North and in Great Britain, where it was made into cloth and sold all over the world.

Between 1740 and 1810, about 60,000 enslaved Africans were sent to the New World (North and South America) every year. This was higher than the number of European immigrants. In spite of the importance of the slave trade, many Americans opposed it. In 1807, the U.S. Congress passed a law that prohibited people from importing slaves. However, owning slaves remained legal in many states. Everyone profited from slavery – the cotton farmers, the clothing factory owners, the rum producers, the slave traders, the ship owners, and people who bought cotton clothing – everyone except, of course, the slaves themselves.

Slaves in Alabama, 1855

The lives of slaves

Unlike most of the people who have come to America, these Africans were brought against their will. From 1500 to 1900, between 10 and 16 million came to North or South America, and many more died either in Africa or during the journey, which lasted about seven weeks. They were brought in dreadful conditions, often chained side by side inside the ships. Between 10 and 25 percent of the slaves died on the journey. The ones who survived were sold. Husbands and wives, children and parents were often separated. They became the property of the people who bought them, with no rights of their own. They were forced to work long hours; most worked in the cotton fields, up to 16 hours a day during the harvest. They received poor food, and rough clothing and housing. If they disobeyed orders or tried to escape, they were severely punished. Women were expected to work up until childbirth and to return to work immediately afterwards. Children began working at the age of five and many died early. Some slaves, especially those who worked inside their owners' houses, lived in better conditions. These "house slaves" still had hard lives, however, and they had no freedom. The average life of a slave was very short – just 22 years – half that of whites at that time.

The end of slavery

The slaves were finally freed at the end of the American Civil War (1861– 1865). Disagreement about slavery was one of the major causes of the war. The antislavery side won, and in 1865 the Thirteenth Amendment to the Constitution made slavery illegal. (You will learn more about this topic when you read "The Legacy of the Civil War," on page 104.)

4

Slave Narratives

After the end of slavery, some slaves began to tell their stories. Here is part of one of these *slave narratives*. This narrative is from an interview with a slave named Fountain Hughes. Notice that it was written in nonstandard English, which was just the way Hughes spoke.*

FOUNTAIN HUGHES

. . . Now I couldn't go from here across the street, or I couldn't go to nobody's house without a note, or something from my master. Whoever he sent me to, they would give me another pass and I'd bring that back . . . to show how long I'd been gone. We couldn't go out and stay an hour or two hours or something like that. . . . I couldn't just walk away like the people do now, you know. We were slaves. We belonged to people. They'd sell us like they sell horses and cows and hogs and all like that. They'd have an auction bench, and they'd put you on, up on the bench and bid on you just same as bidding on cattle.

---

* You can read and hear the original narrative at http://xroads. virginia.edu/~hyper/wpa/hughes1.html

After you read

Task 1 USING A GRAPHIC TO SHOW A SEQUENCE OF EVENTS

> Using a graphic to show a sequence of events can help you visualize a set of facts and see how they are connected. It can also help you analyze and remember what you have read.

1 Discuss the following questions with a partner:

1 How are all of the items on the lists below related?

2 Where were each of these items picked up?

3 Where were they shipped?

Triangular trade
- Slaves
- Molasses
- Rum

Cotton trade
- Raw cotton
- Cotton cloth

2 Draw arrows and write labels on the map below to show the relationship and economic connections among trading partners in the Triangular Trade. One example has been done for you.

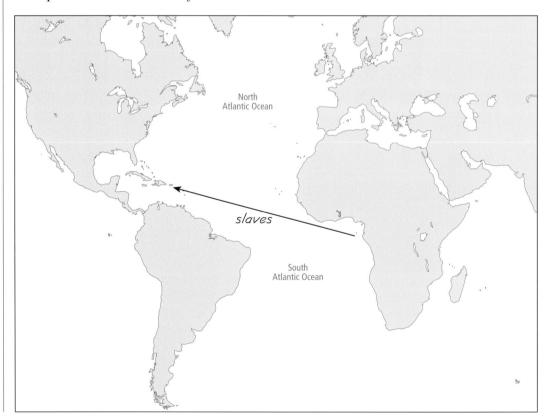

Task 2 READING PRIMARY TEXTS

Primary texts are authentic original documents. Learning to understand them is an important part of academic study.

Discuss these questions in a small group:

1 How is the primary text in the box on page 59 different from the main text?
2 What can you learn from this narrative that you cannot learn from the main text?

Task 3 LANGUAGE FOCUS: RECOGNIZING THE PASSIVE IN A TEXT CHAIN

The passive can be used to create a text chain that makes the text flow smoothly. For this reason, it is often used to explain a process or a series of related events. In a text chain, using the passive allows a key word in the last part of one sentence to appear near the beginning of the next sentence.

In the example below, the chain begins with the key word *cotton* at the end of the first sentence. *Cotton* then appears at the beginning of the next sentence, which is in the passive. The key words are in bold and the passive form of the verb is underlined.

The slaves did the most difficult work; they picked the raw **cotton** from the fields. The raw **cotton** was fed into a machine called a cotton gin, which separated the seeds from the cotton fibers, which are called **lint**. Then the **lint** was packed into **bales**, or large bags, that weighed 500 pounds or more. These **bales** were carried in wagons to seaports, where ships waited to take them to factories in Great Britain.

The description of Triangular Trade below is an example of a text chain. Circle the three key words that are repeated. Underline the passive forms of the verb.

Ships sailed to Caribbean ports and picked up molasses, a raw syrup made from sugar, and brought it to northern cities such as Boston and New York. The molasses was made into rum, an alcoholic drink, and then was shipped to Africa. In Africa, the rum was sold in exchange for slaves. The slaves were then shipped to the Caribbean and southern states, where they were sold, and the cycle began again.

Preparing to read

SKIMMING

> Skimming a text before you read it will make the text easier to under-stand. Skimming means looking quickly over a text to get an idea of what it is about and of how it is organized. You should not read every word. Instead, you should quickly read the introduction, the headings, and the first sentence of each paragraph. Do not spend too much time skimming. Remember that you just want to get a general idea about the text.

1 Quickly read the following parts of the text:

- the short introductory paragraph at the beginning of the text
- the headings
- the first sentence of each paragraph

2 In a small group, discuss the following question: What do you think the text "A Country of Immigrants" will be about?

THINKING ABOUT THE TOPIC BEFORE YOU READ

1 Look at these photographs of immigrants to the United States.

2 For each photograph, discuss the following questions in your group:

1 When do you think these people came to the United States?
2 Why do you think they came?
3 Do you think the people in the two photographs have anything in common?
4 Do you know about any people who immigrated to another country at the same time as the immigrants in the photographs? Why did they immigrate?

Now read

Now read the text "A Country of Immigrants." When you finish, turn to the tasks on page 65.

3 A COUNTRY OF IMMIGRANTS

The United States is a country of immigrants. It has received more immigrants than any other nation in modern history. There have been four major periods of immigration.

1

First period

In the seventeenth and eighteenth centuries, most of the immigrants to the American colonies came from western Europe, primarily England, Scotland, Ireland, the Netherlands, and Germany. Some were looking for adventure; some wanted cheap land to farm. Others were escaping wars, revolutions, or religious persecution. However, most of them were simply poor people hoping for better economic opportunities. Even those who did not have enough money for the voyage found a way to come – as indentured servants. An **indentured servant** signed a contract to work for four to seven years to pay back the cost of the ticket. Over half of all of the immigrants from Europe during the seventeenth century were either indentured servants or prisoners, who were often sent to the colonies as workers. In addition to these Europeans, many black people were brought from Africa as slaves. By 1776, when the War of Independence began, there were more than 600,000 people living in the American colonies.

2

> **indentured servant**
> a person who signs an agreement to work for someone for a certain period of time in return for something, for example, training for a job or payment for a boat ticket

Second period

From 1820 to 1875, more than 7 million newcomers entered the United States. Shorter travel time and cheaper fares made the voyage easier. Most immigrants came from northern and western Europe. Many were escaping from a famine caused by the failure of the potato crop in Ireland. During this period, the United States needed lots of workers and farmers, so the government encouraged this immigration. Also at this time, news of the discovery of gold in California brought many people from China. They hoped to find gold and become rich. Most did not become rich, but many stayed in the country to work. This flood of immigrants began to alarm many American citizens. They believed that the immigrants, who worked for low wages, were taking their jobs away. During the mid-1800s, some Americans began to demand laws to make it harder for foreigners to come to the United States.

3

Third period

Between 1875 and 1920, about 24 million immigrants poured into the United States from almost every part of the world. Until the 1880s, most newcomers had come from northern and western Europe. Beginning in the 1890s, however, the majority of immigrants came from southern and eastern Europe. Increasingly, Americans were afraid that the large number of immigrants coming to the country would take their

4

jobs away. Just as importantly, many American citizens believed that this large number of immigrants threatened the nation's identity.

In response to the fear about the flood of immigrants from so many different parts of the world, Congress passed a law to limit immigration. It allowed only immigrants who could read and write. It also prohibited all immigration from Asia. In 1921, Congress established a system of quotas. Under the **quota** system, limits on immigration from different countries were based on the number of people from those countries in the United States in 1920. Quotas were only for white immigrants; nonwhite immigrants were prohibited from entering the country at that time. 5

Fourth period

In 1965, quotas based on country of origin ended. A new system favored immigrants who had relatives already living in the United States and immigrants who had valuable skills, particularly in engineering, science, and technology. This caused major changes in patterns of immigration to the United States. Immigration from Europe and Canada went down; in contrast, immigration from Asia and the Caribbean rose dramatically. Today, the largest numbers of immigrants come from Mexico, India, the Philippines, and China. 6

quota
a number that is officially permitted

Immigrants being processed at Ellis Island, 1910

Ellis Island

Ellis Island was the location of the U.S. Bureau of Immigration's New York station. The island is in New York Harbor, next to the Statue of Liberty. Between 1892 and 1954, more than 12 million immigrants came through Ellis Island. During its busiest years (1892–1924), thousands of immigrants arrived every day. More than 100 million Americans can trace their family in the United States back to someone who passed through Ellis Island – including the author of this book!*

Ellis Island, 1905

* You can learn more about Ellis Island at http://www.ellisisland.com/indexHistory.html

After you read

Task 1 BUILDING VOCABULARY: USING CONTEXT

> Sometimes you can guess the meaning of a word you don't know from its *context*, that is, the words and sentences surrounding the word. The context can give you some clues, such as whether the word means something positive (good) or something negative (bad).

1 The word *persecution* (par. 2) is probably a new word for you. Study this example of how clues in the text can help you understand the meaning of *persecution*:

> Some were looking for adventure; some wanted cheap land to farm. Others were escaping wars, revolutions, or religious **persecution**.

Is *persecution* positive or negative? The word *escaping* suggests that it is negative. Why would people have to escape because of their religion? Perhaps the immigrants did not like the religion in their old country. Or, perhaps the old country did not like the religion of the immigrants. In either case, *persecution* means *bad treatment*. In other words, the immigrants were treated badly because of their religion.

2 Try to use the context to help you understand the meaning of each word in bold in the sentences below from the text. Follow these steps:

- Decide if the word in bold is positive or negative.
- Underline the word or words in the context that helped you decide.

  1 Many were escaping from a **famine** caused by the failure of the potato crop in Ireland.

  2 This flood of immigrants began to **alarm** many American citizens. They believed that the immigrants, who worked for low wages, were taking their jobs away.

  3 Increasingly, Americans were afraid that the large number of immigrants coming to the country would take their jobs away. Just as importantly, many American citizens believed that this large number of immigrants **threatened** the nation's identity.

  4 A new system **favored** immigrants who had relatives already living in the United States and immigrants who had valuable skills, particularly in engineering, science, and technology.

3 Compare your answers to step 2 as a class.

Task 2 NOTE TAKING: USING A CHART

Taking notes helps you remember new material. Putting your notes into a chart is a good way to see the relationships between parts of a text.

1 Look at the chart below. It is organized to show three themes in the history of immigration to the United States.

Pushes are reasons why people chose to *leave* their countries.
Pulls are reasons why people chose to *come* to the United States.
Barriers are steps that the U.S. government or citizens have taken in order to *stop* or *slow* immigrants from coming.

Time period	Pushes	Pulls	Barriers
	religious persecution in Europe		
1820–1875			
1875–1920			new immigration laws
		relatives living in the United States	

2 Make a chart like the one above on a separate piece of paper. Fill it in with information from the text. (Some information has been filled in for you.) You may not have enough information to fill in all of the boxes.

3 Compare your chart with a partner's.

Task 3 THINKING ABOUT THE TOPIC

Discuss these questions in a small group:

1 Why do you think most people immigrate to the United States today? Are the reasons different or the same as those of immigrants in the seventeenth, eighteenth, nineteenth, and early twentieth centuries?

2 Do you think it is easier or more difficult to immigrate to the United States today than in the seventeenth or eighteenth centuries? Why or why not?

3 Are you familiar with immigration patterns in another country? Who is coming to or leaving from that country? Why?

Preparing to read

BUILDING BACKGROUND KNOWLEDGE OF THE TOPIC

Below is part of a poem that is on the Statue of Liberty in New York. Many American school children learn it. The poet, Emma Lazarus, wrote this in 1883, when many immigrants were coming to the United States from Europe. In the poem, the Statue of Liberty is speaking to the countries the immigrants came from. Some of the words will be new and difficult; it is not important to know all of them. You can understand the ideas in the poem by reading the words that you do know, such as *poor, tired,* and *free.*

1 Underline the words in the poem that you know.

> Give me your tired, your poor,
> Your huddled masses yearning to breathe free,
> The wretched refuse of your teeming shore,
> Send these, the homeless, tempest-tossed to me,
> I lift my lamp beside the golden door!

The Statue of Liberty

2 In a small group, discuss these questions about the poem:

1 Who are the "huddled masses"?
2 What is the "golden door"?
3 What is the Statue of Liberty saying about the immigrants? Is her message positive or negative? Explain.

3 Now discuss these questions:

1 Do you think all Americans felt the same way as Emma Lazarus in 1883? Do you think everyone welcomed the "huddled masses"? Why or why not? (Review "A Country of Immigrants" on page 63 if necessary.)
2 Why do you think that different Americans might have different responses to immigrants?

Now read

Now read the text "Not Always Welcome." When you finish, turn to the tasks on page 70.

➡ Remember to review and update your vocabulary notebook.

4 NOT ALWAYS WELCOME

Immigrants have come to the United States in search of freedom and opportunity, and many immigrants have found them. However, from around the middle of the nineteenth century, immigrants also began to face hostility from people already living in the United States. Two immigrant groups who faced particular hardships were the Chinese and the Irish.

In the nineteenth century, one of the largest groups of immigrants was the Chinese. Many Chinese came as miners when gold was discovered in California in 1849. Often they were treated badly by other miners; some were the victims of violence. The government did not do much to protect them. Chinese people also worked in the construction of the Transcontinental Railroad. This was a huge project that connected the middle of the country to California by railroad. Most of the workers – more than 12,000 of them – were Chinese. They did the most dangerous work, yet they received far lower pay than white workers. Many workers were injured or died. White workers were angry because the Chinese worked for such low wages. Americans also found Chinese customs strange and foreign. For these reasons, the Chinese often became the victims of **discrimination**.

discrimination
| different (usually worse) treatment based on race, ethnicity, sex, or age

The Chinese were not the only group that experienced discrimination. On the East Coast, one of the largest groups of immigrants was the Irish; they were also victims of discrimination. Between 1846 and 1880, nearly two million of them arrived. Most were escaping a terrible economic situation in Ireland, yet when they arrived in the United States, they also faced difficult conditions. Many immigrants were sick and weak after the long, hard journey. Living conditions were crowded, with up to 10 people sleeping in one room. Because so many new immigrants arrived at the same time, they could not all find jobs. Men usually worked as **manual laborers**, for example, building homes, cleaning streets, or working in mines. The work was difficult and sometimes dangerous, and the pay was low. Women worked as servants in American homes or they worked in factories, sewing clothes up to 14 hours a day. As with the Chinese, many Americans believed the Irish were taking away their jobs. Some also believed that this large group of immigrants would be a problem for the rest of the population because they needed government services: schools, running water, and police protection. Many Americans believed that the Irish were dirty, stupid, and lazy. Discrimination against them became common and accepted. Many businesses would not hire Irish workers or would offer them lower pay than other workers. Some restaurants and bars had signs that said, "No Irish Allowed."

manual laborers
| people who do hard, physical work

Each new group of immigrants that comes to the United States faces its own challenges. Latin Americans, Asians, and Africans are the immigrants whose appearance and culture differ the most from the majority, that is, white Americans of European background. Therefore, they are the immigrants who most frequently face anti-immigrant hostility and discrimination. Often the reasons are the same as they have been throughout history: competition for jobs and resources as well as misunderstanding of new and different cultures. It is important to remember, however, that the conditions and opportunities that the immigrants encountered when they arrived in the United States were often better than those they left in their home countries.

The song "No Irish Need Apply" was written during the time when many Irish were immigrating to the United States. It is frequently claimed that businesses hung signs on their doors that said "No Irish Need Apply" so that no Irish would apply for jobs. Historians today say that this probably did not happen often. However, the song is a good example of the strong anti-Irish feeling at the time.

Chinese were often shown as "the bad guys" in cheap detective novels.

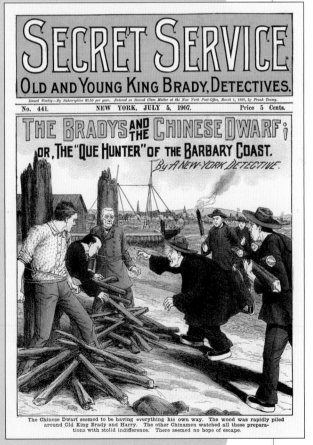

After you read

Task 1 HIGHLIGHTING

> One way to remember what you have read is to highlight important information.

According to the texts "A Country of Immigrants" (page 63) and "Not Always Welcome" (page 68), the three items below are the main reasons for the hostility toward new immigrants. Using a different color for each, highlight evidence from the texts that supports these three main reasons. Then compare your work in a small group.

1 Competition for work
2 The need for increased government services and resources
3 Cultural differences or misunderstandings

Task 2 BUILDING VOCABULARY: USING A DICTIONARY

> Sometimes you will not be able to figure out the meaning of a word, and you will have to look it up in a dictionary. Some words have more than one definition. It is important to choose the right definition for the context.

1 | Read the three definitions below for the noun *service*, which appears in the text in its plural form (par. 3). Circle the number of the definition that fits the sentence in the text.

1 service (noun): the help provided to a customer by someone who works in a restaurant or store
The service in this restaurant is terrible – I've been waiting 15 minutes.

2 service (noun): a system, organization, or business that provides for a public need
There is bus service to the airport every 20 minutes.

3 service (noun): a formal religious ceremony
The wedding service is at 3:00 p.m. on Saturday.

2 | Check (✔) the reason(s) below that helped you choose a definition in step 1.

_____ 1 The things listed in the sentence – schools, running water, and police protection – are public needs.

_____ 2 The other meanings did not make sense.

_____ 3 The things listed in the sentence – schools, running water, and police protection – are similar to the bus example.

_____ 4 Other (explain) _____

3 Make a list of three to six words from the text that are new to you. Look up these words in a dictionary, such as the *Cambridge Dictionary of American English*. (This dictionary is also available online at http://dictionary.cambridge.org/results.asp?dict=A.) Remember to put new words and their definitions in your vocabulary notebook.

Task 3 BUILDING VOCABULARY: COLLOCATIONS

> Collocations are combinations of words that often occur together. The more you are aware of collocations, the easier reading becomes.

1 Underline each use of *victim(s) of* and *face* in the text. Try to figure out the meaning of these words from the context.

2 In the chart below, write the nouns in the text that collocate with *victim of* and *face*. (You will find one noun that is appropriate for both.)

victim of	face
1.	1.
2.	2.
	3.
	4.
	5.

3 Decide what the words in each list in step 2 have in common. Then cross out the words in the chart below that you think will not collocate with *victim of* or *face*.

victim of		face	
cancer	a bombing	many dangers	great happiness
a $1000 prize	a robbery	a threat	a difficult decision
war	a scholarship	fun	a major battle

4 Continue each sentence below with an appropriate word from the chart in step 3. Then complete each sentence by giving a reason or explanation.

1 He was a victim of _____.

2 They faced _____.

Task 4 THINKING ABOUT THE TOPIC

With a partner or group, discuss the following question: Do you know of other countries where immigrants have experienced problems? Explain where the immigrants came from, why they weren't welcome, and what problem(s) they had.

UNIT 2 WRITING ASSIGNMENT A

In this chapter, you have read about the origins of ethnic diversity in the United States. You have learned about the struggles of Native Americans, enslaved Africans, and immigrants. Although the experiences of each of these groups were different, they all faced many hardships. Your assignment is to write a paragraph that describes the similarities in their experiences.

Preparing to write

1 | Make a chart like the one below. Use a whole page for your chart so that you have plenty of room to write in the boxes. Fill in the chart with information from the four texts in this chapter that shows evidence of the hardships stated in the chart headings. One example has been done for you. You will not have information for every box. For some boxes, you may have more than one piece of evidence.

Hardships			
	Discrimination against this group at work	Violence against this group	Cultural misunder-standings between this group and Americans	Other
Native Americans				
Enslaved Africans				
Chinese	*lower pay than Americans*			
Irish				

2 | In a small group, discuss the hardships that each group of people faced. Fill in your chart with any new information and ideas you get from the discussion.

3 | Choose two hardships for which you have evidence for at least two groups of people. Your paragraph will be about the similarities in the experiences of these groups.

Now write

1 Write a sentence to introduce the first hardship. Here are some sample sentences:

- *One problem that ethnic and immigrant groups faced was . . .*
- *They all/Many of them were forced to . . .*
- *There was/were . . . against ethnic and immigrant groups.*

2 Write sentences that give specific examples of the first hardship for at least two groups of people. Use the notes from your chart to help you.

3 Write a sentence to introduce the second hardship. Here are some sample sentences:

- *Another similarity across these groups was . . .*
- *Another problem that these groups had was . . .*
- *They all/Many of them also had bad experiences with . . .*

4 Write sentences that give specific examples of the second hardship for at least two groups of people. Use your chart to help you.

5 Now write a topic sentence to introduce the whole paragraph. You can begin like this:

In the nineteenth century, ethnic and immigrant groups . . .

6 Put your paragraph together. Begin with your topic sentence for the whole paragraph (step 5). Then introduce and explain the two hardships you have chosen (steps 1–4).

After you write

1 Exchange paragraphs with a partner. Discuss the following questions about your paragraphs:

1 What are the two hardships your partner chose?

a _____

b _____

2 Is each hardship introduced with a clear, appropriate sentence?

3 Is the topic sentence of the paragraph clear and appropriate?

2 Discuss any suggestions you have for how your partner could improve his or her paragraph.

3 Although these groups all faced hardships, some of them experienced much more serious hardships than others. As a class, discuss which group of people faced the most serious hardships. Why?

Preparing to read

INCREASING YOUR READING SPEED

Academic courses often require a lot of reading. However, there is not always time to read every text slowly and carefully. Reading speed can be as important as reading comprehension. Here are some strategies for increasing your reading speed:

- Read the text straight through. Do not go back to any parts of it.
- Do not stop to look up any words.
- Skip over words you do not know if they do not seem too important.
- Try to guess the meaning of words that seem important.
- Slow down a little to understand important parts such as definitions and main ideas.

1 Read the text "America's Increasingly Diverse Face" using the techniques described above. Before you begin, fill in your starting time. For this task, do not read Table 4.1 on page 76.

Starting time: _____

2 Fill in the time you finished.

Finishing time: _____

Then calculate your reading speed:
Number of words in the text (530) ÷
Number of minutes it took you to
read the text = your Reading Speed

Reading speed: _____

Your reading speed = the number of words you can read per minute.

3 Check your reading comprehension by trying to answer these questions without looking at the text.

1 What are two recent changes in the immigrant population of the United States?

2 In what way have the changes affected Americans' lives and culture?

3 Give one or two arguments for continued high rates of immigration. Give one or two arguments against the continued high immigration rates.

Now read

Now read the text "America's Increasingly Diverse Face" again. Then check your answers to step 3 above. When you finish, turn to the tasks on page 77.

Diversity in Today's United States

Chapter 4

1 AMERICA'S INCREASINGLY DIVERSE FACE

The 2000 census shows that the United States is more racially and 1
ethnically diverse than at any time in its history. Some school districts
report that they serve immigrant children coming from more than 150
different countries and speaking dozens of different languages. Today,
immigrants do not just go to the traditional immigrant cities on the
coasts, like New York, Miami, Los Angeles, and San Francisco. They
also go to the suburbs and to smaller towns and cities in states like
Georgia, Iowa, Colorado, and North Carolina.

This growing diversity is partly the result of a change in national 2
policy. A 1965 immigration law made it easier to immigrate from places

other than Europe. Since that time, there has been a sharp increase in immigration from Latin America and Asia. Currently, the largest numbers of immigrants come from Mexico, followed by India and the Philippines (see Table 4.1). A new immigrant arrives in the United States every 31 seconds, and approximately 12 percent of everyone now living in the United States was born in another country. Although this is higher than 30 years ago, when the percentage was just under five, it is lower than during the first decades of the twentieth century, when it was closer to 15 percent.

3 In the decade between 1990 and 2000, the U.S. population grew by more than 32 million. Immigration contributed significantly to this growth. The large immigrant presence affects the way the country looks, feels, and sounds. According to the 2000 census, whites are now a minority in half of the nation's 100 largest cities. Latino stars like Jennifer Lopez and Salma Hayek are popular across the entire country. Alex Rodriguez, whose parents were born in the Dominican Republic, is one of America's most famous baseball players. In 2005, the National Basketball Association listed 82 team members from 36 countries playing for the NBA, including the popular Chinese player, Yao Ming, of the Houston Rockets. Thousands of Americans watch Korean television programs. Pharmacies have Chinese medicines on their shelves, and Hindu temples and Muslim mosques are common in many cities and suburbs. Mexican tacos and Greek gyros are almost as popular as hamburgers, Chinese bubble tea competes with milk shakes, and Americans eat more salsa than ketchup.

4 Although America is a country of immigrants, Americans have always had mixed feelings about new immigrants, and this trend continues today. Critics strongly oppose the continued high immigration rate. They claim that immigrants take jobs away from Americans and keep wages low; they argue that immigrants use too many expensive public resources, such as medical services and schools. Supporters of immigration say that many immigrants provide the technological skills that the nation needs. Some of the country's most familiar Internet businesses, such as Yahoo, Hotmail, and eBay, were started by people from other countries. Other immigrants do low-paid work that most Americans do not want, such as picking fruit, cleaning offices, and taking care of the elderly. Supporters also point out that new immigrants contribute to society just as the immigrant grandparents of many Americans did: They increase the nation's productivity and quality of life by buying homes, starting new businesses, and paying taxes.

Table 4.1

Legal Immigration to the United States by country of origin in 2003

Country	Number of immigrants
Mexico	114,984
India	47,157
Philippines	43,258
China	42,415
El Salvador	27,915
Dominican Republic	26,157
Vietnam	21,270
Canada	16,555
Colombia	14,455
Russia	14,286
Guatemala	14,222
Korea	12,177
Haiti	11,948
Ukraine	10,899

Source: 2003 Yearbook of Immigration Statistics.

After you read

Task 1 SCANNING

> Remember that scanning is looking quickly through a text to find specific words or information. You will often need to do this when you study for a test or prepare to write an assignment.

Scan the text, including Table 4.1, to answer the following questions:

1 What percentage of American residents today were born in another country? Is this higher or lower than 100 years ago?
2 Where do the largest number of immigrants to the United States come from today?
3 What was the increase in population between 1990 and 2000?
4 In 2003, how many countries sent more than 20,000 immigrants to the United States?
5 How do immigrants add to American productivity?

Task 2 LANGUAGE FOCUS: REDUCED ADJECTIVE CLAUSES

> Adjective clauses describe nouns or noun phrases. These clauses begin with *that, which,* or *who*.
>
> noun   adjective clause
> There has been an increase in the number of *people* **who live in large cities**.
>
> noun   adjective clause
> The experience of *immigrants* **who come to the United States** has changed since the early twentieth century.
>
> Adjective clauses can be reduced to phrases that begin with an *-ing* word. Reduced adjective clauses are common in academic texts, so you should become familiar with them.
>
>   reduced
> noun   adjective clause
> There has been an increase in the number of *people* **living in large cities**.
>
> noun   reduced adjective clause
> The experience of *immigrants* **coming to the United States** has changed since 1900.

1 In the sentences below, the noun or noun phrase is in bold. Underline the reduced adjective clause that describes the noun or noun phrase. Then rewrite each reduced adjective clause so that it is a full adjective clause. The first one has been done for you.

1 Some school districts are struggling to serve **immigrant children** <u>speaking dozens of different languages</u>. *(who speak dozens of different languages.)*

2 Approximately 12 percent of **the people** living in the United States were born in another country.

3 There are **82 international team members** playing for the NBA.

4 **Many people** working in high technology companies were born in other countries.

5 **Immigrants** hoping for economic opportunity began arriving in the American colonies in the seventeenth century.

2 Underline the reduced adjective clauses in the following sentences. Then complete the sentences by providing your own advice.

1 Students taking important exams should . . .

2 People learning a second language should . . .

3 Tourists visiting (<u>fill in a country or city of your choice</u>) should . . .

4 People earning more than 1 million dollars a year should . . .

Task 3 THINKING ABOUT THE TOPIC

With a partner or small group, discuss the following questions:

1 In the early twentieth century, Americans usually described their country as a *melting pot*. Today, Americans often describe their country as a *salad bowl* or a *patchwork quilt*. What do you think each of these terms means? Why do you think Americans don't use the term *melting pot* anymore?

melting pot   salad bowl   patchwork quilt[3]

2 Do you think increasing diversity in the United States is positive, negative, or both? Explain.

3 Do you think the trend toward increasing diversity in the United States will continue? What might cause it to stop?

---

3 The art on the cover of this book is a patchwork quilt. Read about it in the photographic and illustration credits on page 240.

Preparing to read

EXAMINING GRAPHIC MATERIAL

1 This text is about Latinos, the largest minority group (a group other than the white majority) in the country. The terms *Latinos* and *Hispanics* are used to describe people who have come from Spanish-speaking countries. These terms are sometimes used interchangeably; in general, the word *Hispanics* is often preferred in government publications. With a partner, study the map of the United States below. Then discuss the following question: What part of the country has the highest percentage of Latinos? Why do you think this is true?

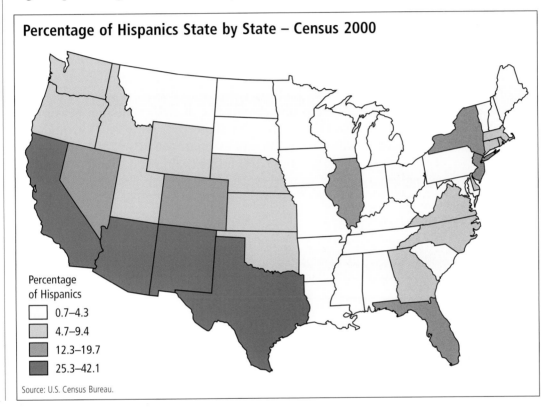

Percentage of Hispanics State by State – Census 2000

Percentage of Hispanics
- 0.7–4.3
- 4.7–9.4
- 12.3–19.7
- 25.3–42.1

Source: U.S. Census Bureau.

2 With your partner, study Figure 4.1 in the text on page 80. What trend does it describe?

Now read

Now read the text "Latinos: The Country's Largest Minority Group." When you finish, turn to the tasks on page 82.

2 LATINOS: THE COUNTRY'S LARGEST MINORITY GROUP

Figures from the 2000 census show that Latinos (Hispanics) are now the nation's largest minority group: 12.5 percent of the population. According to the census, the number of Latinos is now more than 35 million. Between 1990 and 2000, the number of Latinos increased by 58 percent, a rate that is seven times the rate of growth for the rest of the population. In 1990, Latinos represented 18 percent of all foreign-born residents; one decade later, that figure increased to 42 percent. Some of this increase is a result of a high birth rate, but about 40 percent of the increase is due to immigration. Cities with large Latino populations have traditionally been on the coasts: Miami, Los Angeles, and New York, but now at least 28 cities across the country have growing Latino populations of more than 100,000. Some states, such as North Carolina and Georgia, had increases of 300 percent or more between 1990 and 2000. Latinos do not only live in cities. The number of farms owned by Latinos grew more than 50 percent between 1997 and 2002. The United States Census Bureau estimates that by 2050, the number of Latinos will be more than 100 million, almost a quarter of the U.S. population.

1

Latino influence

The increasing number of Latinos is causing cultural, economic, and political change. Perhaps the most obvious influence is in popular culture. Many styles of Latin music are popular throughout the country. Mexican food is a favorite on dinner tables and in restaurants. The economic and political influence of the growing Latino community is also very important. Businesses are beginning to understand the enormous buying power of this group – almost $1 trillion annually. The Latino population is young; the median age is 26.7, almost 10 years younger than the median age of the general population. Businesses are working hard to earn dollars from these young Latinos. Today customers can use a bank machine or make an airline reservation in Spanish. The number of Latino radio and television stations rises every year. Politicians are also working hard to win Latino votes. President George W. Bush often used Spanish in his campaign speeches, and many political analysts believe that Latino voters were an important factor in his victories.

2

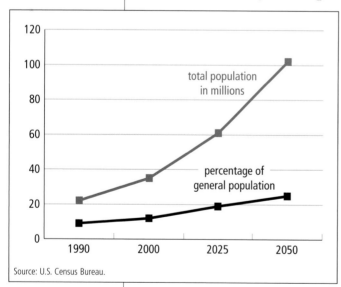

Source: U.S. Census Bureau.

Figure 4.1 Projected growth in Hispanic population

The importance of Spanish

The Spanish language is becoming very important. Many businesses ₃ are looking for Spanish-speaking employees, especially in areas of the country with large Latino communities. Many of them advertise in Spanish as well. Spanish is the most widely studied second language in schools and universities across the country. More than three quarters of a million college students study Spanish every year, an increase of almost 100 percent in 25 years. Spanish expressions such as *¿Qué pasa?* (What's up?) and *loco* (crazy) have become part of the American vocabulary.

The mural tradition

Murals (paintings on walls and buildings) are a tradition in Latin-American culture. The tradition goes back to the time before Columbus and has been an important form of artistic expression, particularly in Mexico. Mexicans have brought this tradition with them to the American cities in which they now live, and it has spread to other Latino communities across the country. In San Francisco, Los Angeles, New York, El Paso, and in many other cities, there are murals painted by Latino artists. Murals are painted for the community, and so they are painted in places where everyone can see them. The themes of the murals include memories of the old country and culture, Latino heroes and history, religious images, and the need for equality for Latino Americans.

After you read

Task 1 TEST TAKING: ANSWERING TRUE/FALSE QUESTIONS

One common question type on tests is the true/false question. Here are some strategies for answering this type of question:

- Most tests with true/false questions have an approximately equal number of true statements and false statements.
- Be careful of statements with negatives in them. These can be confusing. Remember that a negative statement that is correct is true.
- Be careful of statements containing words like *never, always, only,* and *all.* These are often false.
- Statements containing words like *often, many,* and *sometimes* are often true.

1 | Based on the information in the map on page 79 and the text, including Figure 4.1, write *T* (True) or *F* (False) in the blank before each statement.

_____ 1 According to the 2000 census, the highest number of Hispanics is in the southwestern part of the United States.

_____ 2 The 2000 census showed that Texas has more Hispanics than California.

_____ 3 Latinos spend more than $700 billion per year.

_____ 4 Immigration is the reason for more than half of the increase in the Latino population.

_____ 5 The median age of the American population is between 25 and 30.

_____ 6 The Hispanic population will grow faster between now and 2050 than it did between 1990 and 2000.

_____ 7 During the period 1990–2000, the Latino population in Georgia grew by about 100 percent.

_____ 8 The Spanish language is widely studied in the United States.

2 | Next to your answer for each statement in step 1, show where you found the information: Map, Figure 4.1, or Text. (Include the paragraph number of the text.)

Task 2 NOTE TAKING: USING AN OUTLINE

Using an outline can be an effective way to take notes. In this method, numbers and letters show relationships between parts of the text.

1 | Make an outline like the one on the following page. Complete it with the main idea and supporting evidence for each paragraph. Add lines to your outline (*C, D,* etc.) if necessary. Use your own words as much as possible.

Latinos: The Country's Largest Minority Group

I. *There has been a big increase in the Latino population in the United States since 1990.* _____ (par. 1 main idea)

   A. _____ (par. 1 evidence)

   B. _____ (par. 1 evidence)

II. _____ (par. 2 main idea)

   A. _____ (par. 2 evidence)

   B. _____ (par. 2 evidence)

III. _____ (par. 3 main idea)

   A. *Many businesses want Spanish-speaking employees.* (par. 3 evidence)

   B. _____ (par. 3 evidence)

2 Compare your answers with a partner's.

Task 3 LANGUAGE FOCUS: THE *-ING* FORM OF THE VERB AS AN ADJECTIVE

The *-ing* form of the verb frequently appears as an adjective that tells what the noun is doing.

	adjective (-*ing* form of verb)	**noun**	
A	**crying**	child	is a child that is crying.
The	**rising**	sun	is the sun that is rising.

1 The sentences below are from the text. They each include an *-ing* form of a verb used as an adjective. Circle the adjective and underline the noun or noun phrase that it describes.

  1 At least 28 cities across the country have growing Latino populations.

  2 The increasing number of Latinos is causing cultural, economic, and political change.

  3 Many businesses are looking for Spanish-speaking employees.

2 The sentences below all contain the *-ing* form of the verb. Change each sentence to a phrase with an *-ing* adjective that describes the word in bold.

  1 America's **population** is changing. → *America's changing population* _____

  2 The **popularity** of Mexican food is rising. → _____

  3 The **ethnic diversity** is increasing in the United States. → _____

  4 The **economic influence of the Latino community** is growing. → _____

Preparing to read

SKIMMING: FIRST SENTENCES, GRAPHIC MATERIALS, AND ART

> When you skim a text, it is helpful to look at any graphic materials, such as tables or graphs, and at any art, such as photographs or illustrations.

1 | Skim the text by reading the first sentence in every paragraph, looking at Table 4.2, and looking at the photographs and their captions.

2 | Without looking at the text again, make notes about what you remember.

3 | Compare your notes with a partner.

BUILDING BACKGROUND KNOWLEDGE OF THE TOPIC

With a partner, do the activities below. They concern two terms related to illegal immigration that you may not know: *coyote* and *smuggling*.

1 | Read this definition of *coyote*, a kind of animal:

A *coyote* is a small, wild, dog-like animal that is known for its cleverness and fierce behavior. Coyotes live throughout the United States and Mexico.

In the context of immigration, the word *coyote* is used to refer to a person. What kind of person do you think this would be? Why would this type of person be mentioned in a text about illegal immigration?

2 | Look up the word *smuggling* in a dictionary. Then discuss what you think the term *human smuggling* means.

Now read

Now read the text "The Undocumented: Illegal Immigrants." Then review your notes from "Skimming: First Sentences, Graphic Materials, and Art" to see how much you understood when you skimmed. When you finish, turn to the tasks on page 87.

3 THE UNDOCUMENTED: ILLEGAL IMMIGRANTS

In order to live and work in the United States, noncitizens need a special visa. It is difficult to get this kind of visa. Usually they are only given to people with special skills or those with family already in the country. Even these people must wait a long time for permission to come to the United States. For those who have little hope of getting this kind of visa, entering the country illegally may seem like the only choice. Between 10 and 12 million people are living in the United States illegally. The number of illegal residents – sometimes called **undocumented** residents – increases by between 350,000 and 500,000 every year. About 70 percent come from Mexico; most others come from other parts of Latin America and from Asia.

The main reason illegal immigrants come is for jobs. They are willing to do work that pays very little – on farms, in restaurants, and in clothing factories. Many undocumented women care for children or the elderly; many undocumented men work as gardeners or in home repair and construction. For some illegal immigrants, even a job that pays below the **minimum wage** seems like a good opportunity. A recent study showed that many illegal immigrants had jobs in their home countries, but they could not support their families on their wages. They come to the United States for jobs that pay better so they can send money home to their families. It is estimated that five percent of the American workforce is undocumented.

Companies hire undocumented workers because they cost less than legal residents. Because they are undocumented, the workers are afraid to complain if their pay is low, if they are treated badly, or if they are fired. Furthermore, the companies often do not give them **benefits** like health insurance. All of this helps to lower the cost of doing business and makes undocumented workers seem like a good idea to many business owners.

Illegal immigrants take great risks during their journey to the United States. The main route for entering the United States illegally is through the desert across the U.S.–Mexico border. This route has always been dangerous, but since September 11, 2001, the nation has increased security at its borders and crossing illegally has become even more difficult and dangerous. People trying to enter the country through Mexico frequently hire a *coyote* – the term they use for a human smuggler. Business for coyotes has grown dramatically in recent years. In 2003, these smugglers moved about 1 million illegal immigrants from nearly 100 countries across the border. The human-smuggling industry earned $9.5 billion that year, according to immigration officials. Many illegal immigrants have died trying to cross

1

2

3

4

undocumented
| without correct legal papers (documents), that is, papers that prove citizenship or legal residency

minimum wage
| the lowest hourly rate of pay allowed by law

Table 4.2

Country of Origin	Estimated number of illegal immigrants in the United States
Mexico	4,808,000
El Salvador	189,000
Guatemala	144,000
Colombia	141,000
Honduras	138,000
China	115,000
Ecuador	108,000
Dominican Republic	91,000
Philippines	85,000
Brazil	77,000

Source: 2002 Yearbook of Immigration Statistics.

benefits
| payments or services provided for workers in addition to their wages

into the United States. Some tried crossing alone, but got lost and died. Others died of thirst, hunger, heat, or cold when coyotes abandoned them in the desert or in locked railroad cars or trucks. More than 2,500 people died between 1997 and 2004 in attempts to enter the United States illegally.

Once they are in the United States, there are more challenges and risks for undocumented immigrants. They do not have the same legal protection that documented immigrants and citizens have. They cannot complain if they are treated badly. They live with the fear that they will be caught and sent home. Illegal immigrants can also cause problems for the communities where they live. These immigrants need health care, education, and all of the same services that other residents need. Providing these services is expensive, which makes some Americans angry. Some Americans also believe that illegal immigrants take jobs away from citizens and keep wages low. They would like to see better control of the nation's borders. They want strong laws to punish businesses that hire undocumented workers. Some also want laws that punish the immigrants or even the Americans who help them, for example, people who offer food and water to immigrants trying to enter the country or teachers or doctors who help them after they arrive. 5

Although the subject of illegal immigration is controversial, most people agree that as long as there are more jobs and opportunities in the United States than in immigrants' home countries, immigrants will try to enter the country illegally. 6

From *The Devil's Highway,* a novel by Luis Urrea

Five men stumbled out of the mountain pass so sunstruck they didn't know their own names, couldn't remember where they'd come from, had forgotten how long they'd been lost. One of them wandered back up a peak. One of them was barefoot. They were burned nearly black, their lips huge and cracking. . . .

After you read

Task 1 READING LITERATURE ABOUT A TOPIC

Sometimes in academic courses, you may be required to read a work of literature about a topic. Literature is an important part of historical and cultural studies.

Reread the excerpt from the novel *The Devil's Highway* in the boxed text on page 86. You probably don't know all the words, but try to understand the general idea of the excerpt. Then discuss these questions with a partner or in a small group:

1 Who do you think the people described in this excerpt are?
2 What details in the excerpt helped you answer question 1?
3 How did the information in the main text help you understand the excerpt?
4 What can you learn from this excerpt that you can't learn from the main text?

Task 2 THINKING ABOUT THE TOPIC

Discuss the following questions with your partner or group:

1 Do you think it is possible to stop illegal immigration? Why or why not?
2 Is illegal immigration an issue in other countries that you know? If so, what is the government doing about it? Explain.
3 Do you think the current illegal immigration trends in the United States will continue? Why or why not?

Task 3 LANGUAGE FOCUS: WRITING ABOUT HISTORICAL TRENDS

Two tenses that are commonly used to describe historical trends are the present perfect (*have* + past participle) and the simple past (*-ed*).

Use the **present perfect** if:

• There is no specific time reference and the trend may continue.
  Production of laptop computers **has doubled**.

• Only the starting point is given and the trend may continue.
  Production of laptop computers **has doubled** since 1990.

  Note: The preposition *since* requires the use of the present perfect.

Use the **simple past** if a specific time period is given, and that time period is over.
  Production of laptop computers **doubled** last year.

1 The chart below contains sentences from the text. Fill in the chart for each sentence. In the tense column, write *PP* (Present Perfect) or *P* (Simple Past).

	Tense	Time period	Is the time period over?
1a. Since September 11, 2001, the nation has increased security at its borders . . .	*PP*	*September 11, 2001 – present*	*No*
1b. . . . and crossing illegally has become even more difficult and dangerous.			
2. Business for coyotes has grown dramatically in recent years.			
3. In 2003, these smugglers moved about 1 million illegal immigrants from nearly 100 countries across the border.			
4. The human-smuggling industry earned $9.5 billion that year [2003], according to immigration officials.			
5. Many illegal immigrants have died trying to cross into the United States . . .			
6. More than 2,500 people died between 1997 and 2004 in attempts to enter the United States illegally.			

2 Read the facts below about immigration today. Then complete the sentences. (In some cases, you will have to do a little math.)

1 In 2003, there were about 8 million illegal immigrants in the United States. It is estimated that this number increases by about 500,000 every year.
Since 2003, _____
_____.

2 In 2000, about 250,000 Mexicans entered the country illegally. Approximately 250,000 more arrive every year.
Since 2000, _____
_____.

3 In the 1990 census, it was estimated that about half of all illegal immigrants lived in California. Estimates for today are about 33 percent.
Since the 1990 census, _____
_____.

Preparing to read

THINKING ABOUT THE TOPIC BEFORE YOU READ

1 You are going to read a text that discusses the languages spoken in the United States. Read the statements below, and decide whether they are true or false. Base your answers on what you have read in the previous texts in this book and your own ideas. Write *T* (True) or *F* (False) in each blank.

_____ **1** The official language of the United States is English.

_____ **2** You can take a driving test in a language other than English in some American cities.

_____ **3** Some states have an official language.

_____ **4** Many state and city governments provide services in languages other than English.

_____ **5** New immigrants do not learn English.

_____ **6** You must know English in order to vote in elections.

_____ **7** The grandchildren of immigrants often speak only English.

_____ **8** The two most widely spoken languages in the United States, other than English, are German and French.

2 Discuss these questions in a small group or as a class:

1 What percentage of people in the United States do you think speak English?

2 Do you think it is a problem to have more than one language in a country? Why or why not?

3 Is there more than one language spoken in any country you are familiar with? Explain the situation to your classmates.

Now read

Now read the text "Linguistic Diversity or English Only?" Then check your answers to the task above. When you finish, turn to the tasks on page 92.

➡ Remember to review and update your vocabulary notebook.

4 LINGUISTIC DIVERSITY OR ENGLISH ONLY?

English is the most widely spoken language in the United States. It is spoken at home by more than 82 percent of the people in the country. However, there is also great linguistic diversity. In other words, many other languages are spoken in communities across the nation. Spanish, which is spoken by more than 28 million people, is the most widely used, but 12 other languages have more than 500,000 speakers (see Figures 4.2 and 4.3). Some languages are widely spoken in specific areas of the country, such as Arabic in Michigan, Polish in Chicago, Vietnamese in Texas, and Korean in southern California.

In many communities across the United States, English is not necessary for daily life. Newcomers can shop for everything from bread to cars in their own language. Many state and local governments also provide services in other languages. Immigrants in Chicago can vote in Spanish, Polish, Chinese, or Korean. In New York, you can take a driver's test in 21 languages. The courts in California provide interpreters for languages from Armenian to Vietnamese. Multilingual government and medical services in many cities and even in smaller towns allow immigrants to go on with their lives in their new country using their own language.

To some Americans, this situation seems unfair and maybe even dangerous. They contend that English is an important factor in national identity. They also maintain that the use of other languages will cause division among different ethnic communities and slow the adjustment of new immigrants. Although the United States has never had an official language, some citizens would like to change this policy. Many states have already passed laws to make English their official state language. These "English-only" laws have usually not been very strong. Most simply require the use of English in all government business. However, English-only supporters now want to go further; they argue that government services in any language other than English should not be permitted. They want to stop the government from spending tax money on education in other languages as well as on any multilingual public services.

Supporters of linguistic diversity believe English-only laws are based on prejudice against ethnic minorities. They claim that these laws force immigrants to give up their own cultural identity to become American. They argue that multilingual services help new immigrants adjust to life in the United States and become productive members of the community. Just as importantly, they maintain that the language skills of

Bilingual signs are common throughout the United States.

immigrants are a great national resource. The ability to speak other languages is important for economic growth and national security. Those who support linguistic diversity argue that this resource should not be lost. However, this is exactly what frequently happens. *The New York Times* quotes one scholar who contends that the United States is a "language graveyard." When immigrants arrive in the United States, their children often do not want to speak the language of their parents. They prefer to speak the same language as the children in their schools and neighborhoods – English. They may not pass their home language to their own children. As a result, the grandchildren of many immigrants speak only English.

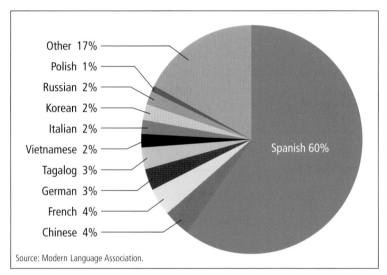

Source: Modern Language Association.

Figure 4.2
Speakers of languages other than English in the United States.

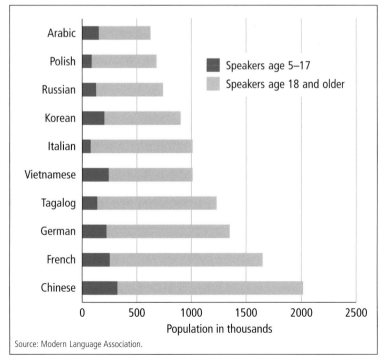

Source: Modern Language Association.

Figure 4.3
Languages spoken in the United States other than English and Spanish, by age of speakers.

After you read

Task 1 THINKING CRITICALLY ABOUT THE TOPIC

Study Figures 4.2 and 4.3 on page 91 and Table 4.1 on page 76. Based on the information in these graphics and the information in the text "Linguistic Diversity or English Only?", discuss the following questions with a partner or small group:

1 Which languages do you think will grow in number of speakers, and which languages will decline?

2 Figure 4.3 shows the percentage of speakers under 18 for each language. Some languages have a larger percentage of young speakers than others. What do you think this means, and why might it be important?

3 How might immigrant languages be important for economic development? For national security?

4 Do you think that language is an important part of cultural identity? Do you think immigrants or minorities lose their cultural identity when they learn the language of the majority?

5 Do you think the government should help immigrant groups keep their cultural identities?

Task 2 LANGUAGE FOCUS: VERBS TO USE INSTEAD OF *SAY* AND *THINK*

If you always use the verbs *say* or *think*, your writing will be repetitive. Some alternatives are *believe, claim, maintain, argue,* and *contend.*

1 Underline examples of alternatives to *say* and *think* in the third and fourth paragraphs of the text, "Linguistic Diversity or English Only?"

2 Review the text, "The Undocumented: Illegal Immigrants" on page 85. Use the information in that text to complete the two opposing arguments about illegal immigration below. Use alternatives to *say* and *think* in your arguments.

a Position 1: It is impossible to stop illegal immigrants from coming to the United States.
Some Americans _argue_ that _we cannot stop illegal immigration_ .
They _____ that illegal immigrants _____ .
They also _____ that _____ .

b Position 2: Illegal immigration must be stopped.
Some Americans _____ that _it is both possible and necessary to limit illegal immigration into the United States_ . These opponents of illegal immigration _____ that undocumented workers _____ .
They also _____ that _____ .

3 Compare your answers to steps 1 and 2 as a class.

UNIT 2   WRITING ASSIGNMENT B

In this unit, you have read about the history of immigration in America. Most Americans are very proud of this history and the multicultural character of their nation. However, many of these same Americans also believe that when new immigrants arrive, they should accept a new American identity. These two attitudes show that many Americans feel *ambivalent* about how diverse and multicultural the country should be. Your assignment is to write a short three-paragraph paper that makes the following claim:

Americans have often been ambivalent about the multicultural character of their nation.

Preparing to write

1 | Look up *ambivalent/ambivalence* in an English dictionary. In a small group, discuss how you think this term applies to the history of immigration and diversity in the United States.

2 | Review the readings in this unit to find supporting information. What are some examples of positive attitudes toward diversity? What are some examples of negative attitudes? Your paper will compare and contrast both attitudes. With a partner, fill in the columns below. One example is done for you. (Make longer columns on a separate piece of paper if necessary.)

Positive attitudes/action	Negative attitudes/action
Pride in ethnic heritage	

Choose two strong examples from each column to write about. You will use these examples to support your claim.

Now write

1 | Write a paragraph about the positive attitudes of Americans toward diversity. Use the examples from step 2 above to support your claim. Here are some possible ways you can begin your topic sentence for this paragraph:

Many Americans . . .
Americans have often been/felt . . .

2 | Write a paragraph about the negative attitudes of Americans toward diversity. Use the examples from step 2 above to support your claim. Here are some possible ways you can begin your topic sentence for your second paragraph:

However, a large number of Americans also . . .
However, Americans have also . . .

3 Write an introductory paragraph that tells the reader what you are going to write about. You can begin your introductory paragraph with this sentence that states your claim:

Americans have often been ambivalent about the multicultural character of their nation.

4 Put all three paragraphs together. The diagram below shows how your paper will look:

Paragraph 1
Americans have often been ambivalent about the multicultural character of their nation.
+
One or two sentences that say what the rest of the paper will be about

↓

Paragraph 2
Topic sentence about positive aspects
+
Two positive examples

↓

Paragraph 3
Topic sentence about negative aspects
+
Two negative examples

After you write

1 Exchange papers with a partner. Discuss the following questions about your papers:

1 Does the first paragraph say what the rest of the paper will be about?

2 Does your partner have good topic sentences for the second and third paragraphs?

3 Does your partner have appropriate, clear examples of the positive side (par. 2)?

4 Does your partner have appropriate, clear examples of the negative side (par. 3)?

2 Discuss any suggestions you have for how your partner could improve his or her paper.

The Struggle
for Equality

In this unit, we look at the idea of equality: how it was viewed in the early days of the nation, how various groups have struggled to achieve it, how it has changed, and how Americans view the concept today. In Chapter 5, we focus on the historical foundations of the struggle for equality, in particular, the struggle of African Americans and women. In Chapter 6, we examine the concept of equality in its current context, especially with regard to groups who are still fighting for equal access and opportunity. We explore how government and society have tried to correct past discrimination and how well they have succeeded.

Previewing the Unit

Read the contents page for Unit 3, and do the following activities.

Chapter 5: The Struggle Begins

In the first chapter of this unit, you are going to read about historical ideas of equality in the United States and some of the effects of these ideas on society.

Discuss the photograph below with a partner or in a small group:

1 What do you think the sign means?

2 When and where do you think the photograph was taken?

3 What do you think the young man might be thinking?

Chapter 6: The Struggle Continues

In the second chapter of this unit, you are going to read about modern ideas of equality and the continuing and new issues in the struggle for equality.

1 | Take this survey about equality. Decide how much you agree or disagree with each statement. You can base your answers on the United States or another country you know well. For each statement, check (✔) the appropriate box.

1 = strongly agree   **5** = strongly disagree

Statements about equality	1	2	3	4	5
1. Everyone is equal at birth.					
2. Everyone has an equal chance of success.					
3. Everyone is treated equally by the government.					
4. Everyone is treated equally in the educational system.					
5. Everyone is treated equally at work.					

2 | Compare your survey results in a small group. Discuss the similarities and differences. What are some of the reasons for the similarities and differences?

Unit Contents 3

Preparing to read

THINKING ABOUT THE TOPIC BEFORE YOU READ

The Declaration of Independence was written in 1776, when the United States was founded. The words in the title of the text you are going to read are the most famous words in the Declaration: "all men are created equal."

Discuss these questions with a partner:

1 What do you think the authors of the Declaration of Independence meant by "all men are created equal"?
2 What does the term *equality* mean to you?
3 Do you think the meaning of *equality* can change?

BUILDING BACKGROUND KNOWLEDGE OF THE TOPIC

1 Read this passage about Thomas Jefferson's ideas.

Thomas Jefferson

Thomas Jefferson wrote the Declaration of Independence. He based the Declaration on the idea of *natural rights,* that is, rights that we have because we are human beings, rights that no government can take away. Such rights include the right to live and to be free. Jefferson believed the government's most important purpose is to protect these natural rights.

In 1801, Jefferson became the third President of the United States.

2 Discuss these questions with your partner:

1 How are Jefferson's ideas connected to the phrase "all men are created equal"?
2 How do you think Jefferson's ideas about the purpose of government were different from earlier ideas?

Now read

Now read the text "All Men Are Created Equal." When you finish, turn to the tasks on page 101.

The Struggle Begins

 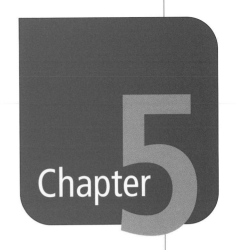
1 ALL MEN ARE CREATED EQUAL

The meaning of equality to the founders of the United States

The idea of equality was essential to the founders of the United States, and it remains important in how Americans view themselves and their nation today. But what did the term *equality* really mean when the nation began? The most famous lines in the Declaration of Independence, written in 1776, are:

> *We hold these truths to be self-evident, that all men are created equal, that they are endowed by their Creator with certain unalienable Rights, that among these are Life, Liberty and the pursuit of Happiness.*[4]

In simpler, more modern language this means:

> *It is clear that all men are equal at birth. God gives them certain rights that no one can take away: the right to live, the right to be free, and the right to try to have a life that will make them happy.*

This idea was revolutionary in 1776, when many people believed that there was a natural inequality in society: Some people were born rich

1

2

3

4

---

4 You can see a copy of the Declaration of Independence in Jefferson's handwriting at http://www.loc.gov/exhibits/treasures/trt001.html

and powerful, others were born poor, and there was not much that people could do to change their place in society.

Thomas Jefferson, who wrote the Declaration of Independence, [5] and the other founders of the United States, rejected this view. They brought together ideas from many different sources including French philosophers and Native-American tribes that had democratic systems of government. In 1789, the Constitution made the democratic idea of "one man–one vote" the law of the land. However, this view of equality did not include everyone. When the Declaration of Independence and the Constitution were written, "men" did not mean "people." It did not include women, enslaved Africans, or Native Americans.

The meaning of equality after the U.S. Civil War

Almost 100 years after the Declaration of Independence, the United [6] States fought a **civil war** that involved the issue of equality. Although most people in the North probably did not believe that white and black people are truly equal, many rejected the idea of slavery. However, the economy of the southern states depended on slaves, and most southerners supported slavery. The disagreements between the North and the South finally resulted in a civil war that began in 1861 and ended in 1865 with victory for the North.

civil war

a war between groups of people living in the same country

President Abraham Lincoln at Gettysburg

In 1863, at a service in Gettysburg, Penn- [7] sylvania, to dedicate a cemetery for northern soldiers, President Abraham Lincoln made one of the most famous speeches in American history, the Gettysburg Address.[5] He reminded the American people of the famous words, "all men are created equal." He stated that "this nation, under God, shall have a new birth of freedom" and asked if the country was ready to keep the promise of the words in the Declaration of Independence.

Could the country accept the idea that all [8] men, regardless of race, are created equal? The country is still struggling to answer Lincoln's question. The Fourteenth Amendment to the Constitution was passed just after the Civil War. It guarantees equal protection of the law to everyone living in the United States. Yet, many Americans still did not receive equal treatment at work, at school, or in the courts. Thus, from the beginning of the nation, the idea of equality has been a cause of controversy, and the fight for equality for all people has been long and difficult.

---

5 You can see a copy of the Gettysburg Address in Lincoln's handwriting at http://www.loc.gov/exhibits/treasures/trt034.html

After you read

Task 1 READING FOR MAIN IDEAS

1| Answer the questions below about the main ideas of the text. Work with your partner from the "Preparing to read" tasks on page 98.

   1 What did the authors of the Declaration of Independence mean by the words *all men are created equal*?

   2 Why was this idea new and different in 1776?

   3 How did the meaning of *equality* change after the Civil War?

   4 Were all people in the United States treated equally after the Civil War?

2| Did any information about equality in the text surprise you? Why or why not?

Task 2 BUILDING VOCABULARY: SUFFIXES THAT CHANGE VERBS AND ADJECTIVES INTO NOUNS

Many verbs and adjectives can be changed to nouns by adding a *suffix,* or ending.

Common suffixes that change verbs into nouns:

      • *-ment*   • *-ation/-ition*

Verb	Noun	Noun
argue	argu*ment*	
define		defin*ition*
establish	establish*ment*	
compete		compe*tition*
celebrate		celeb*ration*

Common suffixes that change adjectives into nouns:

      • *-(i)ty*   • *-ance/-ence*

Adjective	Noun	Noun
diverse	divers*ity*	
ethnic	ethnic*ity*	
minor	minor*ity*	
tolerant		toler*ance*
excellent		excell*ence*

1 The noun forms of these verbs are in the text in the paragraphs indicated. Find the noun form in the text, underline it, and then write it next to the verb below.

1 declare / _____ (par. 1) **4** amend / _____ (par. 8)
2 govern / _____ (par. 5) **5** protect / _____ (par. 8)
3 disagree / _____ (par. 6)

2 Find the noun form of each of these adjectives in the paragraph indicated. Underline it in the text and write it next to the adjective below.

1 equal / _____ (par. 1)   **2** independent / _____ (par. 1)

3 In the following sentences, do nouns, verbs, or adjectives belong in the blanks? The clues in italics can help you make the right choice.

1 The United States has become *more* _____ in the last 20 years. (diverse/diversity)

2 New immigrants make *an important* _____ to society. (contribute/contribution)

3 Many scholars have tried *to* _____ equality. (define/definition)

4 The Fourteenth Amendment guarantees that all people living in the United States receive _____ *treatment*. (equal/equality)

4 Here is a list of word roots from texts in Unit 2. Complete each sentence with the correct word form: verb, noun, or adjective, created from one of these roots. (Be careful to use the correct form of the verb.)

significan-   violen-
punish-   persecut-
hostil-   settle-
popular-

1 In the seventeenth century, most people _____ on the East Coast or along rivers.

2 During the nineteenth century there was _____ against immigrants because they worked for very low wages.

3 Unfortunately, sometimes these negative feelings led to _____ against the new immigrants.

4 There was a _____ increase in immigration between 1880 and 1920.

5 The _____ of Latino music and food in the United States has grown recently, partly because of the increase in the Latino population.

6 Many people still come to the United States to escape _____ in their own countries.

7 Some Americans want the government to _____ businesses that hire illegal immigrants.

5 As a class, discuss the clues that helped you determine the correct word forms in step 4.

Preparing to read

BUILDING VOCABULARY: PREVIEWING KEY TERMS

1 | Working in a small group, review the following words or look them up in a dictionary:

- discriminate / discrimination
- disenfranchise

- segregation / segregated
- separate / separation

2 | Look at the photograph, and discuss the following questions in your group:

1 Which word or words from step 1 describe the situation in the photograph?

2 What is the difference between *separation* and *segregation*?

3 What are some forms of *discrimination* that you are familiar with?

4 What groups in addition to African Americans have been *disenfranchised* in the history of the United States? (Review Chapter 1 to find the answer if necessary.)

The word *colored*, on the sign over the smaller water fountain, was commonly used for African Americans until the 1960s. Today we often use the words *black* or *African American* interchangeably.

3 | The title of the text you are going to read is "The Legacy of the Civil War." Look up the word *legacy* in your dictionary. Then discuss with your group what you think the text will be about.

Now read

Now read the text "The Legacy of the Civil War." When you finish, turn to the tasks on page 106.

2 THE LEGACY OF THE CIVIL WAR

From 1861 to 1865, the American North and South fought a civil war. 1 These two areas of the country had become very different. The North was more industrial; it had a diverse economy, a large middle class, and few slaves. The economy of the South was based mainly on agriculture. The South also had a more unequal social structure, that is, a small upper class and a large class of people on the bottom – poor farmers and slaves. The Southern economy depended heavily on slave labor. As the nation expanded to the west, the interests of the North and South were in conflict. The South wanted to have slavery in the new territories and states; the North did not. Soon the conflicts grew into a war, which lasted four years, destroyed much of the South, and resulted in the death of more than 600,000 Americans, the highest number of any war in American history.

After the Civil War ended with victory for the North, Congress 2 passed the Thirteenth Amendment to the Constitution, freeing all slaves. Then the Fifteenth Amendment gave African-American men the right to vote. For a short time, the lives of African Americans improved. However, the civil and political rights of African Americans were gradually taken away because states in the South began to pass laws that limited these rights. These new laws became known as **Jim Crow laws**.[6] They created a system of segregation and discrimination in the South that continued through the 1960s.

Jim Crow laws affected voting, education, and the use of public 3 facilities. Starting in the 1880s, most Southern states passed laws that disenfranchised African Americans by making them pass **literacy tests** or pay a **voting tax**. Literacy tests required voters to read a text and answer questions about it. Often these texts were very difficult and confusing. Because most African Americans had little or no education at that time, many of them failed the test. The voting tax was one or two dollars. This was equal to several days' wages and was too expensive for many African Americans.

In addition, many southern states passed **grandfather laws**, which 4 stated that anyone with a family member (such as a grandfather) who had voted before 1867 did not have to pass the literacy test or pay voting taxes. This allowed uneducated white voters to avoid these tests and taxes. Because the parents and grandparents of African Americans had been slaves and therefore unable to vote, the grandfather laws prevented many African Americans in the South from voting.

Racial inequality and discrimination were not limited to the South, 5 however; they were common across the nation. Many states had Jim Crow laws requiring whites and African Americans to use segregated public facilities, such as restaurants, waiting rooms in train stations, drinking fountains, and public toilets. On trains and buses, African

---

Jim Crow laws

laws that created a system of segregation and discrimination in the Southern United States after the U.S. Civil War

literacy test

a test that shows if a person can read and write

voting tax

money that has to be paid before you can vote

grandfather laws

laws that allow exceptions to the rule based on past situations

---

6 Jim Crow was the name a popular white comic actor used when he played the character of a poor, uneducated black man. He played the role in a way that made Jim Crow seem stupid.

Americans had to sit in separate sections in the back. Most importantly, African Americans could not go to the same schools as whites. Instead, they went to separate schools for African Americans only. These schools were usually not very good because they did not receive as much money from the government as white schools did. The courts supported these segregation laws. In a famous case in 1896, the Supreme Court ruled that segregation was legal if facilities were "separate but equal."

Finally, there were frequent threats against African Americans, even physical violence, to prevent them from voting and to maintain their low position in society. African Americans who tried to work against this system, even in small ways – for example, by arguing with a white person – might be severely beaten, or worse, *lynched*. A **lynching** is a murder that occurs, usually by hanging, when an angry individual or group decides that someone is guilty of a crime or misbehavior and kills the suspect without a trial. It is estimated that there were almost 5,000 lynchings between 1882 and 1968.

6

lynching
the murder, usually by hanging, of a suspect by an angry individual or group

Madam C. J. Walker

In spite of the hardships, the period between the Civil War and the 1960s was a time of great cultural and artistic activity in the African-American community. There was also an increase in the number of businesses operated by and for African Americans. Madam C. J. Walker ran one of the most successful businesses during this time.

Walker saw a business opportunity in her own community. There were not very many businesses that served African Americans. Her idea was to develop and sell hair-care products that were made specifically for African Americans. Starting in 1905, she went door to door to sell her products. Five years later, she had a factory that provided employment for some 3,000 people. By the time of her death in 1919, Walker was one of the first American women to become a millionaire.

Madam C. J. Walker

After you read

Task 1 READING TO FIND SUPPORT FOR MAIN IDEAS

1 Find and highlight supporting evidence for these ideas in the text. (Be careful; the items below do not follow the order of the text.).

1 Physical violence against African Americans was widespread between 1882 and 1968.
2 The South favored slavery for economic reasons.
3 Separate facilities for blacks and whites were not really equal.
4 Before Madam Walker started her business, there were few products made specifically for African Americans.
5 The end of slavery did not bring equality for Southern blacks.

2 Compare your answers in small groups.

Task 2 BUILDING VOCABULARY: KEY TERMS

In academic texts, key terms are often in bold. Sometimes, they are defined in the margins as well as explained in the text.

1 With a partner, review these key terms from the text that are in bold and defined in the margins. Take turns explaining what each term means in your own words.

1 Jim Crow laws
2 literacy tests
3 voting tax
4 grandfather laws
5 lynching

2 Write a short definition for each term. Write your definitions without looking back at the text. (Review the XYZ format for definitions on page 26 if necessary. However, you may need to add another sentence or two to fully explain each term.)

1 **Jim Crow** laws were laws that . . .
2 **Literacy tests** were . . .
3 A **voting tax** was . . .
4 **Grandfather laws** were . . .
5 A **lynching** is . . .

3 Write one sentence that summarizes the purpose of literacy tests, a voting tax, and grandfather laws. Here is an example of how you can begin your sentence:

These were all steps that . . .

Preparing to read

READING LITERATURE ABOUT A TOPIC

1 | Read this passage about Langston Hughes. Then read his poem, "Dream Deferred."

Langston Hughes in Harlem, New York City, 1958

Langston Hughes (1902–1967) was a poet and journalist who wrote about the lives of ordinary African Americans. He is one of the greatest American poets of the twentieth century. "Dream Deferred," written in 1951, is probably his most famous poem.[7]

Dream Deferred

What happens to a dream deferred?
Does it dry up
like a raisin in the sun
Or fester like a sore –
And then run?
Does it stink like rotten meat?
Or crust and sugar over –
Like a syrupy sweet?

Maybe it just sags
like a heavy load.

Or does it explode?

---

2 | Discuss the questions below in a small group or as a class:

1 Whose dream do you think Hughes is writing about?

2 What do you think Hughes means by saying that the dream is "deferred"?

3 Hughes compares *a dream deferred* to five things. What are they? Why do you think he chose those five things?

4 What do *you* think happens to dreams that are deferred for too long?

Now read

Now read the text "The Battle for Civil Rights." When you finish, turn to the tasks on page 110.

---

7 To hear the poem read aloud, go to http://www.learner.org/catalog/extras/vvspot/video/hughes.html

3 THE BATTLE FOR CIVIL RIGHTS

During the 1950s and 1960s, African Americans continued their struggle for equality. They brought legal cases to court but also protested in the streets. Their efforts became known as **the civil rights movement**. The leaders of the movement wanted all forms of protest to be peaceful and nonviolent.

the civil rights movement
the struggles in the 1950s and 1960s to get equality for African Americans

In the courts

The U.S. Supreme Court had decided in 1896 that "separate but equal" facilities for blacks and whites were legal. By the 1950s, 21 states had segregated public schools. Most of the black schools were not as good as the white ones.

Oliver Brown of Topeka, Kansas, decided to challenge the 1896 Supreme Court decision. He asked the local school board to let his daughter attend a nearby white school. When the board refused, Brown sued them. The case of *Brown versus Board of Education of Topeka* (1954) eventually reached the Supreme Court and is one of the most famous legal cases in U.S. history. The defenders of school segregation argued that states had a right to make decisions about social and educational issues and that segregation was not harmful to blacks. Lawyers for Brown argued that black and white schools were not equal and that federal laws prohibit unequal treatment. The Supreme Court ruled in Brown's favor. The Chief Justice noted, "Separate educational facilities are inherently unequal." In other words, the fact that the schools are separate means that they must be unequal. A year later, the Court ordered all schools to be desegregated.

Brown versus Board of Education of Topeka
a famous legal case that helped stop the segregation of African-American and white schools

Many communities followed the court's order, but in other places, local and state governments refused. In 1957, the Arkansas governor tried to prevent African-American students from attending the all-white high school in the state capital, Little Rock. President Dwight Eisenhower had to send in soldiers to protect the black students. Some communities closed their public schools because they did not want black children to attend. Some white families took their children out of public schools and sent them to private schools. By 1960, in spite of the Supreme Court decision, less than one percent of black children in the South attended school with white children.

In the streets

Meanwhile, discrimination and segregation continued in many other areas of daily life, for example, in public transportation. In 1955, a black woman named Rosa Parks was riding a crowded bus in Montgomery, Alabama. The driver ordered her to give her seat to a white man and move to the back of the bus. Parks refused. She was arrested. In response, African Americans in Montgomery decided to **boycott** the bus company, that is, not use the company's buses. The boycott lasted

boycott
to refuse to buy a product or take part in an activity as a form of protest

for more than a year. In the end, the Supreme Court ruled that the segregation on buses was illegal.

Many college students, both black and white, joined the civil rights movement. In one famous incident at an all-white restaurant in North Carolina, black and white students staged a protest called a **sit-in**. They simply sat in the restaurant until the African-American customers were served. There were many sit-ins. Sometimes they lasted for days. Sometimes white customers in the restaurants shouted at the students, threw food at them, or hit them, but the students continued their protests. Sit-ins and other forms of protests spread across the South.

Still, discrimination and segregation existed in many places, and the civil rights movement continued with protests and demonstrations. The largest demonstration took place in 1963 in Washington, D.C. The main speaker at this demonstration was Dr. Martin Luther King, Jr., who became a national hero because of his leadership during the civil rights movement.

As protests increased, the government was forced to act, and Congress passed two important laws. In 1964, the Civil Rights Act prohibited segregation in schools and public places and prohibited discrimination by employers. In 1965, the Voting Rights Act gave the federal government the power to make sure that African Americans were allowed to vote in elections. Within a year, there were 230,000 new black voters. Thus began the long process of gaining equality for African Americans, an effort that continues today.

sit-in

sitting and refusing to leave as a form of protest

A sit-in at a lunch counter in Jackson, Mississippi, 1963

I have a dream

On August 28, 1963, in Washington, D.C., Dr. Martin Luther King, Jr., made his famous "I have a dream" speech. More than 200,000 demonstrators joined him in demanding voting rights for African Americans and an end to segregation. This is a short excerpt from his speech:

. . . And so even though we face the difficulties of today and tomorrow, I still have a dream. . . . I have a dream my four little children will one day live in a nation where they will not be judged by the color of their skin but by the content of their character. I have a dream today!

Dr. Martin Luther King, Jr., August 28, 1963

* You can read and hear the entire speech at http://www.americanrhetoric.com/speeches/mlkihaveadream.htm

After you read

Task 1 NOTE TAKING: HIGHLIGHTING

Highlighting important information in a text is helpful as a first step in taking notes.

- When you read a text for the first time, read it all the way through without highlighting.
- Read the text a second time. As you read, highlight main points, supporting details, and key terms. If possible, highlight each main point in a different color. Don't highlight every sentence! A text with more than half of the sentences highlighted will not be useful.
- Go back over the material you have highlighted. Make notes in the margin to help you remember what issues the highlighted information relates to.

Reread the text, highlighting main points, supporting details, and key terms. Make notes in the margins about which issues your highlighting relates to. (You will use your notes to help you do Tasks 2 and 3.)

Task 2 TEST TAKING: UNDERSTANDING THE LANGUAGE OF TEST QUESTIONS

Certain verbs are common in academic test questions. It is important to understand what these verbs ask you to do.

Verb	What the verb asks you to do
Analyze	Divide something – for example, an idea, an event, or a series of events – into parts. Explain these parts. Say how they are related to each other.
Describe	Discuss in detail the characteristics of an idea, event, etc.
Compare / Compare and Contrast	Examine at least two ideas, events, etc. Say how they are similar or different.

1 Read these examples of test questions based on information in this chapter:

1 **Analyze** the arguments for segregation in the *Brown versus Board of Education of Topeka* case.
2 **Describe** the strategies of the civil rights movement.
3 **Compare and contrast** the economies of the North and South before the U.S. Civil War.

2 Write one new test question for each of the verbs in step 1. You may use your notes from Task 1 or material from any of the texts in this chapter to help you.

Task 3 TEST TAKING: ANSWERING TEST QUESTIONS

> When you answer test questions, it is a good idea to begin your answer by using the language of the question. This will help you focus on the information you need to provide.

1 Read the statements below. These statements could be the first sentences of answers to the questions in step 1 of Task 2.

   1 The lawyers defending segregation in the *Brown versus Board of Education of Topeka* case offered two main arguments.

   2 The strategies of the civil rights movement consisted of court battles and street protests.

   3 The economies of the Northern and Southern states before the U.S. Civil War were very different.

2 Notice that each statement in step 1 contains two elements:

- the language of the original question
- additional information that shows how the writer will answer the question

In each statement in step 1, underline the language from the question and circle the new information.

3 Exchange your sample questions from step 2 of Task 2 with a partner. For each question, write just the first sentence of your answer. Be sure to use the language of the question and include enough additional information to show how you would answer the question.

4 Explain to your partner what you would say in the rest of your answers to his or her sample questions.

Task 4 THINKING CRITICALLY ABOUT THE TOPIC

Discuss the following questions in a small group:

   1 How do you think Hughes's "Dream Deferred" (page 107) is related to King's dream (page 109)?

   2 Do Hughes and King have the same view about dreams?

   3 How are these dreams connected to the struggle for equality?

Preparing to read

THINKING ABOUT THE TOPIC BEFORE YOU READ

1 | Look at the photographs below, and read the captions. Then discuss the following questions with a partner:

   1 Do you think men and women are treated as equals in the United States?

   2 Do you think the situation today is different from the situation 50 years ago? If so, in what ways do you think the situation is different?

Ruth Bader Ginsburg, the only woman of the nine justices on the Supreme Court

Senator Barbara Boxer, one of 16 women among 100 U.S. Senators

2 | Look at the sayings on the buttons and T-shirts in the boxed text on page 114. They are meant to be funny comments about relationships between women and men. Discuss the following questions with your partner:

   1 What do you think "a fish without a bicycle" means? How is this idea related to the relationship between men and women?

   2 What is the writer's opinion of high-heeled shoes? Why do you think she feels this way?

3 | Choose the saying you like best, and explain to your partner what it means and why you like it.

Now read

Now read the text "The Women's Movement." Then turn to the tasks on page 115.

➡ Remember to review and update your vocabulary notebook.

4 THE WOMEN'S MOVEMENT

Women in the United States began to fight for their equality around the time of the U.S. Civil War. The women who had fought against slavery were pleased when the Fifteenth Amendment, allowing black men to vote, was passed in 1870, but they were angry that they had not received the same right. They had to wait 50 years, until 1920, for the Nineteenth Amendment, which gave women the right to vote.

The role of women in society changed very little between 1920 and the beginning of World War II. During the war (1939–1945), thousands of women joined the workforce because they were needed in the factories while the men were away at war. After the war, most women were asked to leave their jobs and let the men return to work. During the 1950s, when the nation's economy was good, they were encouraged to stay home and maintain the traditional role of wife and mother. During the 1960s and 1970s, however, many things changed in American society. The civil rights movement and opposition to the Vietnam War led to protests across the nation. Many women, particularly young women, began to question their traditional roles and their unequal treatment. They saw the advances made by African Americans and began to protest for rights for themselves.

In 1960, many colleges and professional schools only admitted men, and employers were permitted to choose among job applicants based on their gender. Less than 40 percent of women who graduated from high school went on to college. Only about 10 percent of medical students were women. Even women who finished college often did not join the workforce; instead they married and had families. Women married at an average age of 20 and had an average of three or four children. Only 30 percent of women worked, and they were limited to a very small set of jobs, such as teachers and secretaries. Usually, they earned less than half of what men earned.

During the 1960s, women began to use many of the strategies that had been successful in the civil rights movement: protests, boycotts, and political pressure. In 1961, the **National Organization for Women (NOW)** was established to fight for equal rights for women. Since that time, women have achieved some degree of equality in the home and the workplace. For example, before the women's movement began, far more men than women attended college. Today slightly more women than men attend college; the number of men and women attending law, medical, and business schools is almost equal. Women today make up more than half of the labor force, and some have become leaders in government and business. By law, employers may no longer discriminate

Elizabeth Cady Stanton and Susan B. Anthony were leaders in the struggle for women's right to vote. In 1848, Stanton wrote "We hold these truths to be self-evident: that all men and women are created equal."

National Organization for Women (NOW)

an organization established in 1961 to fight for equal rights for women based on gender; in fact, they may not specify gender in job advertisements. Women now marry later, at the average age of 25, and have fewer children; many husbands share more of the work in the home.

Nevertheless, there is still a gap between men and women, particularly in the workplace. Women earn an average of 87 cents for every dollar that men with equal experience earn for equal work. Although women make up half of the labor force, 80 percent of them work in just 5 percent of job categories, generally the jobs that have the lowest pay. There have been many improvements in the status of women, but inequalities remain. Perhaps the most important achievement of the women's movement is that girls who are born today expect an equal chance for success.

These are some sayings that were popular during the women's movement and are still popular today:

A woman's place is in the House – *and the Senate.*

If high heels were so wonderful, men would be wearing them.

Elect a woman for a CHANGE.

A woman without a man is like a fish without a bicycle.

WOMEN MAKE POLICY, NOT COFFEE.

THE BEST MAN FOR THE JOB MAY BE – A WOMAN.

How about HERstory for a change?

After you read

Task 1 SCANNING

Scan the text for the details you need to fill in the chart below. Be careful. The text does not provide information for every box.

	1960	Today
Average age of marriage for women		
Average number of children for women		
Percent of working people who are women		
Percent of college students who are women		
Percent of medical students who are women		

Task 2 LANGUAGE FOCUS: TIME CONNECTORS

> *Before, after, while,* and *during* are time connectors that say when an event took place. When a time connector signals a connection between two clauses, it is called a **subordinator**. When a time connector signals a connection between a noun phrase and a clause, it is called a **preposition**.
>
> | Subordinators | Prepositions |
> |---|---|
> | before | before |
> | after | after |
> | while | during |
>
> Notice that *before* and *after* can be either a subordinator or a preposition, but *while* can only be a subordinator and *during* can only be a preposition. Here are some examples:
>
> | clause 1 | subordinator | clause 2 |
> |---|---|---|
> | Women had little influence | *before/after* | they got the vote. |
> | Men went to work | *while* | women stayed home. |
>
> | preposition | noun phrase | clause |
> |---|---|---|
> | Before/After/During | the 1960s, | women's lives changed. |

1| Find one example in the text of a time connector used as a subordinator and one example of a time connector used as a preposition.

2 In the following sentences, circle the correct choice. If both are correct, circle both. Pay attention to the meaning of the time connectors.

1 *After the Civil War / After the Civil War ended,* Congress passed the Thirteenth, Fourteenth, and Fifteenth Amendments.

2 *While / During* the 1960s, there were many demonstrations to protest discrimination against women and African Americans.

3 *Before World War II / Before the war began,* fewer women worked in factories.

3 Write four sentences about your own life using each of these time connectors: *before, after, while,* and *during.*

Task 3 EXAMINING GRAPHIC MATERIAL

1 Study the graph below. It compares men's and women's pay.

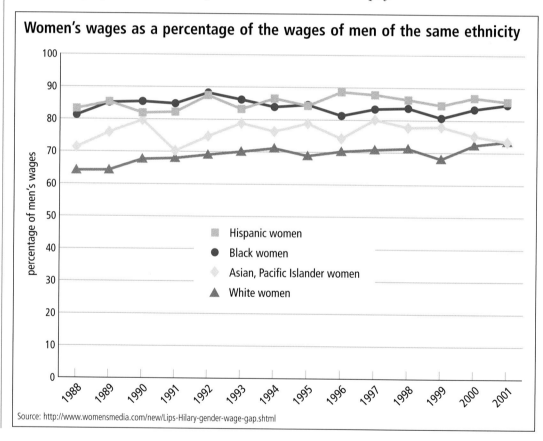

Women's wages as a percentage of the wages of men of the same ethnicity

Source: http://www.womensmedia.com/new/Lips-Hilary-gender-wage-gap.shtml

2 Work in a small group, and do the following:

1 Make a general statement about the earnings of white women.

2 Make a statement about *all* women's earnings compared to men's earnings.

3 Describe the progress women made toward wage equality with men between 1988 and 2000.

UNIT 3   WRITING ASSIGNMENT A

This writing assignment refers to information you have read in Chapter 5. In 1870, the Fifteenth Amendment granted the right to vote to African-American men. In 1920, the Nineteenth Amendment granted the right to vote to women. You will write a three-paragraph paper explaining your answer to the following question: Did the right to vote make African Americans and women equal with the rest of society?

Preparing to write

1 With a group of classmates, discuss the questions below. Take notes on your discussions. You will use your notes for reference as you write.

1 Discuss these questions about voting:

   a What are the advantages of the right to vote?

   b Why did African Americans and women fight so hard to get the vote?

   c Why have people in countries around the world fought for free elections?

2 Discuss these questions about the equality of African Americans with the rest of society:

   a Have African Americans achieved equality since they got the vote? Why or why not?

   b What are some examples to support your answer?

3 Discuss these questions about the equality of women with the rest of society:

   a Have women achieved equality since they got the vote? Why or why not?

   b What are some examples to support your answer?

2 Decide on your point of view. Did these groups become equal members of American society when they got the vote? Your point of view will probably be one of the following:

- Both groups have achieved equality.
- Neither group has achieved equality.
- Both groups have achieved equality in some areas but not in others.
- One group has achieved equality but the other group has not.

Now write

Paragraph 1
Begin your first paragraph by clearly stating your claim, that is, your argument or point of view. Here are two possible ways to begin.

- *The right to vote was an important step for African Americans and women. It . . .*
- *The right to vote was an important step for African Americans and women. However, it . . .*

Complete your first paragraph by explaining why the right to vote is so important. Use your notes from step 1 of "Preparing to write."

Paragraph 2
The first sentence(s) of this paragraph must have a logical connection to your first paragraph. It (They) should reflect the claim that you made in that paragraph. Here are two possible ways to begin:

- *African Americans have achieved equality in many areas.*
- *The right to vote was significant, but . . .*

Complete your second paragraph with evidence to support your claim. Use your notes from step 1 of "Preparing to write."

Paragraph 3
Now present your argument and evidence about equality for women.

After you write

1 | Reread your paper. Review the instructions in "Now write" and make sure that you have followed them correctly.

2 | Choose one area of grammar that can be a problem for you, for example, subject and verb agreement or correct choice of tense. See if you made any mistakes in the area you chose and correct them.

3 | Exchange papers with a partner and do the following:

  1 Underline or highlight the sentence(s) in your partner's essay that states his or her claim.
  2 In a different color, underline or highlight the evidence in your partner's essay that supports his or her claim.

4 | With your partner, discuss the following questions about your papers:

  1 Is the claim clearly stated? If not, how could it be written so that it's clearer?
  2 Do the second and third paragraphs each have clear topic sentences? If not, how could they be written so that they are clearer?
  3 Is there enough evidence to support the claim? If not, what other evidence could be included?
  4 Are there any grammar or spelling errors in the essay? If so, how could they be corrected?

The Struggle Continues   Chapter 6

Preparing to Read

BUILDING VOCABULARY: PREVIEWING KEY TERMS

1 Read these sentences and think about what the words in bold might mean. Use the context to help you. All the words in bold appear in the text you are going to read, "What Does Equality Mean Today?"

_____ **1** The university's admission policy was **biased** against minority students.

_____ **2** Many people believe that hiring decisions should depend only on applicants' **merit**, not their race or gender.

_____ **3** Many critics of the government believe there is unequal **access** to educational opportunities in the United States.

_____ **4** Equal opportunity does not guarantee equal economic **outcome**.

_____ **5** Everyone should have an equal opportunity to compete for **resources**, such as housing, education, and jobs.

2 Chose the best definition below for each word in bold in step 1. Write the letter of the definition on the line before the sentence.

a something useful or valuable that can be used for an advantage [_noun_]

b the right or opportunity to use something, do something, or enter a place [_noun_]

c a result or effect [_noun_]

d showing an unreasonable preference towards or against something or someone [_adjective_]

e good qualities that deserve praise [_noun_]

3 With a partner or in a small group, discuss how _merit, access,_ and _resources_ could relate to the issue of equality.

Now read

Now read the text "What Does Equality Mean Today?" When you finish, turn to the tasks on page 122.

Chapter 6

The Struggle Continues

1 WHAT DOES EQUALITY MEAN TODAY?

What does equality mean in American society today? Does it mean that there are no differences among Americans? Does it mean that Americans should all have an equal opportunity to compete for resources, such as jobs, housing, and education? Or does it mean that all Americans should end up equal – in other words, that resources should be spread equally across all people in the country, regardless of who they are?

It is fairly easy to reject the first idea; Americans are clearly not all the same. There are differences based on race, ethnicity, social class, gender, and religion.

Does equality mean equal opportunity?

The second view says that although we are all different, none of those differences matters; everyone should have an equal opportunity to succeed and equal access to resources. Therefore, any difference in success is a result of how well each person uses those opportunities and resources – in other words, a difference in merit. Consider an example: If a school with mostly white children has better teachers and equipment than a school with mostly African-American children, this will hurt the African-American children's chances to succeed because there is unequal access to resources and opportunities.

This is a problem the government can try to correct by distributing resources more fairly. What if the government provides the two schools with equal resources? Will that ensure equality? History suggests that equal opportunity does not always guarantee equal outcomes. To continue the example, providing better schools has not necessarily led to equal success for African Americans. This could be a result of larger problems of social and economic inequality in society. Perhaps the African-American children are from poor families who cannot give them the support they need to succeed in school. Perhaps they have no quiet place to study; they may not get healthy meals. Their parents may not have the time or ability to help them with their work. As a result, the children may not be able to take advantage of the new and better resources. We therefore need to consider a third perspective on equality.

Does equality mean equal results?

Should the government try to ensure that there are not only equal opportunities but equal results, too? If so, how should they do this?

Consider this example: A city police department has a training program and test for officers that is biased against women. As a result, few women become police officers. Then the department develops a program that is fairer to women, but still there are few women officers. Equal opportunity has not resulted in equal outcomes, again, perhaps as a result of broader social conditions. Perhaps the women still do not think they would be treated fairly by their bosses or other officers. Perhaps they have already experienced some form of discrimination in their jobs, so they choose not to take the test. Or perhaps even among those who pass the test, more men than women are chosen to become officers. Should the city ignore the program and simply guarantee a certain number of positions in the police department to women? This type of policy would encourage equal outcomes but require stronger action from the government. Opponents argue that this is not equality because it means some groups actually receive better treatment than others. Americans are still trying to find the best ways to ensure equality across society.

After you read

Task 1 SUMMARIZING

> Summarizing is one of the most important academic skills. It can help you check your understanding of a text and prepare for tests and writing assignments. A summary includes only the most important information from a text. It does not include details or examples.

1 Choose the best ending to complete this introductory sentence to a summary. *The text, "What Does Equality Mean Today?"* . . .

    a provides the American definition of the term *equality*.
    b presents three different interpretations of the term *equality*.
    c shows that women and minorities do not have equality in the United States.
    d gives the best definition of the term *equality*.

2 Write a sentence that summarizes each of the definitions given in the text. You can begin your sentences like this:

    1 *One interpretation of equality is* . . .
    2 *A second definition* . . .
    3 *A third view* . . .

3 Combine your sentences from steps 1 and 2 to complete your summary. Then compare your summary with a partner's.

Task 2 LANGUAGE FOCUS: *SHOULD*

> The modal verb *should* is used to give advice and make recommendations. *Should* is commonly used in academic writing to express the idea that there is a practical or logical reason for doing something.
>
> • Tax money *should* be used to support education.
> • Women *should* have the same pay as men for similar work.
>
> *Should* is more common in academic writing than *must* because *must* is considered too strong for most situations.

1 Review the text and underline all the uses of *should*. Study how *should* is used.

2 Write two statements using *should* to describe steps that the government, businesses, or other institutions can take to make sure that all citizens are treated equally.

3 Write two statements using *should not* to describe steps you think are *not* a good way to ensure equal treatment.

Task 3 BUILDING VOCABULARY: SYNONYMS

> Synonyms are words that have similar meaning. Using synonyms avoids repetition and can make your writing more interesting.

1 Find and underline these words in the text. Then find and circle a synonym for each one.

1 ensure	**3** spread	**5** led to
2 chance	**4** outcome	**6** view

2 Choose three of the synonyms, and use them to write your own sentences.

Task 4 LANGUAGE FOCUS: MARKERS OF DEPENDENCY

> *Markers of dependency* are prepositional phrases that make the relationship between facts clear. Three common markers of dependency are *based on, depending on,* and *regardless of.* Here are examples of how each marker is used:
>
>   X   Y
> - Discrimination is often *based on* race and gender.
>   (If X is *based on* Y, then Y is a source of X.)
>
>   X   Y
> - Choose one of the two topics *depending on* your point of view.
>   (If X will happen *depending on* Y, then X will vary according to what Y is or does.)
>
>   X
> - Should employers hire employees *regardless of* race and gender?
>   ("*Regardless of* X" means that X does not matter.)

1 Complete the following sentences with one of the markers of dependency.

1 Everyone should have access to a good education _____
   race.
2 The economic success of minority groups varies _____
   the part of the country in which they live.
3 Unfortunately, some employers make hiring decisions _____
   the ethnicity of the applicant.

2 Complete these sentences with your own words.

1 His decision was *based on* _____.
2 *Regardless of* your opinion, _____.
3 *Depending on* the weather, _____.

Preparing to read

BRAINSTORMING

> Brainstorming is one way to activate your background knowledge about a topic before you read. When you brainstorm, try to think of as many ideas as you can about the topic. Do not try to organize or evaluate them.

You have read about the struggle for equality in the United States and how various groups, specifically minorities and women, have not always received equal treatment.

In a small group, brainstorm about ways in which you think inequality in society could be remedied, in other words, how past mistakes could be corrected. Make a list of your ideas.

BRAINSTORMING: ORGANIZING YOUR IDEAS

> After you brainstorm, it is useful to organize the ideas you have generated into categories. This will help you think, talk, and write about the ideas in a logical way.

In your group, organize the ideas you brainstormed using a chart like the one below.

Areas in which inequality needs to be corrected	Ideas for correcting inequality
Education	
Employment	
Housing	
Other	

Now read

Now read the text "Affirmative Action." When you finish, turn to the tasks on page 127.

2 AFFIRMATIVE ACTION

Two high school students applied to the same college. Jim had high grades, and his college entrance exam scores were excellent. Charles had average grades and his scores were disappointing. Jim, who is white and middle class, was rejected by the college. Charles, who is African American and poor, was accepted and also received a scholarship. 1

Did the college make a fair decision? Was the decision unfair to Jim, but justified anyway? Without help, Charles might have had no chance of a college education. Jim, because he is middle class and has more resources, will probably get into another college and be successful anyway. Colleges and employers often make these difficult decisions as part of a policy called *affirmative action*. 2

The meaning and goal of affirmative action

Affirmative action is a term for policies and actions that help to reverse the effects of current and past discrimination. Affirmative action programs are designed to increase the number of women and ethnic minorities, especially African Americans and Latinos, in employment and education. 3

Affirmative action is based on the idea that groups should participate in business, in government, in education, and in other activities in proportion to their numbers in the general population. According to this view, if a group is not well represented, this is a form of discrimination. This would mean, for example, that women should fill half of the management jobs and half of the classes at universities because they are half of the general population. 4

The goal of affirmative action is different from the goal of the civil rights movement and the women's movement. The goal of both of these movements was equality. The goal of affirmative action is not to treat everyone equally. Instead, the goal of affirmative action is to bring all 5 groups to the same level, that is, to achieve equal outcomes – even if this means treating individual members of each group unequally.

Affirmative action programs have been quite successful in reversing past discrimination. Between 1990 and 2000, the number of African-American police officers grew by 35 percent. In 2000, there were over 50,000 black police officers in American police forces, or almost 12 percent. 1.3 million blacks now work in government service. An approximately equal number of women and men go to college and many professional graduate schools. All of these numbers represent big increases following the establishment of affirmative action programs. Yet affirmative action has caused serious disagreement across the nation. 6

Arguments for and against affirmative action

Supporters argue that affirmative action is necessary because there is still discrimination against women and minorities, especially in the workplace. Furthermore, affirmative action is essential for the nation's future, when two out of three workers will be women or members of a minority. These workers need to be educated and prepared. Finally, supporters maintain that a diverse workforce and school population benefits everyone and is essential in a multicultural society. 7

Opponents claim that the discrimination no longer exists, and therefore, affirmative action should end. Merit should be the only factor in hiring and school admission. They argue that the losers in affirmative action are often struggling white students and workers, who also deserve a chance to succeed. Finally, affirmative action can even hurt minorities and women. It encourages the idea that they succeed only because they receive special treatment, and therefore they are considered by others – and sometimes even by themselves – as inferior, that is, not as good as others. 8

Affirmative action is controversial because it puts basic values in conflict: On the one hand, most Americans believe that everyone deserves an equal opportunity. On the other hand, they believe that hard work and merit – not membership in a specific group – should be the reason one person does well and another person does not. 9

Reverse Discrimination

In 1978, Allan Bakke, a white man, claimed that he was the victim of *reverse discrimination*. He argued that he was rejected by a medical school because he was white, and that his grades were better than those of African-American students who had been accepted.

In the legal case *Bakke versus University of California*, the Supreme Court decided against the medical school and its affirmative action program that reserved 16 out of 100 places for minority students. The court ordered the university to give Bakke a place in the medical school class.

After you read

Task 1 UNDERSTANDING THE FUNCTION OF DIFFERENT PARTS OF THE TEXT

A text will often contain different parts that have different functions, or purposes. These are some common functions:

- to give a definition
- to argue a point of view
- to describe an example

Recognizing the function, or purpose, of each part will help you understand the text as a whole.

1 Match each section of the text with its main function by writing the correct paragraph number in the blank that follows each function. In one of the blanks you will need to write *BT* for *boxed text*.

1 Explains the argument in favor of affirmative action _par. 7_
2 Gives a definition of affirmative action _____
3 Describes an example of affirmative action _____
4 Expands the definition of affirmative action _____
5 Describes an example of a successful fight against affirmative action _____
6 Explains the goals of affirmative action _____
7 Explains an argument against affirmative action _____
8 Discusses the difficulties of making affirmative action decisions _____
9 Gives reasons for the controversy about affirmative action _____
10 Describes the success of affirmative action programs _____

2 With a partner, take turns answering the following questions:

1 The first text in this chapter, "What Does Equality Mean Today?", presented three different interpretations of *equality*. Affirmative action is based on one of them. Which one is it?
2 What are the arguments for affirmative action?
3 What are the arguments against it?
4 Why are affirmative action programs so controversial?
5 What was Bakke's argument?

Task 2 APPLYING WHAT YOU HAVE READ

Read these quotations. Then discuss the questions below in a small group.

> In order to get beyond racism, we must first take into account* race. There is no other way. And in order to treat some persons equally, we must treat them differently.
>
> – Harry Blackmun, Former Supreme Court Justice, 1978

* think about

> It is morally wrong to treat people as members of groups rather than individuals.
>
> – Stephan Thernstrom, Professor of History, Harvard University, 1998

1 In the first quotation, how can the two parts of the last sentence both be true? How can people be treated equally *and* differently?
2 What does Professor Thernstrom mean when he says society should not treat people "as members of groups"? Which groups do you think he means?
3 How are these quotations related to affirmative action?
4 Which of the two authors would be in favor of special treatment for African Americans and women? Which author would be against it?

Task 3 DEBATING THE TOPIC

Debating is an academic activity that helps you explore different sides of an issue.

1 Read the following two positions on the topic of equality:

• Society must correct past injustices against minority groups and women, even if this means giving them special help. In order to establish equality, it may be necessary to treat people unequally.
• Society must treat everyone equally. This means that all people must be treated on the basis of their individual merit. To treat minority groups and women differently is not fair.

2 Which position do you agree with? Work with a partner who shares your view, and make notes about all the arguments you can think of that support your position. Take turns explaining your point of view and your supporting reasons.

3 Find a pair of classmates who don't agree with you, and debate the topic with them. Try to convince them of your position. You may use phrases like these:

• I believe that / I am convinced that . . . • It's well known that . . .
• The point is that / It's clear that . . . • It is unreasonable / unacceptable / unfair because . . .

Preparing to read

THINKING ABOUT THE TOPIC BEFORE YOU READ

Look at these pictures. Then discuss the questions below in small groups or as a class.

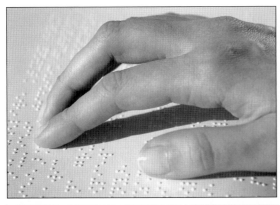

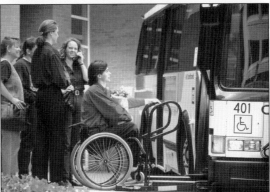

1 What do the pictures have in common?
2 Are there any scenes in these pictures that are familiar to you? Where have you seen them?
3 The pictures show ways of accommodating (helping) people with disabilities in everyday life. How would you describe or define someone who is disabled?
4 What other sorts of accommodations for the disabled can you think of?
5 Are there similar accommodations for the disabled in other countries that you know?

Now read

Now read the text "Trying Not to Be Special: Americans with Disabilities." When you finish, turn to the tasks on page 132.

3 TRYING NOT TO BE SPECIAL: AMERICANS WITH DISABILITIES

When we consider prejudice, discrimination, and the fight for equality, we usually think of racial and ethnic minorities and women. However, there are other groups that have faced challenges in their struggle for equal treatment. One group that has made progress in the United States recently is the disabled. 1

It is estimated that more than 50 million Americans have some form of physical or mental disability. Historically, some people have believed that the disabled cannot live and work with other people. They have not thought the disabled can be integrated into society. Therefore, it has not always been easy for the disabled to gain access to education and employment. There is a strong relationship between disability and low income, low levels of education, and unemployment. Over the past 35 years, people with disabilities have fought for equal protection and treatment. Their battle has been difficult but has had positive results. Today, federal and many state laws prohibit companies, governments, and institutions from discriminating against people with disabilities. 2

In 1990, President George H. Bush signed the *Americans with Disabilities Act* (ADA) into law. In a speech, he declared it was "the world's first comprehensive declaration of the equality of people with disabilities and evidence of America's leadership internationally in the cause of human rights." The law has several important parts: 3

Employment: It prohibits discrimination against people with disabilities at work. If they are qualified to do a particular job, the employer must offer reasonable assistance to those workers. For example, if a qualified computer programmer is blind, the company might have to provide software for the blind that reads the information on the computer screen aloud.

Government: State and local government programs must provide equal opportunities to people with disabilities. For example, a program for children at a city park must allow children in wheelchairs to participate.

Public facilities: Public places must provide access for people with disabilities so that they can participate in daily life. For example, office buildings and restaurants must provide accommodations such as accessible bathrooms and ramps for people in wheelchairs.

Telecommunications: Telephone and Internet services must be accessible to people who have problems hearing, seeing, or speaking. For example, telephone companies must provide special communication systems for the deaf.

It is possible for many disabled people to participate in the workplace.

Transportation: The disabled must have access to public and private transportation. For example, bus companies must provide services for customers in wheelchairs.

What exactly is a disability? According to the ADA, a person with a disability is someone who has "a physical or mental impairment [that is, problem or weakness] that substantially limits one or more major life activities." What do "substantially limit" and "one or more major life activities" mean? The ADA says that three factors determine a "substantial limitation": (1) the seriousness of the disability, (2) how long it will last, and (3) its effects. For example, someone who wears glasses does not have a disability; someone who is blind does. A condition such as pregnancy is not a disability because it is normal and temporary. A person with an injury that prevents him from lifting heavy objects might be considered disabled if he was a builder before his injury, but not if he worked in an office. "Major life activities" include walking, seeing, hearing, speaking, learning, standing, or reading. If an injury or illness prevents people from doing one or more of these things, they may be considered disabled.

Although the ADA may seem to be about special treatment for the disabled, most disabled people would disagree. They argue that it is really about allowing them to be just like other people: to live independent and productive lives, to work, to play, and to go to school along with everyone else. In other words, it is about *not* being special.

4

5

Christopher Reeve

Christopher Reeve (1952–2004) was an actor. His most well-known role was Superman, which he played in four films. He is perhaps even better known for his work for the disabled. In 1995, he fell off a horse, his spine was broken, and he became

paralyzed below the neck. He could not move anything except his head; even breathing and speaking were difficult. After his accident, he worked very hard to help others with similar spinal injuries. He raised money for research and established a center to help people with spinal injuries learn to live productive lives with their disabilities. His life and his work have inspired people all over the world.

Christopher Reeve presenting a Tony Award, New York City, June 8, 2003

After you read

Task 1 APPLYING WHAT YOU HAVE READ

For each of the accommodations for the disabled listed below, decide which part of the ADA law requires it: Employment (E), Government (G), Public facilities (PF), Telecommunications (TC), and Transportation (TP). Write the abbreviation next to the accommodation.

_____ **1** Elevator signs are written in *Braille,* a writing system that the blind can read by touch.

_____ **2** A university installs ramps in all of its buildings.

_____ **3** A company provides a "text-only" version of its Web site. Special software for the blind reads aloud descriptions of the pictures on the Web site.

_____ **4** A court provides a sign-language interpreter for a deaf person.

_____ **5** A subway station has an elevator for customers in wheelchairs.

_____ **6** A company buys a special chair for an employee with a back injury.

Task 2 LANGUAGE FOCUS: INTRODUCING EXAMPLES WITH *FOR EXAMPLE* AND *SUCH AS*

Examples are often used in academic writing to support main ideas and claims. Two common expressions for introducing examples are *for example* and *such as.*

for example
- can introduce a sentence
- can introduce a noun or a list of nouns, but only if the noun or list of nouns is part of a sentence

Correct: *For example, restaurants must provide accessible bathrooms.*
A business can provide many types of accommodation for the disabled, for example, ramps, special parking places, and accessible bathrooms.

Incorrect: *A business can provide many types of accommodation for the disabled. For example, ramps, special parking places, and accessible bathrooms.*

such as
- cannot introduce a sentence
- can introduce a noun or list of nouns, but only if the noun or list of nouns is part of a sentence

Correct: *A business can provide many types of accommodation for the disabled, such as ramps and special parking places.*

Incorrect: *A business can provide many types of accommodation for the disabled, such as they can build ramps and special parking places.*

1 Decide if the sentences below include the correct use of *for example* and *such as.* Put a check (✔) on the line if the use is correct. Put an ✘ if it is incorrect.

_____ **1** Employers must provide reasonable assistance to disabled workers. *For example,* they must provide special computers, software, and furniture.

_____ **2** Many disabled people, *such as* Christopher Reeve, have led active lives.

_____ **3** The ADA has resulted in considerable progress for the disabled. *Such as* there are laws against discrimination in education and employment.

_____ **4** Major life activities are part of everyday life, *for example,* walking, seeing, hearing, speaking, and learning.

_____ **5** Special accommodation must be made for people who have difficulty communicating. *For example,* the deaf and the blind.

_____ **6** Many stores offer special accommodation for disabled shoppers. *Such as* parking places near the store and special carts.

2 Write two new sentences with examples of accommodations for the disabled that you have seen or heard of. Use *such as* or *for example* in your sentences. Pay attention to where you put the commas.

Task 3 THINKING CRITICALLY ABOUT THE TOPIC

1 Look at these two pictures and read their titles. *Cripple* is an old word for someone with a disability, especially someone whose arms or legs are disabled. *Beggars* are poor people who ask other people to give them money so they can live.

"Cripples (The Beggars)," Pieter Bruegel, 1568

A marathon, 2005

2 Discuss these questions with a partner or in a small group:

1 Describe the pictures. How do they show attitudes toward disability?

2 Do you think that there are some types of work and some activities that people with physical or mental disabilities should not participate in? Why or why not?

3 How much should society do to accommodate people's disabilities?

Preparing to read

REVIEWING WHAT YOU HAVE ALREADY READ

You are going to read a text titled "How Equal Are We Now?" Review the previous texts in this chapter. Then, with a partner or in a small group, describe the state of equality in the United States today.

THINKING ABOUT THE TOPIC BEFORE YOU READ

With your partner or group, look at the photographs below. Do these photographs support the ideas you discussed above? Explain.

Antonio Villaraigosa was elected mayor of Los Angeles, California, in 2005.

Renetta McCann is CEO (Chief Executive Officer) of a large media company.

Barack Obama was elected U.S. Senator for Illinois in 2004.

Now read

Now read the text "How Equal Are We Now?" When you finish, turn to the tasks on page 137.

➡ Remember to review and update your vocabulary notebook.

4 HOW EQUAL ARE WE NOW?

The United States and its citizens take pride in their belief in equality. **1** Most Americans believe their country is an egalitarian society, that is, a society of equals. Americans say they judge others based on their individual merit, not their background. Yet there is a large gap between the rich and poor, and often this gap is related to differences of race or ethnicity. So are all Americans really equal today? How can equality be measured?

The government and many private organizations use statistics to **2** show progress and to compare population groups within the country, specifically the white majority; African Americans; and Latinos, the largest minority group. On educational and economic measures, African Americans and Latinos have historically been lower than whites. These minority groups are also not well represented in government. Statistics from the 2000 census suggest that African Americans and Latinos have made progress in some areas, but there are still ways in which they continue to fall behind the white population.

Education

African Americans have shown a steady increase in high school gradua- **3** tion rates and college attendance. In 1940, only 7 percent of all African Americans finished high school. Census reports show that this figure grew to 51 percent by 1980 and to 79 percent in 2000. However, this rate is still lower than the 89 percent average for whites. The number of African Americans with a college degree has also risen, from 8 percent in 1980 to 14 percent in 2000; again, this is still lower than the 24 percent rate for whites. The figures for Latinos have also shown improvement but remain lower than the African-American figures, perhaps because of the challenge of studying in a second language. According to the 2000 census, only 52 percent of Latino adults have completed high school, up from 32 percent in 1970, and less than 11 percent have graduated from college, up from 4.5 percent in 1970. The difference between the educational levels of whites and minorities may be linked to the kinds of schools that each group attends. A 2005 study suggests that public schools in African-American and Latino neighborhoods serve more students than public schools in other neighborhoods, but they have fewer resources and fewer good teachers.

Economics

The **economic profile** for minorities is also mixed. The **median income** **4** for all minorities has risen substantially in the last 50 years, and fewer minorities live in poverty. Yet according to the 2000 census, the poverty rate for minorities remains considerably higher than for whites. About 25 percent of the African-American and Latino populations live in poverty, compared to 8 percent of the white population. Unemploy-

economic profile
a description that includes the most important economic facts, such as income and employment

median income
the middle point of the income distribution, where half of the population earns more and half of the population earns less

ment figures also show considerable differences; minority workers are two to three times more likely to be unemployed than white workers. Income levels differ significantly as well (see Figure 6.1). This is partly because the white and minority populations have different **job profiles**. There is a higher percentage of whites in high-paying professional jobs, such as managers, doctors, and lawyers, and a higher percentage of minority workers in low-paying jobs. These differences in employment and income have important consequences. Low-paying jobs are less likely to include benefits, such as health insurance. As a result, workers in low-paying jobs may not have access to good health care. These workers may also find it more difficult to save money for important purchases, such as a home. Although home ownership by minorities has increased – in 2000, it reached 43 percent for African Americans and 46 percent for Latinos – this figure is still far below the figure for the white population, 75 percent.

job profile

a description of the range of jobs that are typical for a specific group

Representation in government

Finally, there have been substantial increases in minority representation in the government. Fifty years ago, many African Americans were prevented from voting. Today the number of black elected officials is estimated at 9,040, mostly in state and local government. As of 2004, there were more than 500 black mayors of cities with populations of more than 40,000, up from just 81 in 1970. As of 2007, there were 42 black representatives in Congress, but only one black senator and one black governor. There were 23 Latino representatives, three Latino senators, and over 300 Latino mayors. African Americans and Latinos are also serving in an increasing number of important and powerful appointed positions, for example, Condoleezza Rice, an African American, as Secretary of State, and Dr. Richard Carmona, a Latino, as Surgeon General.

5

Figure 6.1
2000 median household income.

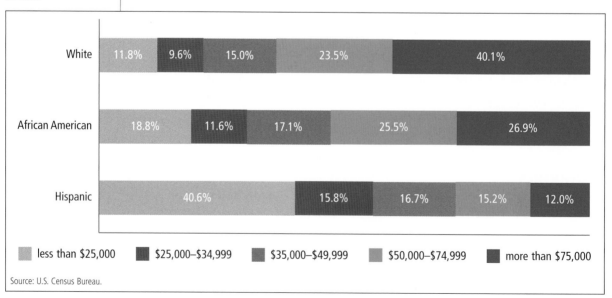

| | less than $25,000 | $25,000–$34,999 | $35,000–$49,999 | $50,000–$74,999 | more than $75,000 |

Source: U.S. Census Bureau.

After you read

Task 1 UNDERSTANDING STATISTICS

Academic texts often use statistics as supporting evidence. If a text has
lots of statistics, it is a good idea to organize them in your notes in
some way, such as a chart or a graph, so that you can see the relationships and patterns in them. This will help you understand the points
the author is using the statistics to make.

1 Scan the text and fill in the chart below according to the information in the text.
(Be careful. The text does not provide information for all of the boxes.)

	Percent that . . .	1970	1980	2000
African Americans	graduated from high school			
	graduated from college			
	lived in poverty			
	owned a home			
Latinos	graduated from high school			
	graduated from college			
	lived in poverty			
	owned a home			
Whites	graduated from high school			
	graduated from college			
	lived in poverty			
	owned a home			

2 Now discuss these questions with a partner:

   1 Do you think these statistics show significant progress?

   2 Do you think the progress will continue?

   3 What do you think are some reasons for the changes in the statistics?

Task 2 BUILDING VOCABULARY: SYNONYMS

1 Find synonyms (words with similar meanings) in the text for the words below.
Some synonyms appear more than once. Pay attention to the word form you need.

   1 big (*adjective*)

   (par. 1) *large*

   (par. 4) _____

   (par. 5) _____

   2 a lot (*adverb*)

   (par. 4) _____

   (par. 4) *considerably*

   (par. 4) _____

   3 go up (*verb*)

   (par. 3) _____

   (par. 3) *has risen*

   (par. 4) _____

2 Using three of the synonyms from step 1, write three sentences of your own that describe the trends presented in the text.

Task 3 LANGUAGE FOCUS: USING THE VERB *ESTIMATE* IN THE PASSIVE TO REPORT STATISTICS

> In academic writing, it is often important to say where your information comes from. Sometimes, however, the information is well-known, or the source is not important. In these cases, it is common to use a passive verb to present the information. One verb that is frequently used in the passive to report statistics is *estimate*.
>
> • The population of the United States **is estimated** to be more than 300,000,000.
> • **It is estimated** that more than 150,000 people were killed by the 2004 tsunami.

1 Read these sentences from texts in this book.

• The number of black elected officials **is estimated** at 9,040.
• **It is estimated that** more than 50 million Americans have some form of physical or mental disability.
• **It is estimated that** the number of illegal immigrants increases by about 500,000 every year.

2 Using the information in Figure 6.1, on page 136, write two sentences using the passive construction *it is estimated that*.

Task 4 THINKING CRITICALLY ABOUT THE TOPIC

Discuss the following questions with a partner or in a small group:

1 Consider the text, including Figure 6.1, and the photographs on page 134. Do you think African Americans and Latinos have made progress toward equality? Why or why not?

2 The text mainly discusses the progress of African Americans and Latinos. Are there other groups you know about that have received unequal treatment in the United States or around the world? Which groups are they? (The groups you choose to discuss do not have to be ethnic minorities.)

3 Do you think the groups you discussed in question 2 deserve special treatment? Why or why not?

UNIT 3   WRITING ASSIGNMENT B

This assignment refers to information in Chapters 5 and 6. In "Debating the Topic," on page 128, you discussed what society should do to ensure equal treatment for all. Now you will write a three-paragraph paper on this topic.

Preparing to write

In the first text in Chapter 6, "What Does Equality Mean Today?", a question was raised about the meaning of equality in the United States:

> *Does it mean that Americans should all have an equal opportunity to compete for resources, such as jobs, housing, and education? Or does it mean that all Americans should end up equal; in other words, that resources should be spread equally across all people?*

1 | In a small group, discuss what *you* think equality means. Take notes on your discussion.

2 | On your own, think about which group(s) in the United States need some extra help or protection in order to achieve equality and which group(s) should not receive any special assistance. Possibilities include ethnic minority groups, women, the disabled, poor people, or perhaps some other group you have thought of. Make notes about why you have chosen these groups.

3 | Make notes about what sort of assistance or protection should be provided. Are laws that prohibit discrimination enough? Or should there be specific laws that protect specific groups from discrimination? For example, should there be a law that specifically prohibits discrimination against the disabled? Should there be even more protection for specific groups? For example, should businesses, schools, and other organizations be required to give special treatment to some groups? What kinds of special treatment should they provide?

Now write

- Remember that even though you are expressing your point of view, you should not use the pronoun *I*.
- You may want to review the use of the modal verb *should* on page 122.
- Follow the directions for **Choice A** or **Choice B**, depending on your point of view. Select **Choice A** if you think that some groups should get special treatment. Select **Choice B** if you think that laws prohibiting discrimination are enough and that no groups should get special treatment.

Paragraph 1

For **Choice A** and **Choice B**

Introduce your paper by writing a few sentences about the idea of equality. Include a sentence that states your point of view: A or B.

Paragraph 2

For **Choice A**

Write a topic sentence that states which group(s) need help or protection. Then, give reasons for your choice. Your reasons might include historical events, current discrimination, or other factors.

For **Choice B**

Even though your position is *against* special treatment, you need to explain that you are aware of the arguments *for* special treatment. In this paragraph, you will explain those arguments.

   1 Write a topic sentence. Here are some examples:
- Many people believe that special treatment will help make society more equal.
- Some people have argued for special treatment for minority groups and women.
- Do some groups need extra help and protection? Some people say "yes."

   2 Explain why other people think that special treatment is necessary for certain groups. (Review the arguments for affirmative action on page 126 if necessary.)

Paragraph 3

For **Choice A**

Describe what you think should be done to help the group(s) you think need help or protection. Be sure to begin with a clear topic sentence.

For **Choice B**

In this paragraph, you will give your argument *against* special treatment.

   1 Write a topic sentence that states your disagreement with the point of view you explained in paragraph 2. Here are two examples:
- The view that special treatment for some people will make society more equal is wrong.
- Special treatment for some people means unfair treatment for other people.

   2 Explain your position against special treatment.

After you write

1 Exchange papers with a partner, and discuss the questions below. If the answer to any question is "no," discuss how the paper could be improved.

   1 Did your partner state his or her point of view clearly in paragraph 1?

   2 Do paragraphs 2 and 3 each have an appropriate topic sentence?

   3 Does the evidence support your partner's point of view? Is the evidence convincing?

2 Check each other's papers for grammar and spelling errors.

American Values

In this unit, we look at some of the fundamental values that are the basis of much of American social, economic, and political life. In Chapter 7, we see how these values are connected to the historical development of public education and business. We also explore Americans' romantic views of the frontier – the "Wild West." In Chapter 8, we consider how these values are reflected in contemporary American life at home, on the road, and in the workplace. We also examine an idea that is often referred to as "the American Dream."

Previewing the unit

Read the contents page for Unit 4, and do the following activities.

Chapter 7: American Values from the Past

In this chapter you are going to read about some traditional American values in business, in education, and in everyday life.

At the end of the nineteenth century, the United States was on its way to becoming the most powerful nation in the world. Based on the texts you have read and these pictures of the United States in the nineteenth century, discuss this question: What do you think was responsible for the United States' success?

Chapter 8: American Values Today

In this chapter, you are going to learn about how some traditional American values are connected to life in the United States today.

Read this list of generalizations that have been made about the United States and Americans. Then discuss the questions below with a partner or small group.

- The United States is a land of opportunity, where anyone can succeed.
- Americans believe in hard work.
- Your family background is not important in the United States.
- You can make a new start in the United States.
- Everything moves fast in the United States; you have to move fast, too.
- Americans are free to do what they want.
- Everyone is equal in the United States.
- Americans are interested in what is new and different.

1 Have you heard these generalizations before? If so, which ones have you heard? Where did you hear them?

2 Do you think some of these generalizations are true? Do you think all of them are true? Why or why not?

Preparing to read

INCREASING YOUR READING SPEED

1 Review the strategies for increasing your reading speed on page 74.

2 Enter your starting time. Then read "The Roots of
American Values," using the speed-reading strategies.
For this task, do not read the boxed text on page 146.

Starting time: _____

3 Fill in the time you finished.

Finishing time: _____

Then calculate your reading speed:
   Number of words in the text (562) ÷
   Number of minutes it took you to
   read the text = your Reading Speed

Reading speed: _____

Your goal should be about 150–180 words per minute.

4 Check your reading comprehension by trying to answer these questions without
looking at the text.

1 In the list below, check (✔) the items that are basic American values according
to the text.

_____ **a** hard work

_____ **b** the importance of freedom

_____ **c** the importance of your
family's position in society

_____ **d** self-reliance

_____ **e** individual rights

_____ **f** self-discipline

_____ **g** the belief that good things will
happen

_____ **h** the equality of all individuals

_____ **i** the belief that you will never
get a second chance to succeed

2 Decide whether the statements below are true or false according to the text. Put
T (True) or *F* (False) in the blank before each statement.

_____ **a** The authors of the Declaration of Independence and the Constitution
got their ideas for these documents from European traditions.

_____ **b** In its early days, the United States did not have a strong class system.

_____ **c** The settlers who came to the United States saw endless natural
resources.

_____ **d** The values that the text discusses are only American. People from other
countries do not share these values.

Now read

Now read the text "The Roots of American Values" again. Then check your answers to
step 4 above. When you finish, turn to the tasks on page 147.

American Values from the Past

Chapter 7

1 THE ROOTS OF AMERICAN VALUES

There are consistent themes in many areas of American social and political life as well as in the personal behavior and attitudes of Americans. Many people believe that these themes are based on fundamental American values. However, it is important to remember that although these values do reflect the historical experiences and beliefs of many Americans, they have not always reflected the real lives of all Americans.

Many American values have their origins in the early history of the country and the people who settled it. They include the importance of freedom, hard work, self-discipline, and self-reliance. They stress the significance of individual rights, responsibility, and choice; the power of individuals to control their own lives; and the basic equality of all individuals. There is a deep belief in the equality of opportunity, that is, the idea that all people should have an equal chance to succeed and that everyone should have an equal say in what the country does. Indeed, this is at the root of the American idea of democracy. Finally, Americans are often seen as full of energy, optimism, and the willingness to take risks in order to succeed.

Certainly, these values are not exclusively American, but there are historical reasons for the presence of these consistent themes in American society, and they have consequences in public and private life. The founders of the nation, the men who wrote the Declaration

1

2

3

of Independence and the Constitution, put their egalitarian beliefs into these documents. They believed in the fundamental equality of all men, and that individuals should be judged by their achievements. At that time in Europe, family background and class were more important than individual achievement. If you were from an upper-class family, your world was secure and comfortable; if you were poor, you had little chance of success. In the New World, the settlers found a society without a strong class system that would limit their dreams. Many of the first settlers were Protestants,[8] who shared a belief in the power of hard work and self-reliance. They believed these were ways of improving themselves in the eyes of God, who would reward them for their discipline. This attitude toward life is sometimes referred to as "the Protestant work ethic." The significance of individualism was also apparent in many aspects of Americans' lives, in their desire to make their own choices, in their wish for privacy, and in their wish for others, including the government, to stay out of their lives. Finally, the settlers came to a land that seemed to have endless resources, such as land, food, wood, and water. This natural wealth encouraged their optimism and made them feel confident of success in their new country.

All of these circumstances came together to make American society somewhat different from the societies that preceded it. Because of their faith in the basic equality of all men and in the equality of opportunity in America, the early settlers believed that they controlled their own lives. This idea – that with hard work and courage, all people can achieve their goals – is often called "the American Dream." This view has both positive and negative consequences. Americans believe that individuals are responsible for their own success; they also tend to believe that those who fail simply have not worked hard enough. However, they don't see failure as an end; there is always a second chance, and there is always a way forward if you keep trying.

4

Benjamin Franklin

Proverbs and sayings that illustrate traditional American values
- The early bird gets the worm.*
- God helps those who help themselves.*
- Idle hands are the devil's workshop.
- The show must go on.
- If you can't stand the heat, get out of the kitchen.
- Today is the first day of the rest of your life.
- Little strokes fell mighty oaks.*
- If life hands you lemons, make lemonade.
- Where there's a will, there's a way.
- There is no free lunch.

* Attributed to Benjamin Franklin (1706–1790): scientist, philosopher, printer, inventor, statesman, and signer of the Declaration of Independence

8 Protestants are members of a branch of the Christian religion.

After you read

Task 1 BUILDING VOCABULARY: KEY TERMS

1 Match the key words from the text in the left column with their meanings in the right column. Write the appropriate word in the blank below its meaning.

values

risks

self-discipline

individualism

egalitarianism

self-reliance

optimism

1 ability to make yourself do things that you should even when you don't want to

_____

2 hopefulness and belief that good things will happen

_____

3 belief in the importance of individual and personal independence

_____

4 beliefs about what is right and wrong and what is important in life

_____

5 actions or situations that might turn out badly

_____

6 belief that all people are equally important

_____

7 ability to succeed without the help or support of others

_____

2 Fill in the missing words in the following sentences. Use the words from the left column in step 1.

1 The settlers were famous for their _____. They lived alone in the wilderness and rarely asked for help from their neighbors.

2 The men who wrote the Constitution believed in _____, that is, the fundamental equality of all men.

3 Many new Americans had to take _____ in their efforts to make a new life. Some found success; some failed.

4 The immigrants who landed on Ellis Island were filled with _____ about starting a new life in a new country.

5 Many Americans believe that hard work and _____ are the keys to success. Many new Americans have done work they do not like in order to succeed.

6 Americans' belief in _____ means they think people should make their own choices. It also means that each person's independence is very important.

7 _____ such as hard work and self-discipline were especially typical of the Christians who were the majority in the first waves of immigrants.

Task 2 THINKING ABOUT PROVERBS

> Proverbs and sayings illustrate basic values and ways of behaving in a culture. Understanding the proverbs of a culture can deepen your understanding of that culture.

1 As a class, discuss the meaning of the proverbs in the box at the end of the text. They are reprinted in step 2 below. Look up any words you don't know.

2 What basic value do you think each proverb illustrates? Write the letter of the value in the blank before the proverb. Some proverbs may illustrate more than one value.

a The importance of hard work

b The importance of continuing to try even though there are challenges and problems

c The need for independence and self-reliance

d Optimism about the future

_____ **1** The early bird gets the worm.

_____ **2** God helps those who help themselves.

_____ **3** Idle hands are the devil's workshop.

_____ **4** The show must go on.

_____ **5** If you can't stand the heat, get out of the kitchen.

_____ **6** Today is the first day of the rest of your life.

_____ **7** There is no free lunch.

_____ **8** Little strokes fell mighty oaks.

_____ **9** If life hands you lemons, make lemonade.

_____ **10** Where there's a will, there's a way.

3 Discuss any proverbs that you may know from other cultures. What values do they illustrate?

Preparing to read

THINKING ABOUT THE TOPIC BEFORE YOU READ

Look at the picture on page 145, and look at these pictures. All three pictures are of the American West in the early days of the country. Then discuss the questions below:

1 What do these pictures make you think of?
2 Have you seen films or television programs that use similar images?
3 Do you think these pictures show what life was really like in the old American West?

BUILDING VOCABULARY: PREVIEWING KEY TERMS

The words in bold on the left are from the text. Find the definition on the right for each word in bold, and write the word in the blank after its definition.

The **pioneers** left their towns in the east and began to move west, where the country was still wild.

Only a few white people lived on the western **frontier**.

The pioneers believed it was their **destiny** to develop and live on the new land.

The pioneers built homes in the **wilderness**, which was full of forests and animals.

The idea of the western frontier is part **myth** and part truth.

1 a border between developed land where white people live and undeveloped land where Native Americans live _____

2 an idea that is incorrect but that many people believe is true _____

3 people who are among the first to do something _____

4 events that are going to happen in the future; events that no one can control _____

5 land that has not been farmed or developed _____

Now read

Now read the text "The American West." When you finish, turn to the tasks on page 152.

2 THE AMERICAN WEST

Few images have as powerful a place in the American imagination as the symbols of the American West, such as the covered wagon, the log cabin, and the cowboy. Why are these images so powerful? One reason is that these images of the West are deeply connected with the traditional values that many Americans believe give their nation strength and character. It is important to remember, however, that the idea of the western frontier is partly a myth; it includes what Americans want to believe happened. What really happened as Americans moved west was not always what they would like to remember.

Large numbers of pioneers from Europe and the Eastern part of the United States began moving west in the nineteenth century. For these people, the West, which meant land west of the Mississippi River, seemed to be a place of unlimited opportunity and resources: excellent farmland and land rich in minerals, thick forests, and lots of animals for hunting. The land and the sky seemed to stretch without end, waiting for them. Many people also moved west to get away from the cities. They dreamed of a freer life in a wilder place.

However, this search for a new life had a cost. The journey west and life in the West were difficult. There were many physical hardships and few comforts or conveniences. Only the toughest and most self-reliant pioneers did well in these circumstances. They had to be able to build houses for themselves, farm, raise animals, hunt for food, and protect themselves and their property. A final important characteristic of the frontier was its social equality. In the struggle to survive, success depended on individual strength and resourcefulness, not on money or family background.

Throughout the nineteenth century, the pioneers moved west. The pioneers and the American government believed it was the destiny of Americans to populate the land from one coast to the other. They believed they were bringing civilization to the wilderness. However, this movement westward – often called the **westward expansion** – had some terrible consequences. It contributed to the death of thousands of Native Americans and the destruction of native communities. (See "America's First People," page 53.) Furthermore, as more people moved west, the frontier became less and less like the wilderness of their dreams, and more and more like the communities they had left back in the east.

Over time, Americans developed a romantic, but limited and not always accurate, picture of the old West. This picture is of strong, tough, and independent pioneers; of wide open spaces; of freedom and endless opportunity. Although the western frontier disappeared long ago, these ideas have been kept alive in books, art, movies, and advertising.

westward expansion
the movement of settlers to the western United States in the nineteenth century

Pioneer Diaries

Many of the pioneers kept diaries of their experiences on the journey west. This is from the diary of Amelia Stewart Knight, on her journey to Oregon in 1853. She was pregnant with her eighth child.

May 17th

We had a dreadful storm of rain . . . It killed two oxen. I never saw such a storm. The wind was so high that I thought it would tear the wagon to pieces. The rain beat into the wagons so that everything was wet. In less than two hours, the water was a foot deep all over our camp grounds. We could pitch no tents at all so we all had to crowd into the wagons and sleep in wet beds with wet clothes, without supper.

June 6th

Still in camp, husband and myself being sick (caused we supposed by drinking the river water).

June 11th

We crossed this afternoon over the roughest . . . piece of ground that was ever made. Not a drop of water, not a spear of grass to be seen. Nothing but . . . bare and broken rock, sand and dust.

July 4th

It has been very warm today. I never saw mosquitoes as bad as they are here. Sick all day with fever, partly caused by mosquito bites.

July 25th

A calf took sick today and died before breakfast. Soon after . . . one of our best cows was taken sick and died in a short time. Cattle are dying off very fast all along this road.

"Death Scene on the Plains"

A home in the West around 1900

After you read

Task 1 READING TO FIND SUPPORT FOR MAIN IDEAS

> Many academic assignments ask you to look for evidence in a new text that supports ideas you have read about previously.

1 Review the values that you learned about in "The Roots of American Values," page 145.

2 Now highlight evidence in "The American West" that supports each of the values below. Use a different color for each value if possible.

- self-reliance
- taking risks
- optimism
- egalitarianism

Task 2 THINKING CRITICALLY ABOUT THE TOPIC

Discuss the following questions in a small group:

1 Why do you think Americans, as well as people from other countries, have romantic views of the West?

2 How are these romantic views related to the values you have learned about in this chapter?

Task 3 READING PRIMARY TEXTS

1 Review the diary entries in the boxed text. You do not need to understand every word. Try to understand the general ideas.

2 In a small group, describe what you think life was like for pioneer families.

- For men
- For women
- For children

3 With your group, compare the diary entries and pictures on page 151 with the pictures of the American West on pages 145 and 149.

1 In what ways are they similar?

2 In what ways are they different?

3 How do the facts you have read about in the diary compare to the romantic image of the West that you discussed in Task 2?

Task 4   LANGUAGE FOCUS: *FEW* / *A FEW*

Few and *a few* are both ways of describing quantities. However, their meanings can be different.

few = not many or not enough

- **Few** of the children can read or write yet.
- **Few** things give me more pleasure than spending an evening with friends.

a few = some; a small number of

- I need to get **a few** things at the supermarket.
- We've been having **a few** problems with the new computer.

1 The word *few* appears in two sentences in "The American West." Scan the text to find the word each time it appears, and underline it.

2 With a partner, answer this question for each use of *few* in the text: Is its meaning closer to "not many," or is it closer to "some"? What clues helped you decide?

3 Discuss the difference in meaning between the sentences below. What clues helped you decide?

1 Kate was sad because she had made *few* friends at her new school – just Diane, Jane, and Nancy.

2 Kate was pleased because she had made *a few* friends at her new school – Diane, Jane, and Nancy.

4 Fill in the blanks in the following sentences with *few* or *a few*.

1 There are _____ symbols that seem more American than the cowboy.

2 You can still visit _____ places in the American West where you can find wilderness.

3 The American pioneers had to depend on their families and _____ neighbors for help in emergencies.

4 Life in the new western settlements offered many resources but _____ comforts or conveniences.

Preparing to read

NOTE TAKING: USING A MAP

> Some people take notes by making a "map." One way to do this is to draw lines and circles to show relationships between parts of the text.

1 Look at the illustration below. It is the beginning of a map of the text you are going to read, "The Marketplace." Notice that the circle in the center is large and its content is general. As the circles move away from the center, they become smaller and their content becomes more specific.

Read the content of the circles, and discuss what you think the text will be about.

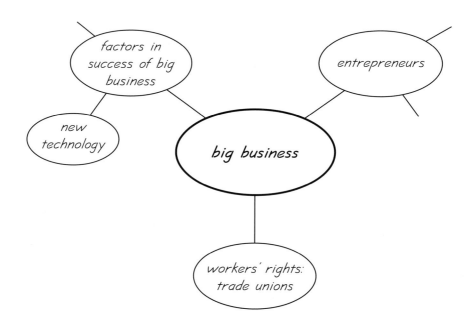

2 As you read the text, finish the map by adding more lines and circles. (You may prefer to draw your map on a separate sheet of paper.)

Now read

Now read the text "The Marketplace," and complete your map. When you finish, turn to the tasks on page 157.

3 THE MARKETPLACE

Americans admire people who take risks. Throughout the nation's history, the biggest success stories have been about people who took risks. These people started with very little and, with a good idea and hard work, became successful. In the business world, we call such people *entrepreneurs*.

The rise of big business

In the middle of the nineteenth century, the United States seemed to be a land of endless opportunity for someone with a good idea and the willingness to take risks and to work hard to make the idea successful. The country was rich in natural resources such as coal, iron, oil, and wood. The **Industrial Revolution**, which began in Europe in the late eighteenth century, had reached the United States, and there were small factories all across the country. It was a time of opportunity for entrepreneurs. Two entrepreneurs who were extremely successful during this period have become known as symbols of American big business. These men were Andrew Carnegie and John D. Rockefeller.

Andrew Carnegie came to the United States from Scotland when he was 12. His family was very poor. His first job was working in a factory for $1.20 a week. He saved his money carefully, invested it in various businesses, and made more money. While he was still in his thirties, Carnegie decided that the future of the country was in steel. He learned about a new process of manufacturing steel. He built a factory and began production using this new process. His business was very successful, but Carnegie was not satisfied. He knew that if he reduced his competition, he would make even more money, and so he bought other steel companies. He also used a strategy called *vertical integration* to control all aspects of steel production: he bought iron mines that supplied the steel mills, and he bought railroad companies that shipped the steel. In this way he could control and profit from all parts of the manufacturing process. Carnegie's company was the first to achieve this level of vertical integration. His profits rose, and he became the richest man in America.

The life of John D. Rockefeller offers a similar "rags-to-riches" (poor to rich) story. At the age of 16, he started to work for a shipping company. He saved his money and invested it in the oil business. Like Carnegie, he understood the importance of vertical integration and of reducing competition. He controlled all phases of the oil industry: drilling, refining, and transportation. He wanted to decrease competition and increase his profit, and so he bought every small oil company that he could. By 1877, when Rockefeller was only 38 years old, his company, Standard Oil, controlled 90 percent of the oil industry in the country.

Industries that are controlled almost entirely by one company, such as the steel industry (controlled mainly by Carnegie's company)

> **Industrial Revolution**
> the introduction into the economy of machines to do work that had previously been done by hand

Children of workers in front of a steel mill

and the oil industry (controlled mainly by Rockefeller's company), are called *monopolies*. In the 1890s, the federal government took action to limit the power of monopolies. However, the businesses of Carnegie, Rockefeller, and other important entrepreneurs still remained large and successful. These huge industries were partly responsible for helping to make the United States the most important economic power of the twentieth century.

Workers' rights: The rise of trade unions

The rise of big business in the nineteenth century was often at the workers' expense. Many successful industrial entrepreneurs of the time believed that any business strategy was fair in the race for higher profits. Frequently they did not treat their workers well, demanding long hours and paying low wages. 6

A magazine cover showing the violent conflict over unions and workers' rights at one of Andrew Carnegie's steel factories in Homestead, Pennsylvania, in 1892

One aspect of the Industrial Revolution was new technology that allowed machines to take the place of skilled craftsmen who had done much of the work by hand. The machines needed fewer and less-skilled workers to operate them, which meant that factories hired fewer people, and wages usually decreased when new technology was introduced. The large number of immigrants coming into the United States and looking for factory work increased the competition for jobs and also helped to keep wages low. 7

Low wages were not the only problem facing workers. Industrial workplaces were often dangerous: hot metal in the steel factories and dust in the mills caused injuries and disease. Workers had no protection and lost their jobs if they became sick and could not work. In the second half of the nineteenth century, the combination of these dangerous and difficult conditions and low wages encouraged the establishment of the labor movement, that is, the creation of trade unions to fight for and protect workers. The struggle to create unions and expand their power was difficult and sometimes violent. Factory owners were often opposed to the unions because they knew that strong unions would demand better pay and working conditions for their members, and better pay for workers would lower the company's profits. 8

In spite of the opposition of owners, however, unions continued to fight for the rights and protection of workers against powerful businesses. They won many of these battles, increasing pay and benefits, such as health insurance and pensions, and making workplaces safer. Many of the favorable workplace conditions in the United States today are a result of the efforts of trade unions. 9

After you read

Task 1 NOTE TAKING: CHECKING YOUR NOTES

Your notes will only help you if they are complete and accurate. One way to check your notes is to ask yourself questions about the text. If your notes do not provide the answers, go back to the text, find the missing information, and add it to your notes.

1 Look at the questions below. Can you answer them with information from your map? If not, find the necessary information in the text and add it to your map.

1 What are two main reasons for the success of entrepreneurs like Carnegie and Rockefeller?
2 What were some of the difficulties that workers faced as a result of the Industrial Revolution?
3 How was the success of big business related to these difficulties?
4 What were some of the positive effects of big business?
5 What were some of the negative effects?

2 Compare your answers to step 1 with a partner or in a small group.

Task 2 BUILDING VOCABULARY: KEY TERMS

Each sentence below describes a key term introduced in the text. Write the name of the terms in the blanks.

1 Control of all stages of a manufacturing process, from raw materials to shipping of the finished product

_____

2 An organization or company that has complete control of the sale of a product, for example, oil

_____

3 An organization that represents and protects workers

_____

4 A person who starts a new business, especially one that involves risk

_____

5 Something extra besides money that workers receive as part of their job

_____

Task 3 BUILDING VOCABULARY: VERBS OF DIRECTION

Some verbs show the direction of an action, that is, whether the action is upward or downward. Some of these verbs show who or what controls the direction. Other verbs do not. Some can do both.

Controller must be stated		Controller must never be stated	
raise (↑)	cut (↓)	go up (↑)	fall (↓)
	lower (↓)	rise (↑)	go down (↓)
	reduce (↓)		

        controller

- Andrew Carnegie **reduced** his workers' pay in order to keep his steel mills profitable.

  INCORRECT: Steel industry profits **reduced** at the end of the twentieth century.

        [controller is not stated]

- Union membership **rose** in the first half of the twentieth century.

  INCORRECT: Unions **rose** workers' wages.

Controller may or may not be stated	
increase (↑)	decrease (↓)

        controller

- Vertical integration **decreases** competition.

        [controller is not stated]

- Competition **decreases** if there are monopolies.

1 Find these verbs of direction in the text. State what went up or down and, if possible, who or what controlled the upward or downward direction. If the controller is not stated, write an X.

Verb of direction	What went up or down?	Who/what controlled it?
reduce (par. 3)		
rise (par. 3)		
decrease (par. 4)		
increase (par. 4)		
decrease (par. 7)		
lower (par. 8)		

2 Write three sentences of your own. Use any of the verbs in the box at the top of the page or in the chart in step 1. Describe trends you have read about in this chapter or in earlier chapters. You might consider trends in immigration (Unit 2) or progress made by women and minorities (Unit 3).

Preparing to read

BUILDING BACKGROUND KNOWLEDGE OF THE TOPIC

Horace Mann was a politician in the early nineteenth century. He helped to change the education system in the United States, starting in one state – Massachusetts. In the quotation below, he contrasts European values regarding education with new ideas in the United States.

1 | Read this quotation from Horace Mann:

> According to the European theory, men are divided into classes – some to toil* and earn, others to seize** and enjoy. According to the Massachusetts theory, all are to have an equal chance for earning, and equal security in the enjoyment of what they earn.
>
> – Horace Mann, *Report No. 12 of the Massachusetts School Board*, 1848

* do hard, tiring work
** take

2 | Discuss the following questions as a class:

1 What differences does Horace Mann describe between the European tradition and the ideas in Massachusetts?
2 How do you think these differences could affect education?
  a What do you think education was like for the "toil and earn" class in Europe?
  b What do you think education was like for the "seize and enjoy" class?
3 What clues in the quotation helped you answer 2a and 2b?
4 How do you think education could help to promote equality?
5 How are Horace Mann's ideas connected to some of the basic themes that were introduced in "The Roots of American Values," page 145?

Now read

Now read the text "Education for All." When you finish, turn to the tasks on page 162.

➡ Remember to review and update your vocabulary notebook.

4 EDUCATION FOR ALL

Poor children in New York City around 1900

In the early nineteenth century, education in urban areas was mostly for the rich. The public did not want to pay to educate poor children; only churches were willing to provide schools for the poor. These schools were generally open for just a few hours a day and a few months a year. **1**

Gradually this situation changed. One reason for the change was necessity. The cities were filled with thousands of uneducated poor children, and people were afraid that the children would make trouble if they were left alone. In addition, immigrants were pouring into the cities from all over the world. They needed to learn the new language and culture. People began to see schools as the solution to these problems. In school, children learned not only reading and arithmetic, but moral and cultural lessons as well. **2**

The first public schools

The middle building is one of the first public high schools in New York City.

By the middle of the nineteenth century, a new kind of school was established in some eastern cities, and these schools soon spread to other parts of the country. The education in these schools was based on several important ideas that are at the heart of American values. First, education is essential for democracy. Only the educated can participate as full citizens in a democratic society; therefore, it is essential that all citizens receive a basic education. Another central principle was the belief that education could provide a reliable workforce and contribute to the strength and stability of the nation. **3**

The general public's view of the power and function of education was also beginning to change. People began to understand that without an education, it would be difficult for children to succeed. They saw education as a way of providing equal opportunity to all citizens. It was the ladder to economic success, but just as importantly, it was a way for individuals to have some control over their own future. It was a path to the American Dream. This was the beginning of American **public schools** that were free for all children. **4**

public schools

schools that are paid for by taxes and that are free to the students who attend them

private schools

schools that are not free; schools that charge tuition

Supporters of public education saw these schools as a reflection of a democratic society. All children in the community went to school together. It is important to note, however, that this did not include African Americans, who were mostly excluded from public education. There were also some rich parents who did not want their children to go to school with poor children and instead, sent their children to **private schools**, that is, schools that charge tuition. Despite some opposition, public schools soon became an established part of American society. Today, most American children still get their education in public schools. **5**

Higher education

Higher education, that is, college and university education, also reflects the broad, egalitarian value that all people are equally important and have equal rights. The United States has a system of state and local colleges with low-cost tuition that has encouraged a large percentage of Americans to get a college education. The goal of this system has been to provide a college education to as many people as possible. Many older adults, as well as recent high school graduates, take advantage of these educational opportunities. The result has been a continuing rise in the number of people attending colleges and universities.

Today, a college degree is increasingly necessary for success. Fifty years ago, there were good jobs in factories for workers without a college education; however, many of those factories have now closed because manufacturing is cheaper in countries where workers earn less money. Most good jobs in the twenty-first century in the United States require at least some higher education. Therefore, more Americans are going to college than ever before. In 2004, 18.34 million high school graduates enrolled in college, a rate more than nine times higher than in 1950.

The average pay for a college graduate is more than 60 percent higher than for a high school graduate. Lifetime earnings for a person with at least a college degree are $1 million more than the lifetime earnings of a worker with no college education (see Figure 7.2). Statistics suggest that there are also differences in many other measures of success. People with more education tend to have better health, are less likely to become unemployed or go to prison, and are more likely to vote and participate in their community. The difference affects the next generation, too; children of college graduates tend to do better in school than children of high school graduates. Finally, children of college graduates are far more likely to complete their own college degree. As in the nineteenth century, education is a major factor in success. A difference in today's world is the increasing importance of higher education.

6

7

8

Figure 7.1 Enrollment in higher education

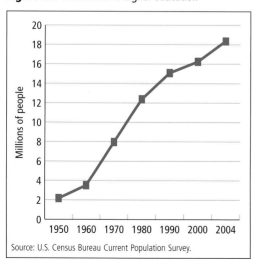

Source: U.S. Census Bureau Current Population Survey.

Figure 7.2 Expected lifetime earnings by educational level (2003)

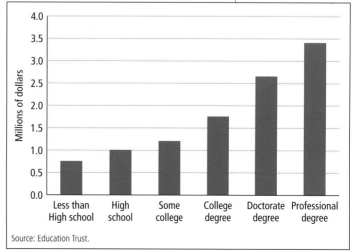

Source: Education Trust.

After you read

Task 1 TEST TAKING: USING YOUR NOTES TO PREPARE

Using your notes helps you prepare for a test. Here are some guidelines for using your notes effectively.

- Take notes using a method of your choice.
- Review your notes and decide how the information in them could be organized into categories.
- On separate paper or in a separate e-file, organize the information in your notes into the categories you have chosen.
- Use your organized notes to predict test questions.

1 Skim "Education for All," and think about the best way to take notes on this text. You will probably want to use one of the note-taking techniques you used in earlier chapters: using a chart (page 66), highlighting (page 70), using an outline (page 82), or using a map (page 154).

2 Reread the text carefully, and take notes using the technique you chose in step 1. Be sure to take notes on Figures 7.1 and 7.2.

3 Review your notes and organize the information into categories. Some categories that you might use for this text are listed below. You may decide to add other categories.

- reasons for public education
- history of public schools
- colleges and universities
- reasons to get higher education
- American values related to education for all

4 Use your notes to predict test questions.

1 For each of your categories, predict one test question. (Review "Test Taking: Understanding the Language of Test Questions" on page 110 if necessary.)

2 Exchange questions with a partner, and give an oral response to your partner's questions.

3 Compare your questions in a small group. If your questions were similar, you probably did a good job of predicting the test questions.

Task 2 BUILDING VOCABULARY: WORDS THAT DESCRIBE TRENDS

Academic writing frequently includes descriptions of trends or generalizations about beliefs or behavior. These descriptions often use words that indicate things that will probably happen or probably not happen. Describing trends with these words allows you to make generalizations that are not too strong. Here are two common examples:

- **tend (not) to**
  Voters in cities **tend to** vote for Democrats.
  Voters in farming communities **tend not to** vote for Democrats.

- **be (un)likely to**
  Rainstorms **are likely to** occur during the summer months.
  Snow **is unlikely to** occur during the summer months.

Here is a way to show tendencies when you make a comparison:

- X is *more/less likely to* do Z than Y.
  Today, women **are more likely to** go to college than men.
  Today, men **are less likely to** go to college than women.

1 Read this excerpt from the text, and fill in each blank with an appropriate expression of tendency. Then look at paragraph 8 in the text to check your answers.

People with more education _____ have better health, _____ become unemployed or go to prison, and _____ vote and participate in their community. The difference affects the next generation, too; children of college graduates _____ do better in school than children of high school graduates. Finally, children of college graduates are far _____ complete their own college degree.

2 Complete the following sentences with information from the text, including Figures 7.1 and 7.2. Use expressions of tendency.

1 People with only a high school education _____
2 College graduates _____
3 People with a professional degree _____
4 _____ vote.
5 _____ go to college.

3 Write two sentences of your own to describe group tendencies that you have observed in your own life.

UNIT 4   WRITING ASSIGNMENT A

In this chapter, you have read about the historical context of some traditional American values. In the next chapter, you will read about how these values relate to American life today. Your assignment is to write about how fundamental American beliefs are connected to historical events and the lives of contemporary Americans. You will begin your paper for this assignment and finish it for the writing assignment at the end of the next chapter.

Preparing to write

1| With a partner or a small group of classmates, discuss which of the themes in this chapter you think are the most important or influential. Some themes are listed below. You may think of others, too. Take notes on your discussion.

- equal opportunity
- self-reliance
- optimism
- hard work

- risk taking
- individual achievement
- basic equality of all individuals

2| Choose one theme to write about. We will call this "Theme X."

3| In what areas of American life and history has Theme X had a strong influence? Review the topics that have been discussed in this chapter or in earlier chapters to find evidence of the influence of your theme. Possibilities from this chapter include:

- education
- business
- attitudes toward the land

4| Choose two examples of evidence that can help you illustrate the influence of your theme. Explain the examples to your partner or group.

Now write

You will write two paragraphs, one to explain each of your two examples. You can use information from any of the texts, but don't copy the sentences. If you refer to your notes instead of looking at the text, it will make it easier for you to use your own words so that you don't plagiarize.

Introduce each paragraph with a topic sentence that connects your theme with your example.

<u>Example</u>
Theme X:
    equality of opportunity
First example of evidence:
    education
Topic sentence for paragraph 1:

    The history of **American education** shows the influence of the American belief in **equality of opportunity**.

Paragraph 1

Write a topic sentence. Then include some details about how your example shows the influence of your theme.

Paragraph 2

In your topic sentence for this paragraph, use a signal word, such as *also* or *another*. This will show your readers that this is a second example.

<u>Examples</u>

- Another example of the importance of (<u>Theme X</u>) is _____.
- This history of _____ also shows the influence of (<u>Theme X</u>).

Then include some details about how your second example shows the importance of your theme.

After you write

Exchange papers with a partner, and answer these questions about his or her paragraphs.

1 What theme did your partner choose?

    _____

2 What two examples did your partner use to illustrate the influence of the theme?

    (1) _____

    (2) _____

3 Underline the topic sentence in each paragraph. Does it state what the paragraph is about? If not, how could it be improved?

4 Is your partner's explanation of each example clear? If not, how could it be improved?

5 Did your partner provide enough details for you to understand the influence of the theme? If not, what more could he or she add?

6 Are there any grammar or spelling errors in your partner's paper? If so, how could they be corrected?

Preparing to read

BUILDING VOCABULARY: PREVIEWING KEY TERMS

1| Read the title of the text and the titles of the headings.

2| Discuss the following questions with a partner:

1 What "rights and responsibilities" do you think the title refers to?

2 Both headings contain the word *versus*. What does this term mean? (Is this term in your vocabulary notebook? Review your notes from "Building Vocabulary: Previewing Key Terms" on page 42 if necessary.)

3 What do you think the text under each heading will be about?

THINKING ABOUT THE TOPIC BEFORE YOU READ

Discuss the following questions with your partner or in a small group:

1 What is an example of a situation in which the rights of an individual might conflict with the interests of a larger group of people?

2 Most people agree that individuals should show some self-reliance and not always depend on the assistance of others. Are there some situations in which this is *not* true? Discuss some examples.

3 Are there some situations in which individuals should expect the assistance of other people? Discuss some examples.

4 Are there some situations in which individuals should expect the assistance of their government? Discuss some examples.

Now read

Now read the text "The Individual and Society: Rights and Responsibilities." When you finish, turn to the tasks on page 169.

American Values Today

A work program created by the U.S. government during the Great Depression

1 THE INDIVIDUAL AND SOCIETY: RIGHTS AND RESPONSIBILITIES

Individual rights are so important to Americans and so fundamental to the nation that they are part of the Bill of Rights, which was written to protect and defend the rights of individuals against their own government and against the rule of the majority. Yet a nation that allows all individuals to do whatever they want will soon fall apart. The good of the whole society must also be considered. Therefore individuals have rights but they also have responsibilities.

A balance between the rights of individuals and the good of society, that is, the good of the whole nation, has been required throughout American history. Sometimes, however, circumstances make it impossible for individuals to accept their responsibilities, and society must act to help those individuals who cannot help themselves. This is one of the most important functions of government. Thus, the United States government has had to find a balance in two situations: (1) between protecting the rights of the individual and protecting the good of society, and (2) between encouraging self-reliance and providing support and assistance to people who need them.

Individual rights versus the good of society

Two situations in which the rights of the individual have conflicted with the good of society involve **eminent domain** and national security. The principle of eminent domain states that private individuals may

> **eminent domain**
> the government's right to take private property for the public good

be required to sell their property, including their homes, if the land is needed for a project that is for the good of society. For instance, the government might want to build a railroad, a school, or a park on land where there are homes. The owners of those homes receive a payment, but they must give up their property.

The second situation concerns the balance between the need to protect national security and people's freedom of speech and their expectation of privacy. Most citizens do not expect the government to read their e-mail or listen to their telephone conversations. By law, if government officials want to do this, they must first persuade a judge to give them permission. Since September 11, 2001, however, the government has limited individual rights in these areas in order to allow for greater protection of national security. Today, when government officials think there is a danger to national security, they may sometimes read or listen to communications without first getting permission from a judge.

Self-reliance versus government support and assistance

An important example of the need to balance self-reliance and government assistance is the federal government's response to the problems of the **Great Depression** (1929–1940). During this time, almost a quarter of the population was unemployed. People lost their farms, their businesses, and even their homes. They could not rely on themselves; they needed help from the government. In 1933, President Franklin Roosevelt established the **New Deal**, which included many programs and new laws to provide economic security for all members of society, especially the retired, the unemployed, and the poor. To provide jobs, the government paid unemployed workers to build roads, schools, and government buildings; it paid unemployed artists to paint, take photographs, write books, and perform plays and music.

Thirty years after the Great Depression, there were still people struggling to succeed. Once again, the government helped people who were unable to help themselves. In the 1960s, the aim of the **Great Society** programs, under President Lyndon Johnson, was to end poverty in the United States by providing jobs, health care, housing, and better education for the poor – especially for African Americans, who had limited access to these services. The Great Society programs had some success but did not reach the goal of ending poverty.

The New Deal and the Great Society programs increased government assistance to individuals, but they also increased people's reliance on the government. Today there has been a return to support for the value of self-reliance and a growing opposition to the high cost of government assistance, which relies on tax dollars. Today's government assistance programs are more likely to provide training for those who want to improve their job skills and assistance for those who want to complete or continue their education – in other words, for those who have shown some self-reliance.

Great Depression

a period in history (1929–1940), during which economic activity slowed dramatically, prices fell, and people lost jobs

New Deal

a set of government programs that were established to help the United States recover from the Great Depression

Great Society

a set of government programs that were established in the 1960s to help end poverty and racial inequality in the United States

4

5

6

7

After you read

Task 1 VISUALIZING THE MAIN IDEAS

> Sometimes visualizing difficult or complicated ideas can help you to
> understand them better.

1 The drawings below show two situations that illustrate the main ideas in the text.
Fill in the blanks with the appropriate terms.

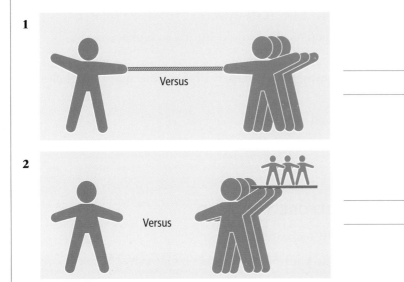

1

Versus

_____

_____

2

Versus

_____

_____

2 Work with a partner. Take turns explaining one example from the text for each of
the situations illustrated above.

3 Look through the previous texts in this book, and find at least two situations that
involve a conflict between the individual and society. As a class, discuss what
happened in each situation. Was the conflict resolved? Explain.

Task 2 UNDERSTANDING THE FUNCTION OF DIFFERENT PARTS OF
THE TEXT

Read the functions listed below. Match each one to a paragraph in the text. Write the
paragraph number in the blank before each function. In one case, several paragraphs
match a single function.

_____ **1** Establishes and explains the main idea

_____ **2** Provides and explains an example

_____ **3** Reviews previous information about the topic and provides background
for the main idea

_____ **4** Brings the topic into the present time

Preparing to read

SCANNING

1 Scan the text "The Open Road" to find the following numerical information. The relevant paragraph is given in parentheses.

   1 How many cars were on American roads in 1930? (par. 2) _____

   2 What percentage of American families owned a car in 1960? (par. 3) _____

   3 What percentage of American families own a car today? (par. 3) _____

   4 How many miles of road were on the original interstate highway? (par. 3) _____

   5 What percentage of Americans drive their own cars to work? (par. 4) _____

   6 How many cars are on the road in the United States today? (par. 6) _____

2 Based on the information you gathered in step 1, discuss the questions below with a partner:

   1 What do you think the text will be about?

   2 How important do you think cars are to people in the United States? What makes you think this?

THINKING ABOUT THE TOPIC BEFORE YOU READ

Discuss the following questions with a partner:

   1 Do you own a car? If so, what kind of car do you own? Why? What do you use your car for?

   2 Do you think a car is mainly a convenience, a symbol of how much money you have, or both?

Now read

Now read the text "The Open Road." When you finish, turn to the tasks on page 173.

2 THE OPEN ROAD

The road and the automobile have always been symbols of Americans' love of the freedom of wide-open spaces. Americans feel that having a car means the freedom to come and go wherever they want, whenever they want. Rising gasoline prices, traffic jams, and air pollution have not kept Americans off the road.

Model T

At the beginning of the twentieth century, cars were for rich people and roads were rough and not well maintained. Over the next several decades, several factors made it possible for millions of Americans to participate in "car culture." First, the price of cars dropped significantly because of Henry Ford, an extremely successful entrepreneur. Ford introduced new technology and new methods for manufacturing cars that resulted in lower prices. Soon the price of cars was so low that even the people who worked in Ford's factories could buy cars. The discovery of oil in the state of Texas brought down the price of gasoline as well. Still, in 1930, there were fewer than 5 million cars on American roads.

After World War II, the economy of the United States began to grow. The soldiers came home and they wanted to start families, buy houses, and buy cars. Many of them chose to live outside of the cities, in the suburbs. Those who lived far from their jobs needed to drive because there was little public transportation from the suburbs to the city. This situation created the need for more roads. In 1956, Congress established the Interstate Highway System, with more than 42,000 miles of roads. More roads meant more people could reach their jobs from the suburbs, so more people moved to the suburbs. The number of cars on the road went up by 50 percent from 40 million to 60 million. By 1960, 77 percent of all American families had at least one car. Today the figure is over 90 percent. In fact, in most American homes, there are more cars and trucks than drivers!

Thunderbird

Today stores and services are often in large shopping malls that may be miles away from people's homes, which means more car trips. A recent survey by the Department of Transportation found that the average American takes four car trips per day, and nearly half of them are for shopping. The survey also showed that more than 90 percent of Americans drive their own cars to work. In the last 50 years, federal and local governments have built more roads and less public transportation.

Cars are not just for transportation, however. The kind of car you have can say a lot about who you are – or who you want to be. During the 1950s, American cars became bigger and more stylish. Drive-in restaurants and movie theaters became popular. Young people in small towns and suburbs spent

SUV (sport utility vehicle)

their evenings in cars, driving up and down the streets. Books and movies made cars and life on the road seem glamorous. Today this association of cars with lifestyle continues. One example is the popular SUV (sport-utility vehicle). This car reminds Americans of a traditional image: a self-reliant individual with an active life. SUVs are for mountain climbers, hikers, and for life in the wilderness. Of course, most SUV owners simply drive their cars to work every day. As in the past, cars are often not just for transportation; they can symbolize who you are.

With 200 million cars across the country, Americans are still in love with cars and the open road; they drive more than 2 trillion miles every year.

6

Drive in, drive through

In the 1950s, people wanted to be in their cars. Drive-in restaurants were popular places to eat. Waiters brought food out to the car and the family ate inside the car. Drive-in movie theaters were even more popular. Huge outdoor screens showed movies to an audience sitting in their cars. In 1958, there were almost 5,000 drive-in movie theaters across the country. One theater in the state of Michigan had space for 3,000 cars.

The Whitestone Bridge Drive-In, New York, 1951

Today, the "drive-through" or "drive-up" is popular, not because people want to be in their cars, but because they want to save time. There are drive-throughs available so you can stay in your car while you:

- withdraw money from the bank
- get medicine from a pharmacy
- buy lunch
- hear a church service
- get married

A Valentine's Day wedding at a drive-through in Las Vegas, Nevada, 2004

After you read

Task 1 THINKING CRITICALLY ABOUT THE TOPIC

1 With a partner or small group, discuss this excerpt from the text. What does it mean? Do you agree? Why or why not?

> . . . cars are often not just for transportation; they can say a lot about who you are – or who you want to be.

2 Think about the American cars on the road today. What kinds of cars do you think are popular? What do these cars say about Americans today?

3 If you are familiar with another country, describe how people there view their cars. Are their views similar to or different than the views of Americans?

Task 2 LANGUAGE FOCUS: *BECAUSE / BECAUSE OF*

Because and *because of* both indicate that a reason will follow, but they have different functions in a sentence:

- *Because* is a subordinator, and it links two clauses.

      clause   clause

  Many factories closed, **because** costs were too high.

- *Because of* is a preposition, and it links a clause with a noun phrase.

      clause   noun phrase

  Many factories closed **because of** the high costs.

1 Find one sentence in the text with *because*; circle *because* and underline the clause that follows it. Find one sentence with *because of*; circle *because of* and underline the noun phrase that follows it.

2 Complete the following sentences with *because, because of,* or your own words. If you need more space, write your answers on a separate piece of paper.

  1 Some Europeans immigrated to the United States *because of* _____.

  2 Some businesses hire undocumented workers _____ they can pay them lower wages.

  3 Many African Americans could not vote _____ literacy tests and voting taxes.

  4 After the legal case of *Brown versus Board of Education of Topeka,* some communities closed their public schools *because* _____.

  5 Some people argue that affirmative action is necessary *because of* _____.

  6 Andrew Carnegie opposed the trade unions _____ he knew they wanted higher pay for workers.

Preparing to read

SKIMMING

Skim the reading for one minute to answer the two questions below:

1 What is the topic of the reading?
2 What two businesses does it discuss?

THINKING ABOUT THE TOPIC BEFORE YOU READ

With a partner or group, discuss what you know about the two businesses.

1 Do you use Google? If so, what do you use it for?
2 What do you know about Google? Have you read and heard about it in the news?
3 Have you ever been to a Wal-Mart? If so, do you prefer shopping at Wal-Mart or at smaller stores?
4 What do you know about Wal-Mart, either from your own experience or from reading about it?
5 Why do you think the author chose to discuss Google and Wal-Mart in a text called "The Twenty-First-Century Marketplace"?

Now read

Now read the text "The Twenty-First-Century Marketplace." When you finish, turn to the tasks on page 177.

3 THE TWENTY-FIRST CENTURY MARKETPLACE

American business has changed a great deal since the days of Andrew   1
Carnegie and John D. Rockefeller. Monopolies are prohibited, and the
government has passed laws to make sure that workplaces are safe.
Trade unions continue to protect workers' rights, although these unions
are not as strong as they were in the past. Some in the business world
argue that these changes have made it more difficult for entrepreneurs
to be successful. Yet there have been many examples of extremely successful entrepreneurs in recent years. Surprisingly, the factors in their
success are not very different from the factors in the success of the
business leaders in the past. The founders of these modern businesses
all had good ideas for a new product or service or simply a new and
better way of running an old business. They combined their ideas with
a good education, hard work, and an understanding that their business would have to adjust constantly to changes in the market and
in technology. Not surprisingly, many modern success stories involve
technology.

Three modern entrepreneurs

Larry Page and Sergey Brin met when they were students at Stanford   2
University in the 1990s. They realized that many of the Internet search
engines that were available at that time did not deliver the information
that people were looking for. They also realized that the most popular
Web pages were usually the most useful. Therefore, they created a new
system: They put the Web sites that people visit the most first on the
search results page.

Page and Brin worked out of a friend's garage and borrowed money   3
from friends and family to develop their business. In 1998, they for-
mally introduced their search engine, Google. When it began, Google
got about 10,000 inquiries a day; the number of inquiries quickly grew
to more than 200 million a day. Today Google is the most successful search engine in the world, and it performs an enormous variety
of searches in dozens of languages. It has also begun to offer other
services, such as shopping guides, news, satellite maps, e-mail, photo
sharing, translation, and even help with dating.

Sam Walton's success story is different. Walton did not even have   4
a specific product or service to sell. He had a concept – **discounting** – which he applied to a huge variety of products. With this concept,
he created Wal-Mart, a discount **retail chain**. Walton also used new
business practices: He bought products in such large quantities that he
could demand very low prices from his suppliers; he bought directly
from manufacturers all over the world; he built enormous stores that
sold everything from toys to light bulbs at such low prices that smaller
stores could not compete. Finally, Wal-Mart was one of the first retail
businesses to completely computerize its operations, significantly
increasing efficiency. The only computer system in the country that is

discounting
offering something for sale
at a lower price than usual

retail chain
a group of stores in
different locations that
have the same name and
are owned by the same
company

larger than Wal-Mart's belongs to the U.S. Department of Defense. Wal-Mart was so successful that Sam Walton became one of the richest men in the country. Many people say that Wal-Mart has hurt small businesses and has not always treated its workers and suppliers fairly; however, it remains very successful in the United States and around the world.

Superstores versus small business

Until recently, stores in the United States were small stores. Even after the success of big business in the time of Carnegie and Rockefeller, the majority of businesses remained small. Often a family owned a small store, and it was passed from the parents to the children. In smaller cities and towns, the owners often knew all their customers. Large stores like Wal-Mart are relatively new, but their numbers have grown quickly. Today there are many of these "superstores," such as Best Buy, Home Depot, and Office Max. These kinds of stores are different because of their size and the relatively low cost of their products. Many of them follow Wal-Mart's example of buying in large quantities so they can offer low prices. Unlike Wal-Mart, many specialize in one particular kind of product, for example, computers, products for pets, or office supplies.

Superstores are convenient for customers because they can find everything they need in one place. However, they do not offer the personal connection between the salespeople and the customers that was common in the days of small, family-owned stores. The small stores have struggled since the appearance of superstores because small stores cannot compete. They cannot match the prices or the variety of the products in the superstores. Many shoppers have gradually stopped going to the small stores, and as a result, many of these businesses have had to close. Some Americans regret these changes, and today there are communities that have decided they do not want superstores. They prefer the personal connection and service they get at small stores, even if the prices are higher.

Inside a Wal-Mart superstore

Small stores

After you read

Task 1 READING FOR MAIN IDEAS

1 Name three important factors for success in the twenty-first-century marketplace.

1 _____

2 _____

3 _____

2 Name the new idea that was the basis for each of the two businesses described in the text.

1 Google: _____

2 Wal-Mart: _____

3 Give two reasons why customers prefer Wal-Mart over small stores.

1 _____

2 _____

Task 2 READING FOR DETAILS

Read the phrases in the left column. Put a check (✔) under the name of the company that the phrase describes. In some cases, the phrase applies to both companies.

	Google	Wal-Mart
1. started with a good idea		
2. pioneered new business practices		
3. began in a garage with borrowed money		
4. uses computer technology		
5. can help you find a date		
6. has been very successful		
7. has many stores		
8. is used more than 200 million times a day		
9. offers services in many languages		

Task 3 LANGUAGE FOCUS: *SO . . . THAT / SUCH . . . THAT*

So . . . that and *such . . . that* appear in expressions of degree. They introduce a clause that shows a result.

so . . . that
So can be followed by an adjective or an adverb.

                     adjective   result clause
The price of cars was **so** low **that** many people could buy them.

         adverb   result clause
He did **so** well on the test **that** he got into a good college.

So can also be followed by an expression of quantity, for example, *many / much* + **noun.**

               noun   result clause
There were **so many** people **that** he couldn't get on the bus.

          noun   result clause
She made **so much** money **that** she bought a new house.

such . . . that
Such is followed by an adjective + noun; if the noun is singular, it is always introduced by the indefinite article, *a(n).*

          adjective + noun   result clause
The store had **such** beautiful dresses **that** it was difficult to choose one.

       article + adjective + noun   result clause
He had **such** a small apartment **that** he could not have a desk.

1 | Find the expressions below in the text, and complete the sentences.

    1 _____ such large quantities that _____ .

    2 _____ such low prices that _____ .

    3 _____ so successful that _____ .

2 | Complete the following sentences based on the information in the text.

    1 Google works so well that _____ .

    2 Wal-Mart's prices are so _____ that _____ .

3 | Write two new sentences of your own using the expressions of degree *so . . . that* or *such . . . that.*

Preparing to read

CONDUCTING A SURVEY

Surveys are frequently used in academic research to gather information about people's opinions and behaviors.

1 | The text you are going to read, "Is the American Dream Still Possible?", concerns factors that are important for success in life. With a partner, discuss what factors you think are important for success.

2 | Conduct a survey to find out your classmates' views. You will use the same questions that were used for a survey that appeared in a major American newspaper, *The New York Times*.

On a separate piece of paper, make a chart like the one below. Ask each classmate how important he or she thinks each factor is in getting ahead, that is, in becoming successful. Put a check (✔) in the appropriate box for each response.

Factors in getting ahead	Essential	Very important	Somewhat important	Not very important	Not important at all
wealthy family					
knowing important people					
natural ability and talent					
good education					
hard work					

3 | Count up your results, and report a percentage for each factor in the chart. For example, what percentage of your classmates said a wealthy family is essential for getting ahead?

Now read

Now read the text "Is the American Dream Still Possible?" When you finish, turn to the tasks on page 182.

➡ Remember to review and update your vocabulary notebook.

4 IS THE AMERICAN DREAM STILL POSSIBLE?

Is it still possible to achieve the American Dream? The answer depends on how you define "American Dream." Americans generally explain its meaning in one of two ways. Some say it means having freedom and living in a society based on equality; however, most think it means achieving economic security and success. In other words, the American Dream means having upward economic and social mobility, that is, improving your financial and social situation. Americans have always believed that success is a result of a person's individual ability and hard work as well as access to education and opportunity. They see the United States as a meritocracy, or a system in which individuals are rewarded for their ability and effort, not for their family background, wealth, or connections to powerful people. Generally, Americans believe people can control their own success.

In the history of the United States, almost every generation has been able to achieve upward mobility; each generation has been more successful than the previous one. Today, however, upward mobility has become more difficult because of changes in the job market and inequalities in the educational system. There is also considerable evidence that the income gap between rich and poor has increased in the last 25 years. In other words, the poor are getting poorer and the rich are getting richer.

Owning your own home has always been a symbol of "the American Dream."

Until recently, the United States was a major producer of goods, with many natural resources, plentiful labor, and advanced technology. All of these made the country an efficient and powerful economic and political force in the world. Today, however, the United States' role has changed. It is now a major consumer nation. Many of the good jobs that gave people the opportunity for upward mobility were in manufacturing, but these jobs are gone now.

There has been another important change – in the educational system. Americans have always thought of education as a democratic process, allowing children of all backgrounds equal access to opportunity. They have seen education as a path to economic success. Today, more than ever, an education is necessary to get a job that pays well. It may no longer be true, however, that every child gets an equal education and the chance to succeed that education can bring.

The American educational system does not always provide as much support for poor children as for children from high-income families. Public schools are paid for mostly with property tax dollars from states and cities. The taxes are based on property values, which means that people pay taxes based on the value of their homes. Sadly, as poor communities become poorer, the value of their homes decreases and these communities cannot collect enough tax money to pay for good schools. Thus, the poor lose an important path to economic success – a good education.

Americans have begun to ask if it is still possible for each new generation to move up the economic ladder, that is, to have a better life than their parents. According to a recent report in *The Economist*, upward mobility in the United States has slowed significantly. A 1978 survey found that 23 percent of adult men from the bottom fifth of the population (in social and economic terms) had moved to the top fifth in one generation. In 1998, a professor at Indiana University repeated this survey; he found that there was very little upward mobility. Nearly 70 percent of the people in his study were either at the same level or were doing worse than their parents. Two other recent studies had similar results. For the first time, many Americans are poorer and less successful than their parents. Some scholars claim that upward mobility is still possible, but most agree that it is not keeping up with the growing gap between the rich and the poor.

In spite of this trend, Americans continue to show their traditional optimism. Many still believe that things will get better for them and for their children. In a 2004 survey by *The New York Times* (see Figure 8.1), Americans were asked if they thought their standard of living, that is, their economic level, was better than that of their parents; 66 percent of them replied "yes." When they were asked if they thought their children's standard of living would be better than theirs, again, the majority said "yes." The survey also showed that most Americans still believe that individuals control their own success and that the most important factors in getting ahead are ability, hard work, and a good education.

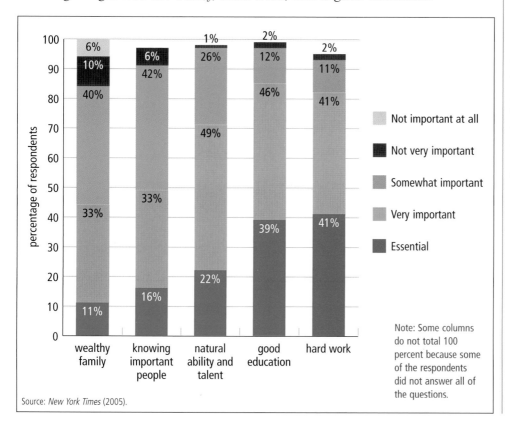

Source: *New York Times* (2005).

Figure 8.1 Factors in getting ahead.

The New York Times asked 1,764 Americans to rate the importance of various factors in getting ahead. The results are shown in this graph.

Note: Some columns do not total 100 percent because some of the respondents did not answer all of the questions.

After you read

Task 1 EXAMINING GRAPHIC MATERIAL

1 Review Figure 8.1 on page 181. Put *T* (True) or *F* (False) in front of each statement below based on the information in the graph.

_____ **1** Most people responded that education is an essential or very important factor in getting ahead.

_____ **2** Some people said that hard work is not important in getting ahead.

_____ **3** About half of the respondents said that knowing important people is essential or very important.

_____ **4** Most people responded that a good education and hard work are about equally important factors in getting ahead.

_____ **5** A wealthy family background is one of the most important factors in getting ahead.

2 Write two statements of your own based on the information in the graph.

3 Review the results of the survey you conducted in "Preparing to Read." As a class, discuss how the results of your survey compare to the results of the survey conducted by *The New York Times*.

TASK 2 WRITING DEFINITIONS: THE XYZ FORMAT

1 Review the instructions for writing definitions using the XYZ (X is a Y that Z) format in the Writing Assignment for Chapter 1 on page 26.

2 Write a one-sentence definition of each of these key terms from the text using the XYZ format. Use your own words.

1 A **meritocracy** is a system that _____

_____

_____.

2 A **property tax** is a tax that _____

_____

_____.

3 A **consumer nation** is a country that _____

_____

_____.

Task 3 WRITING DEFINITIONS: USING *MEAN* + A GERUND

Remember that gerunds (the *-ing* form of the verb) are used when the meaning requires an action, but the grammar requires a noun. Therefore, gerunds are used in definitions that describe actions. Such definitions often use the verb *mean*.

term | definition using gerund

Self-reliance means depending on yourself, not other people.

term | definition using gerund

Poverty means not having enough money for the basic necessities, such as food and shelter.

1 | Review the text and underline the three definitions of "American Dream" that use *mean* + a gerund.

2 | Write a one-sentence definition for each of the terms below using *mean* + a gerund.

1 *upward economic and social mobility*

_____

_____

2 *optimism*

_____

_____

3 *success*

_____

_____

4 *freedom of expression*

_____

_____

5 *self-discipline*

_____

_____

6 *vertical integration*

_____

_____

Task 4 UNDERSTANDING THE USES OF PARENTHESES

Parentheses ( ) can be used in several ways, so it is important to understand their different uses:

- To add extra information – something that the author wants the reader to know but that is not essential
- To give a definition
- To give a reference – the source of the information – or the date of a source

Scan the texts listed in the left column, and find the passage that is quoted. Put a check (✔) in the appropriate box to show the purpose of each parentheses.

Chapter and text	Passage from the text	Purpose of parentheses		
		extra information	definition	source or date of source
Ch. 7, Text 1 (page 146)	1. *Benjamin Franklin (1706–1790)*			
Ch. 7, Text 2 (page 151)	2. *Still in camp, husband and myself being sick (caused we supposed by drinking the river water).*			
Ch. 7, Text 3 (page 156)	3. *Industries that are controlled almost entirely by one company, such as the steel industry (controlled mainly by Carnegie's company) and the oil industry (controlled mainly by Rockefeller's company), are called monopolies.*			
Ch. 8, Text 1 (page 168)	4. *An important example of the need to balance self-reliance and government assistance is the federal government's response to the problems of the Great Depression (1929–1940).*			
Ch. 8, Text 2 (page 171)	5. *One example is the popular SUV (sport-utility vehicle).*			
Ch. 8, Text 4 (page 181)	6. *A 1978 survey found that 23 percent of adult men from the bottom fifth of the population (in social and economic terms) had moved to the top fifth. . . .*			
	7. *The New York Times (2005)*			

UNIT 4   WRITING ASSIGNMENT B

In this writing assignment, you will finish the paper that you began in Chapter 7.
In Chapter 7, you developed examples of evidence to illustrate the importance of a
theme. Now you will write an introductory paragraph that presents your theme and
makes a claim about it.

Preparing to write

1 How has the theme you chose continued to be important in American life? Think
about the examples that you read about in this chapter. Discuss these examples
with the partner or group you worked with for the Chapter 7 writing assignment.
Can any of the information in Chapter 8 make your examples stronger? Take notes
on your discussion.

2 Review your notes from step 1. Decide what claim you will make about your
theme.

Now write

1 Begin your paragraph by writing a general statement to introduce your topic. Look
at the example below. Notice that it introduces the topic, but does not make any
specific claim.

- Every culture has a set of beliefs that guides behavior and attitudes. There are
many specific values and beliefs that are important in American history and
culture.

2 Now write your position statement, or claim. Here are some examples.

- (Theme X) has played an important role in _____.
- Many aspects of American _____ are based on (Theme X).
- (Theme X) has been an important theme in _____.
- (Theme X) was an important influence in _____, but now it
is _____.

Notice the use of the present perfect (*has played / has been*) in some of the
statements. Using the present perfect allows you to talk about something that
started in the past and continues in the present.

3 Finish your paragraph by telling the reader the specific examples of Theme X that
you will explore. Here are two possible ways to do this.

- The influence of (Theme X) in the history of American _____ and
_____ has been very _____.
- (Theme X) has been extremely important in the development of American
_____ and _____.

4 Review the paragraphs you wrote for Chapter 7. Can you add any details from Chapter 8 to make them stronger or clearer?

5 Organize your paper:

```
┌─────────────────────────────────────────────────┐
│  ┌───────────────────────────────────────────┐  │
│  │              Paragraph 1                  │  │
│  │          Introduce your topic.            │  │
│  │   Position statement: Make a claim.       │  │
│  │ State the specific examples you will discuss. │
│  └───────────────────────────────────────────┘  │
│                      ↓                           │
│  ┌───────────────────────────────────────────┐  │
│  │              Paragraph 2                  │  │
│  │ (This is paragraph 1 from Writing Assignment A │
│  │             on page 164.)                 │  │
│  │        Give evidence: Example 1           │  │
│  └───────────────────────────────────────────┘  │
│                      ↓                           │
│  ┌───────────────────────────────────────────┐  │
│  │              Paragraph 3                  │  │
│  │ (This is paragraph 2 from Writing Assignment A │
│  │             on page 164.)                 │  │
│  │        Give evidence: Example 2           │  │
│  └───────────────────────────────────────────┘  │
└─────────────────────────────────────────────────┘
```

After you write

1 Reread your paper and make sure that it has the following:

- An introduction that provides a claim, or position statement, and states the examples you will explore
- Two paragraphs, each with different examples of evidence to support your position
- An appropriate topic sentence for each of the two supporting paragraphs

2 Choose one area of grammar that can be a problem for you, for example, subject and verb agreement or correct choice of tense. See if you made any mistakes in this area, and correct them.

3 Exchange papers with the same partner you worked with for Writing Assignment A. Read your partner's paper, and do the following:

1 Underline the claim. Highlight each example and its evidence in a different color.

2 If you think your partner's paper could be improved, offer him or her specific suggestions.

3 Check each other's papers for grammar and spelling errors.

Unit 5

Spotlight on Culture

In this unit, we will explore ideas and innovations in popular culture that either began in the United States or developed as a result of the United States' interactions with other countries of the world. In Chapter 9, we focus on historical aspects of American culture, particularly in the first half of the twentieth century. In Chapter 10, we examine the process of globalization, in particular the changes that happen to ideas and practices as they cross borders. We look at some examples of the globalization process in relation to American culture.

Previewing the unit

Read the contents page for Unit 5, and do the following activities.

Chapter 9: American Innovations

1 The United States is often considered a country of innovations. An innovation is something that is new or is used in a new way: a new idea or a new way of doing something. For example, when humans started using animals, such as oxen and horses, to help them farm, this was a new way of doing something, an innovation. When musicians experimented and developed what we now call rock and roll, it was also an innovation, a new style of music. Social scientists also use the term *innovation* to include specific inventions, that is, devices such as television or space rockets.

Give three or four examples of innovations.

2 Check (✔) the items listed below that you think were American innovations. Then, check your answers at the bottom of this page.

_____ **1** basketball		_____ **6** frozen food	
_____ **2** seatbelt		_____ **7** movies with sound	
_____ **3** elevator		_____ **8** microwave oven	
_____ **4** tin can		_____ **9** rap music	
_____ **5** cigarette		_____ **10** plastic	

Chapter 10: Global Transformations

This chapter introduces the subject of cultural globalization. It examines the transformation (changes) that certain aspects of American culture undergo when they travel to other countries and are influenced by the culture of those countries.

1 With a partner, make a list of things you think are typically American, that is, things that are symbols of American culture. Use the photographs on page 187 to help you get ideas.

2 Discuss the following questions with your partner:

1 Are you familiar with any countries outside the United States where there are features of American culture? Explain.

2 Are you familiar with influences of other cultures that exist within the United States? Explain.

5. ✔; 6. ✔; 7. ✔; 8. ✔; 9. ✔; 10. ✔ (The inventor was originally from Belgium.)
1. ✔ (The inventor was originally from Canada.); 2. Sweden; 3. ✔ 4. England;
Answers to Chapter 9, step 2.

Unit Contents 5

Preparing to read

THINKING ABOUT THE TOPIC BEFORE YOU READ

Discuss these questions as a class or in a small group:

1 Have you ever listened to the blues or jazz? If so, where?

2 How would you describe these styles of music? What do you think of when you think of the blues? What do you think of when you think of jazz?

3 Where do you think the blues comes from? Where do you think jazz comes from?

READING PRIMARY TEXTS

1 Read the excerpt below from an article that was published at the beginning of the Jazz Age (the 1920s) in the *Ladies' Home Journal*. This magazine was for young women, and it is still published today. You do not need to understand every word. Try to determine the author's point of view without looking up any words you do not know.

Does Jazz Put the Sin in Syncopation?*

The National Dancing Masters' Association realizes the evil influence of this type of music and dancing and has adopted this rule:

"Don't permit vulgar cheap jazz music to be played. . . . it is harmful and dangerous, and its influence is wholly bad."

---

* The term *syncopation* refers to the unusual rhythm of jazz.

2 Discuss these questions with a partner:

1 What is the *Ladies' Home Journal* author's opinion of jazz?

2 Why do you think that the author (as well as many other people) had this opinion of jazz?

3 Do you know of any other contexts in which new music has been considered a bad influence?

Now read

Now read the text "America's Music: The Blues and Jazz." When you finish, turn to the tasks on page 193.

American Innovations

Leadbelly (1885–1949), blues singer

Billie Holiday (1915–1959), jazz singer

Duke Ellington (1915–1974), jazz musician and composer

1 AMERICA'S MUSIC: THE BLUES AND JAZZ

Many people consider popular music to be one of America's finest cultural achievements. American popular music includes many styles, but there are two – both with origins in African-American culture – that have had a profound impact on later forms of music in the United States and around the world: the blues and jazz. Soul, rock, rap, and even some classical music all have links to the blues or jazz. African-American musical styles, particularly the blues, have had a deep influence on rock musicians from Elvis Presley to the Rolling Stones. Many current artists, such as Erykah Badu and the Black Eyed Peas, use jazz rhythms in their hip-hop performances. Some rappers include *samples,* or short sections of music, by jazz and blues artists in their own work.

1

The blues

The blues has deep roots in African-American culture and history. Music historians believe it has origins in earlier types of black music, mostly in religious songs, that go back to the time of slavery. In the United States and many other western countries, the color blue is associated with sadness. The style of music called the blues began as the musical expression of the experience of African Americans, the pain

2

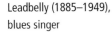

191

of slavery and racism, and the African-American struggle for survival and respect. Blues songs have a predictable, consistent structure, and they are often about loss – loss of love, loss of respect, loss of money, and loss of trust.[9]

Jazz

Jazz developed later than the blues. Jazz, as a distinct style of African-American music, began in the South, in New Orleans, around the beginning of the twentieth century. In the 1920s, when many African Americans started to move North in search of jobs and a better life, they brought their music with them. In cities like New York, Chicago, and Detroit, the African-American population tripled during that period, and jazz became popular in these northern cities. From the 1920s to the 1940s, jazz was particularly popular. It was heard in clubs and dance halls across the nation and around the world.

There are many different styles of jazz. In the beginning, jazz was closely connected to the blues, but as it developed, it became more complex and diverse. It brings together elements of many different types of music. An important characteristic of jazz is that it emphasizes individual performances. In jazz bands, the musicians each have a chance to play alone for a short time and show their skill. In addition, jazz encourages improvisation, that is, unplanned stretches of music that make every performance unique.

The rise of jazz had social as well as artistic importance. Jazz clubs were one of the few places where whites and blacks mixed in the first half of the twentieth century. As the popularity of jazz grew, whites came to clubs in black neighborhoods, such as Harlem in New York, to hear the new music. Although at first all the musicians were black, white musicians who were attracted to the exciting sound soon began to play jazz. Jazz bands were also the first to mix white and black musicians. Until the 1940s, many clubs and concert halls, especially in the South, prohibited integrated bands; therefore, many bands played in Europe where they were welcome.

The presence of white jazz musicians increased the popularity of the music among white listeners, but it also demonstrated the deep inequality between blacks and whites. Whites usually earned better salaries and played in more popular locations. Today, people of all races and backgrounds play and enjoy jazz together, and salaries are more equal. Filmmaker Ken Burns has called jazz "the purest expression of American democracy: a music built on individualism and compromise, independence and cooperation."[10]

3

4

5

6

---

9 You can hear examples of the blues from different parts of the United States at http://www.pbs.org/riverofsong/artists/e3-home.html

10 To hear some classic examples of jazz, go to:
http://www.pbs.org/jazz/biography/artist_id_holiday_billie.htm
http://www.pbs.org/jazz/biography/artist_id_ellington_duke.htm
http://www.pbs.org/jazz/places/spaces_cotton_club.htm
http://www.si.edu/ajazzh/audio.htm#Big%20Band%20Treasures%20Live

After you read

Task 1 NOTE TAKING: USING A CHART

Remember that putting your notes into a chart is a good way to see the relationships between different parts of a text.

Fill in the chart below with the topic and details of each paragraph. The first one has been started for you. Notice that you don't have to use complete sentences. If you need more space, make your own chart on a separate piece of paper.

Par.	Topic	Details
1	*intro – importance of blues and jazz*	• *influence on soul, rock, rap, and classical* •
2		
3		
4		
5		
6		

Task 2 TEST TAKING: USING YOUR NOTES TO PREPARE

1 | Review the three common types of test questions described in "Test Taking: Understanding the Language of Test Questions" on page 110.

2 | Use your notes to write three test questions, one of each type.

3 | Exchange questions with a partner, and answer your partner's questions orally.

Task 3 BUILDING VOCABULARY: SYNONYMS

> Your writing will be more interesting if you use synonyms instead of always expressing the same idea in the same way.

For the second sentence in each pair, find different words in the text that have a similar meaning to the underlined words in the first sentence. The paragraph number in parentheses tells you where to find the words.

1 These words show the *beginnings* of the blues and jazz.

The blues has its _____origins in_____ African-American culture and history.

Jazz has _____ the African-American community. (par. 2)

2 These words show the *relationship* of the blues and jazz to other musical forms and traditions.

Several musical styles have ___connections to___ the blues or jazz.

Early jazz had close _____ the blues. (par. 1)

3 These words show the *effect* of jazz and the blues on other musical forms and traditions.

Jazz and the blues have had a profound ___influence on___ different forms of music all over the world.

African-American musical styles have had a strong _____ many rock musicians. (par. 1)

Task 4 THINKING CRITICALLY ABOUT THE TOPIC

1 Reread the quote about jazz by Ken Burns at the end of the text. Then read the dictionary definition of democracy below:

democracy: *the belief in freedom and equality between people, or a system of government based on this belief*

2 Discuss the following questions with a partner or in a small group:

1 How do the four characteristics Burns identifies – individualism and compromise, independence and cooperation – represent "the purest form of democracy"?

2 How do you think jazz is like democracy?

Preparing to read

THINKING ABOUT THE TOPIC BEFORE YOU READ

1 Read the quotation below from Alfred Hitchcock, the famous director of suspense movies (*The Birds, Psycho, Rear Window, To Catch a Thief, Suspicion*).

> Cinema* is life, with the boring bits cut out.
>
> – Alfred Hitchcock, 1995

* the movies

2 With a partner or in a small group, discuss the following questions:

1 What do you think the Hitchcock quotation means?

2 What are some reasons that people go to the movies?

3 Look at the pictures below from old Hollywood movies. Discuss these questions:

1 What do you know about Hollywood?

2 What do these pictures make you think of?

Now read

Now read the text "Hollywood and the Movies." When you finish, turn to the tasks on page 197.

2 HOLLYWOOD AND THE MOVIES

From the 1920s until about 1950, Hollywood and the movies presented an image of glamour, romance, and success that was welcomed across the country and around the world. Beginning with silent films in the first part of the twentieth century and continuing into Hollywood's Golden Age in the 1930s and 1940s, everyone went to the movies. 1

Hollywood's success involved technology and business as well as art. The 1920s and 1930s brought new technology that improved the quality of moving pictures and perhaps most importantly, introduced sound. 2

WORLD PREMIERE NOW SHOWING

This was also the period when a few powerful movie studios controlled the industry. They understood the advantages of vertical integration: they controlled the production and distribution of films, they owned the theaters, and above all, they owned the stars. Movie stars had to sign contracts with studios that made them promise not to work for other studios.

In the 1930s, the Great Depression had a deep impact on the United States. It was difficult for Americans to be optimistic about their lives. Businesses closed, thousands of people lost their jobs, and fortunes were gone overnight. Americans needed something to be happy about. Movies provided a way to escape to a fantasy that was impossible in their own lives – a story with a happy ending. Movies had heroes and heroines, romance, and glamorous stars. Westerns, romantic comedies, horror movies, and movies about gangsters were popular because their characters and stories seemed far away from the lives of ordinary people. Anyone who went to the movies could share the fantasy: people in small towns, people in crowded cities, farmers, secretaries, and businesspeople – all Americans. During the 1930s and 1940s, many Americans went to the movies once or twice a week; children often spent Saturday afternoons in movie theaters. Viewers accepted the messages they saw on the screen, in particular, the idea that the "good guys" always win in the end. 3

The movies of Hollywood's Golden Age created one of the nation's first shared cultural experiences. They created a popular culture that was available to everyone. Young people read magazines about the lives of the movie stars, and they copied the fashions of the stars. Hollywood movies were a major export; people all over the world saw these movies. They saw the tough gangsters, fast cars, beautiful women, and wide open spaces. Everyone in them moved fast and many seemed rich. People in other countries often based their views of Americans on what they saw in movies. 4

American movies are still popular, but by 1950, Hollywood's Golden Age was coming to an end, in part because of a new invention: the television. 5

After you read

Task 1 ASKING AND ANSWERING QUESTIONS ABOUT A TEXT

Remember that asking and answering questions about a text – either by yourself or with a partner – helps you make sure you understand what you have read.

1 For each question below, do the following:

1 Reread the relevant paragraph.

2 Practice saying the answer out loud to yourself without looking at the text.

    a What were the factors in Hollywood's success as a business? (par. 2)

    b Why did Americans spend a lot of time at the movies in the 1930s and 1940s? What was attractive about the movies that were produced during that period? (par. 3)

    c What was the cultural and historical importance of Hollywood's Golden Age? (par. 4)

    d When did Hollywood's Golden Age end? What was one reason? (par. 5)

2 Work with a partner. Take turns explaining the answers to the questions in step 1.

Task 2 TEST TAKING: WRITING A SUMMARY FROM YOUR NOTES TO PREPARE

Writing a short summary from your notes is a good way to prepare for a test. If you can write a summary, you will probably be able to write good answers to test questions.

1 Review the text by making notes based on your discussion with your partner in step 2 of Task 1, above. Do not look back at the text.

2 Using your notes for reference, write a short summary of the text. Your summary should include the following points:

- a brief description of Hollywood's Golden Age, what it was, and when it was
- factors in Hollywood's success
- a brief explanation of the cultural and historical importance of the Golden Age

3 Exchange summaries with a partner. Were your summaries similar? If so, you probably both have included the most important information. You can check your work by looking back at the text.

Preparing to read

THINKING ABOUT THE TOPIC BEFORE YOU READ

1 Work with a partner or in a small group. Look at these pictures, and then answer the questions below.

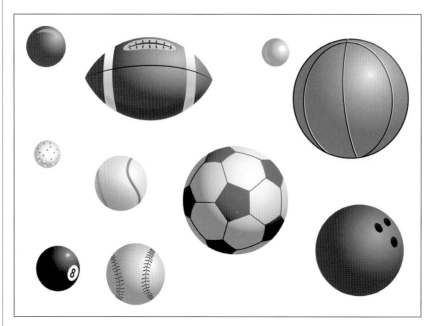

1 Which do you think are the three most popular sports *to watch* in the United States?

Most popular _____

Second _____

Third _____

2 Which sport do you think is the most popular *to play* in the United States?

_____

2 Check your answers to step 1 at the bottom of this page.

Now read

Now read the text "American Sports." When you finish, turn to the tasks on page 201.

Answers to step 1
Most popular to watch = football; second = baseball; third = basketball
Most popular to play = bowling

3 AMERICAN SPORTS

Sports for enjoyment is a relatively new development in the United States. For most of the nineteenth century, few people had time to watch or participate in sports. Their only free time was on Sunday, but that day was traditionally for religious activities. Starting in the mid-nineteenth century, however, American workers began to have more free time. The number of work hours in the day decreased. By the 1920s, many workers only worked five days a week, which gave them more time to relax. Additionally, a series of child labor laws increasingly kept children out of the workforce, so they had more time to play when they were not in school.

Watching and participating in sports appeals to traditional American values. It is consistent with Americans' respect for hard work, competition, and individual achievement. Furthermore, the sports world has produced players who have become popular heroes, many of them with the kind of rags-to-riches life stories that Americans have always loved. Playing sports and watching sports have often brought the country together, uniting Americans across the country and across class and ethnic lines.

Baseball

The sport that probably occupies the most important place in American culture is baseball. Baseball is an American version of a sport that had been played in other countries for years. By the 1860s it had become the most popular sport in America. It seemed that everyone was playing or watching baseball. By the 1980s, football replaced baseball as the nation's most popular sport, but baseball remains an important national tradition, and it has a special place in the national memory. Baseball is connected to a time when Americans' lives were tied to the land. The baseball season follows the farming season. It starts in the spring, at the same time that farmers plant their crops; it ends in the fall, at the time farmers harvest their crops. Baseball games move slowly and have no time limit.

Many older adults think back to ball games of their childhood. They remember a special family time, warm evenings filled with peanuts, hot dogs, and the sounds of the ball park.[11]

Basketball

Today many Americans prefer faster games, such as basketball. Unlike baseball, in basketball the players are always moving, and the games have lots of action. Basketball is the one American sport that was deliberately invented. In 1891, the inventor was looking for a sport that young men could play indoors in the winter, so he nailed fruit baskets

---

11 To hear a traditional song that every American baseball fan knows,
   go to http://www.niehs.nih.gov/kids/lyrics/ballgame.htm

onto two poles. Players threw a soccer ball to one another and then tried to get it into the basket.

Professional basketball is played indoors, but outdoor basketball is also extremely popular as a neighborhood game. In contrast to baseball, it does not require much space or equipment – just a ball and a ring on a pole – and it can be played with as few as two players. The popularity of basketball has spread around the world. It has been an Olympic sport since 1936.

Extreme sports

Some Americans like their games even faster and with more risk; they prefer extreme sports. Many extreme sports, such as skateboarding, snowboarding, and mountain biking, are also American inventions. Most are more dangerous than traditional sports like baseball and basketball. They may include tricks, like turning around in midair, and high speed. Perhaps most importantly, they are usually played by individuals rather than teams.

Some extreme athletes think that traditional sports have too many rules. They prefer the nontraditional and individual nature of extreme sports. In fact, for many years, extreme sports have existed outside of the traditional sports community. However, this may be changing. One extreme sport, snowboarding, was included for the first time in the Olympics in Nagano, Japan, in 1988.

Snowboarding

Snowboarding is a combination of skateboarding, surfing, and skiing. It started in the 1950s but has recently become much more popular. Today, more than 3.4 million people snowboard. Many skiers are switching to snowboarding, and it is predicted that by 2015 there will be more snowboarders than skiers. Like most extreme sports, it has high speed, lots of tricks, and an element of danger. In the 2006 Olympics, an American man and woman, Shaun White and Hannah Teter, each won gold medals in one of the snowboarding events.

Shaun White

Hannah Teter

After you read

Task 1 READING FOR DETAILS

Put an *X* in front of the one statement that is *not* presented in the text to support each of the claims below.

1 Workers had more free time at the end of the nineteenth century because

_____ **a** the work week became shorter.

_____ **b** people didn't attend church as much, so they had leisure time on Sundays.

_____ **c** child labor laws prevented young children from working and gave them more free time.

2 Sports for enjoyment fits in with American tradition because

_____ **a** Americans love competition.

_____ **b** sports stress individual achievement.

_____ **c** sports give equal access to opportunity.

3 Sports that began or were developed in the United States include

_____ **a** baseball.

_____ **b** bowling.

_____ **c** basketball.

4 Baseball

_____ **a** follows the farming calendar.

_____ **b** is as popular today as it was in the past.

_____ **c** has a special place in American culture.

5 Basketball has become popular because

_____ **a** it has lots of action.

_____ **b** it is an Olympic sport.

_____ **c** it doesn't require much space or equipment.

6 Extreme sports are popular in the United States because

_____ **a** they are played by individuals.

_____ **b** they involve risk.

_____ **c** they are less expensive than traditional sports.

7 Snowboarding

_____ **a** is more popular than skiing.

_____ **b** is an Olympic sport.

_____ **c** can be dangerous.

Task 2 THINKING ABOUT CULTURE-SPECIFIC EXPRESSIONS

Words and expressions that reflect important new aspects of culture are created all the time. Some of them remain in the language for many years, even centuries.

1 Read the following words and expressions that are connected to baseball. They are now used in everyday contexts beyond baseball – most often in spoken language.

right off the bat = immediately
ballpark = approximate
touch base = be in contact
out of left field = unexpectedly, as a surprise
strike out = fail
on the ball = quick to understand or respond

2 Fill in the blanks with the appropriate expression. If the expression includes a verb, you may have to change its tense.

1 We'll _____ tomorrow evening and decide which movie to see.

2 We were very impressed with the new manager. He was really _____ .

3 I was completely unprepared. Her question came _____ .

4 He asked three different girls to the dance but he _____ each time.

5 Can you give me a _____ estimate for how much the repairs will cost?

6 I was amazed. He guessed the answer _____ .

Task 3 CREATING A GRAPH FROM A SURVEY

Creating a graph from a survey you have conducted is an excellent way to analyze the results of the survey.

1 As a class, make two charts that you can use to survey each student's opinion about the information listed below.

Chart 1 • favorite sport to watch
         • most popular sport to watch in another country you know

Chart 2 • favorite sport to play
         • most popular sport to play in another country you know

2 Survey your class and fill in the charts.

3 Now create two bar graphs so that you can analyze the results of your survey.

1 Make a bar graph that shows the favorite sports of the class. Here is an example.

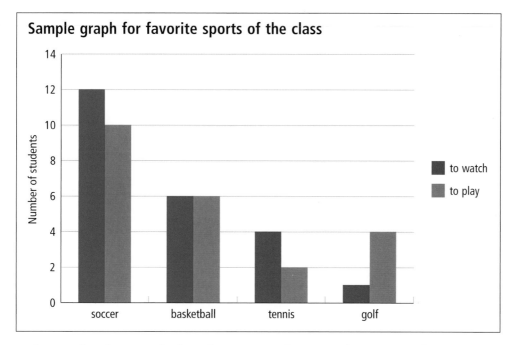

Sample graph for favorite sports of the class

- to watch
- to play

2 Make another bar graph that shows your classmates' opinions of the popularity of sports to watch and to play by country.

3 Discuss the results as a class or in small groups. Did any of the results surprise you? Why or why not?

Task 4 THINKING CRITICALLY ABOUT THE TOPIC

All over the world people love to watch sports. Discuss these questions about people's relationship to sports as a class or in small groups:

1 Why do you think people become so excited and emotional about sports?

2 Are sports just about entertainment, or is there something else that makes so many people love to watch them?

3 Usually more men than women watch sports. Why do you think this is true?

4 Do you think sports have a role in shaping national identity? In local (city or state) identity?

Preparing to read

1 Fill in the chart below. Put a check (✔) in the appropriate boxes to show whether you mostly use the Internet or some other method for the activities listed. If you mostly use other methods, explain what they are, for example, telephone, handwritten letter, or talking in person.

Activity	Mostly Internet	Mostly other methods (explain)
Communicating at work or school		
Communicating with friends		
Taking courses		
Finding out information		
Finding out information about services and products		
Entertainment		
News		
Sharing or publishing your views and opinions		
Shopping		

2 Compare your results in a small group.

3 As a class, discuss the following questions:

1 Do you think the responses would have been different for a class 10 years ago? In what way?
2 What activities do you think will be added to the list of activities that can be performed on the Internet 10 years from now?

Now read

Now read the text "The Development and Impact of the Internet." When you finish, turn to the tasks on page 207.

➡ Remember to review and update your vocabulary notebook.

4 THE DEVELOPMENT AND IMPACT OF THE INTERNET

Throughout the twentieth century, the United States was a leader in developing new technology. One innovation resulted in worldwide changes in communications, education, business, and entertainment. This innovation was the Internet.

1

The development of the Internet

The Internet began as a project in the 1960s to connect researchers at several universities and in government departments. It was based on a new idea about how to send information from one place to another. Traditional communication systems, such as the telephone, send information by circuit switching. In circuit switching, information can move from point A to point B by only one route. If the route is busy, the information has to wait to be sent. The new system, packet switching, divides up information into smaller pieces, or packets. The packets are sent over a network and then put back together. There are many routes over the network. If one route is busy, the packets take a different route. Packet switching makes the network very fast and reliable. (See Figure 9.1) In the beginning, scientists and engineers did not plan the network for personal communication, but soon many of them started using it as an early form of e-mail.

2

Figure 9.1

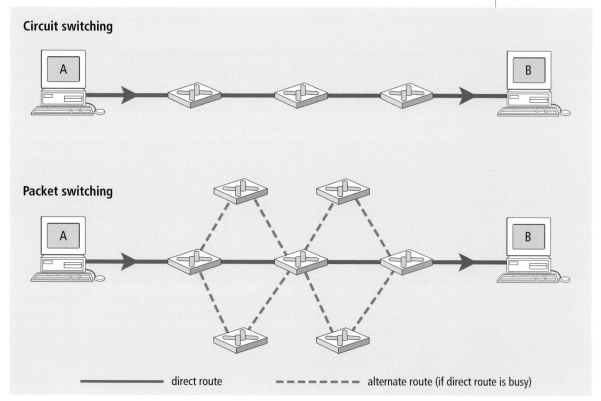

Circuit switching

A → → B

Packet switching

A → → B

———— direct route – – – – – – – alternate route (if direct route is busy)

By the early 1990s, the World Wide Web was in place. The Web is a global space where people can post and exchange information using computers that are connected to the Internet. Users find their way around the Web with a browser. (Currently, we use browsers such as Netscape, Internet Explorer, and Firefox.) By the middle of the 1990s, there was a huge amount of traffic on the Web. E-mail and other forms of communication over the Web had spread throughout the world, and businesses and institutions had created Web sites to communicate with their customers. 3

Today we use the Internet for communication, for commercial and government business, and perhaps most of all, for sharing information and ideas. As technology improves, there is more that can be shared. In the beginning, the Web contained mostly text, that is, words. Very quickly it became possible to post and share images, too. Today this includes not just pictures, but moving images and sound as well. 4

The impact of the Internet

It is hard to imagine life without the Internet. It has permitted the greatest exchange of information in history. People who are miles apart can share their thoughts and interests, as well as music, artwork, and documents. It also allows more people to publish their work and ideas than ever before. Before the Internet, publication was expensive. On the Web, publication is not limited by cost or location. With the invention of the browser, it has also become easy to find information quickly. Many people consider the Internet to be an important democratic institution because it makes information available to anyone with access to a computer connected to the Internet. 5

Although the Web has brought many advantages, it also presents problems. It allows people to share their ideas, but it also allows people to spread hatred and false information. It allows people to read documents from libraries around the world, but it also lets them find instructions for creating bombs. It permits us to stay in touch with the office when we are away, but it makes it hard for us to take time off from work. Finally, the same technology that gives us access to other people's information can give other people access to our private information, such as credit card and bank account numbers. 6

Many people may think of the Web and the Internet as important tools for democracy, but they also create inequalities in society. It is true that anyone with access to a computer connected to the Internet can use all of its resources. Yet a large percentage of the American public and many other people throughout the world do not have this kind of access. This digital divide means that people with higher incomes and educational levels are more likely to have access to the Internet and all the advantages it brings. Fortunately, in the United States at least, Internet use at all economic levels is growing. In 2002, a U.S. Department of Commerce report noted that there were 2 million new Internet users every month. 7

After you read

Task 1 BUILDING VOCABULARY: KEY TERMS

1 Match each term in the left column to one of the definitions in the right column. Write the letter of the correct definition in the blank before each term.

_____ **1** World Wide Web

_____ **2** browser

_____ **3** packet switching

_____ **4** digital divide

_____ **5** e-mail

a a method of sending information electronically that permitted the development of the Internet

b global space where information is stored

c a program that finds information on the Web

d a message that is sent through the Internet

e differences across society in access to technology

2 Compare your answers to step 1 with a partner.

Task 2 EXAMINING GRAPHIC MATERIAL

1 Examine the graph below.

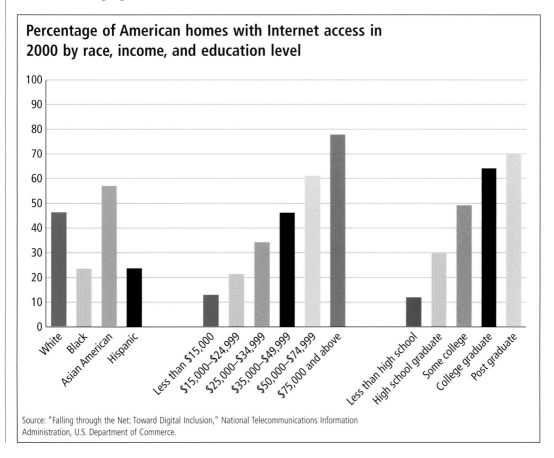

Percentage of American homes with Internet access in 2000 by race, income, and education level

Source: "Falling through the Net: Toward Digital Inclusion," National Telecommunications Information Administration, U.S. Department of Commerce.

2 Based on the information in the graph on page 207, write three sentences about the digital divide. Use at least two words that describe trends (see Chapter 7, page 163).

1 _____

_____

_____

2 _____

_____

_____

3 _____

_____

_____

Task 3 THINKING CRITICALLY ABOUT THE TOPIC

Discuss the following questions:

1 What are two important benefits of the Internet?

2 What are two disadvantages of the Internet?

3 What do you think is important about the information in the graph on page 207?

4 Do you think the Internet can be a tool for democracy? In the United States? Around the world? Explain.

UNIT 5 WRITING ASSIGNMENT A

In this chapter, you have learned about the historical significance of some innovations that began in the United States. In some cases, they may illustrate broader cultural themes that you have explored throughout this book. Your assignment is to write a two-paragraph paper about an innovation that has not been discussed in this chapter. It could be from the United States or from another country. You will describe the innovation and explain why it is important within its cultural context.

Preparing to write

1 | Choose an innovation to write about that you're familiar with. Here are some ideas:

- An innovation that has had a major influence on people's lives, for example, the television or the skyscraper
- An innovation that has an important place in a particular culture, such as a dance, a type of clothing, a type of music, or a game

2 | Make notes about your innovation and why it is important for the culture in which it exists. How is it related to the values of that culture?

3 | Work with a partner.

1 Take turns explaining your choices and why they are important.
2 Ask each other questions so that you can help each other decide what is most important about your topic.
3 Add information from your discussion to your notes from step 2.

4 | Use the Internet or the library to research any details about the innovation you chose that will make what you say clearer and more interesting to your reader.

Now write

Be sure to include a topic sentence in each paragraph.

If you include information that you researched on the Internet or in the library, do the following:

- Write as much of the information as possible in your own words.
- Say where you got your information from.

Remember that copying more than a few key words or phrases from another author's text without giving proper credit is *plagiarism,* and plagiarism has very serious consequences in American academic institutions.

Paragraph 1

Introduce the innovation and state why it is important. Give some background information about it.

Paragraph 2

Explain in more detail the significance or importance of the innovation. Give examples of how it is used or practiced.

After you write

1 | Reread your paper. Make any changes that you think will make your writing clearer.

2 | Think about which type of grammar errors your teacher usually finds in your work. Choose one or two of your typical grammar problems, and check your paper for them.

3 | Exchange papers with a partner. Read your partner's paper and answer the following questions:

　　1 Does each paragraph have a good topic sentence? Highlight it.
　　2 What does the topic sentence in the first paragraph say the paper will be about?
　　3 Has your partner clearly explained what the innovation is?
　　4 Has your partner clearly explained the innovation's importance and how it fits into its cultural context?

4 | Discuss your papers. If the answers to any of the questions in step 3 were "no," how could your partner improve his or her paper? Do you have any other suggestions for improvement?

5 | Check each other's papers for grammar and spelling errors.

Global Transformations Chapter 10

Preparing to read

BUILDING VOCABULARY: PREVIEWING KEY TERMS

1 | Look up the following words in a dictionary:

- adopt
- adapt
- develop

2 | Explain to a partner how you would complete the following definitions:

1 To adopt an innovation means to . . .
   or
   Adopting an innovation means . . .

2 To adapt an innovation means to . . .
   or
   Adapting an innovation means . . .

3 To develop an innovation means to . . .
   or
   Developing an innovation means . . .

3 | Tell your partner an example that you know about of something that was adapted for a new use or situation.

Now read

Now read the text "Global Changes and Improvements to American Innovations." When you finish, turn to the tasks on page 214.

Chapter 10

Global Transformations

1 GLOBAL CHANGES AND IMPROVEMENTS TO AMERICAN INNOVATIONS

American innovations have been adopted and have also been transformed, that is, adapted, developed, or improved, by people, businesses, and organizations all over the world. In many cases, these transformed innovations find their way back to the United States.   1

Technology

One example of an American innovation that has been greatly developed and improved in other countries is cellular phone technology. The basics of cellular technology were developed in the United States in the 1940s, but they could not be put into use until the 1970s when computer chips and other technology became available. Furthermore, the federal government did not actively support the development of cellular phone technology. Therefore, it was Japan and countries in Scandinavia that developed the first cellular networks, not the United States.   2

Today although the United States has a large cellular network and American companies do manufacture cell phones, Japan, Sweden, Finland, and South Korea are the leaders in cellular technology. They are developing the newest innovations. For example, in South Korea, people can already watch live television on their cell phones. In Japan, you can point your cell phone at a building, such as a house for sale or a tourist attraction, and you will receive information about it on your cell phone screen. Japan is also developing a way to allow shoppers to pay for their purchases with their cell phones.   3

Entertainment

Two other examples of global transformation relate to entertainment. Beginning in the 1930s, America's Walt Disney Studios entertained children everywhere with its animated movies like *Bambi* and *Dumbo*. At the same time, American comic books introduced an international audience to superheroes like Superman and Batman. *Anime* and *manga* from Japan were influences on Western animation and comic book art, but these Japanese forms were also influenced by the American ones. Japanese *anime* and *manga* are unique forms of art and entertainment that are hugely popular in the United States today. *Anime* has become a multimillion-dollar business, with television programs, films, Web sites, and toys. It is the fastest-growing area in the DVD rental market in the United States. *Manga* comics now appear in major American newspapers, and bookstores have whole sections of *manga*. It is becoming an increasingly popular area of U.S. publishing.

4

anime

5

manga

6

Sports

Two of America's sports, baseball and basketball, have traveled around the world and been adopted in many other places. Baseball is particularly popular in Japan, Taiwan, the Caribbean, and parts of South America; basketball is played on every continent.

Many athletes from the places that have adopted baseball and basketball have become outstanding players, often better than Americans. To complete the global circle, many excellent players from outside the United States now play on U.S. teams. For example, Ichiro Suzuki, from Japan, has won six Gold Glove Awards and has been voted onto his league's All-Star team six times. Chien-Ming Wang, who is a great pitcher, is a hero in New York, where he plays, and in Taiwan, where he is from. Carlos Delgado, from Puerto Rico, has won many awards, especially for his abilities as a powerful batter. In fact, in 2005 almost 30 percent of the major league baseball players in the United States were from other places. The largest number, 144, were from the Dominican Republic. Pedro Martínez, a Dominican, is considered one of the top pitchers in baseball.

7

Pedro Martínez

Basketball is now played on every continent. Some of the best players on U.S. teams come from South America, Europe, Africa, Asia, and the Caribbean; the largest number come from eastern Europe. Among the best-known international players are Luol Deng from the Sudan, Manu Ginobili of Argentina, Zydrunas Ilgauskas of Lithuania, Steve Nash of Canada, Dirk Nowitzki of Germany, Hidayet Turkoglu of Turkey, and Yao Ming of China.

It seems certain that the processes of innovation and transformation will continue and even increase. Some innovations will continue to come from the United States, but increasingly, they will come from around the globe as all parts of the world become more closely connected.

8

Dirk Nowitzki

After you read

Task 1   READING FOR MAIN IDEAS

1 Work with a partner. Based on the information in the text, give an example of each of the following situations. Explain them to your partner.

 1 an American innovation that has been developed further in other countries
 2 an American idea that has influenced innovations in another country
 3 an American tradition that has been adopted by another country

2 Choose two of your examples from step 1. Write a short explanation of each example. Use the phrases *for example* or *such as*. (Review "Language Focus: Introducing Examples with *for example* and *such as*" on page 132 if necessary.)

Task 2   LANGUAGE FOCUS: *UNTIL / NOT . . . UNTIL*

> *Until* and *not until* are commonly used time connectors. They can be used as prepositions (to introduce a noun or noun phrase) or conjunctions (to introduce a clause).
>
> **until** = up to a specific time
> • **Women had to wait until 1920 for the right to vote. (***until* = preposition)
> • **The students sat in the restaurant until the African Americans were served. (***until* = conjunction)
>
> **not . . . until** = not before a specific time
> • **Women could not vote until 1920. (***not . . . until* = preposition)
> • **The students would not leave the restaurant until the African Americans were served. (***not . . . until* = conjunction)

1 Complete the sentences below based on information in this book.

 1 Americans cannot vote until _____.
 2 African Americans could not vote in the United States until _____.
 3 Segregation in schools was legal until _____.
 4 During World War II, women worked in factories until _____.
 5 Hollywood's Golden Age lasted until _____.
 6 _____ was not an Olympic sport until _____.

2 Write two sentences of your own with *until* or *not . . . until* about something you have learned in this book.

Preparing to read

THINKING ABOUT THE TOPIC BEFORE YOU READ

As a class, discuss the following questions:

1 What is *fast food*? Describe it, and give a few examples.
2 Do you eat fast food? How often? When do you eat it?
3 Do you like fast food? Why or why not?

PREVIEWING ART IN THE TEXT

Looking at photographs and illustrations in a text before you read it can help you understand some of the ideas in the text.

With your group, discuss the cartoon at the end of the text, on page 217.

1 What is the artist trying to say?
2 Do you agree with the artist's message? Why or why not?

Now read

Now read the text "Fast Food." When you finish, turn to the tasks on page 218.

2 FAST FOOD

Americans have always looked for ways to save time and to do things faster. Beginning in the twentieth century, new machines such as washing machines and dishwashers made housework faster and easier. Transportation and communications also became faster and easier. Yet today, Americans still complain that they do not have enough time. In many American homes, both the husband and wife work, and it can be difficult to balance the demands of work and family. The fast-food restaurant provided one way for Americans to save valuable time. Now fast food has an important place in American daily life.

The popularity of fast food

Fast-food restaurants first appeared in the United States in the 1940s. Today there are hundreds of thousands of them. According to Eric Schlosser in his book, *Fast Food Nation,* the amount of money Americans spent on fast food went from $6 billion in 1970 to more than $100 billion in the late 1990s. Twenty-five percent of the population eats at a fast-food restaurant every day. Americans eat an average of three hamburgers and four orders of french fries every week.

Although fast food started in the United States, it has spread across the world and its popularity is growing. For many fast-food chains, the majority of their profits now come from outside of the United States. In 2005, China had more than 600 McDonald's, Korea had more than 300, and there are more fast-food restaurants on the way. According to KFC (Kentucky Fried Chicken), every day, over two million Chinese eat in one of their 900 restaurants. KFC has adapted its menu for different countries. In China, the company offers dark meat chicken instead of the white meat that Americans prefer, and rice porridge instead of mashed potatoes. In India, their menu includes more vegetarian options, which many Indians, particularly Hindus, require.

The influence goes both ways. Fast food in the United States is becoming more international. For example, in the 1990's, McDonald's bought the Chipotle Restaurant chain, which serves Mexican tacos and burritos. Chipotle began in Colorado with just a few restaurants, and by the time McDonald's sold it in 2006, there were almost 500 throughout the United States. Samurai Sam's started with one restaurant in Arizona and now serves Japanese teriyaki at over 70 fast-food restaurants across the western United States.

Another example of international influence in the United States is the establishment of fast-food chains that began in other countries. When American fast-food restaurants arrived in other countries, local businesspeople decided to start their own. Some, such as Nirula's in India, or Gusto in Japan, serve western-style food. Others, such as Pollo Loco in Mexico, Pollo Campero in Guatemala, and Yoshinoya in Japan, serve local food. These last three chains are examples of fast-food restaurants that began in other countries and now also have many locations in the United States. Some of them, such as Yoshinoya, are popular because many Americans like international foods. Others are serving the immigrant market. When Pollo Campero came to Chicago in 2005, 200 people, many waving Guatemalan flags, waited more than six hours in the summer heat for the restaurant to open. Making the trip around the globe complete, Pollo Campero has opened its first restaurant in China and plans to open 500 more there by 2010.

The negative side of fast food

Fast food also has a negative side. Although eating in fast-food restaurants   6
is convenient and less expensive than eating in traditional restaurants, it can have a harmful effect on health. Many studies suggest that the increased consumption of fast food may be one factor in the growing number of overweight and obese people in the United States, which has become a rising threat to health. The Centers for Disease Control reports that one-third of all American adults are obese and about 15 percent of American children and teenagers are obese. Of course, fast-food consumption is not the only reason for the national weight problem; insufficient exercise is another important factor. However, most of the choices at fast-food restaurants are high in fat and calories.

Unfortunately, the problem of obesity has begun to spread across the   7
world, and fast food may be one contributing factor. In some countries, people – especially young people – are replacing their traditional diets, which include lots of fruits and vegetables, with fast food, which contains more fat and sugar. In response to complaints about the health effects of their food, many fast-food restaurants have begun to offer healthier choices, such as fresh fruit and salads. Yet a recent study shows that customers continue to prefer the high-fat, high-calorie options.

Don't you know how bad those things are for you?

After you read

Task 1 NOTE TAKING: USING A GRAPHIC ORGANIZER

> A graphic organizer is a drawing that provides a format in which you can organize your notes. Charts and maps are graphic organizers, but you can also create unique graphic organizers for particular texts.

1 Look at the diagram below. It is the beginning of a note-taking graphic organizer for "Fast Food." Make a larger organizer like the one below on a separate piece of paper. Fill it in with the appropriate information from the text. You can reduce or increase the number of blanks.

Reasons for increase in FF   Effects of increase in FF

```
┌─────────────────────┐         ┌──────────────────┐         ┌─────────────────────┐
│ _____ │         │ Increase in FF   │         │ _____ │
│ _____ │   →     │ restaurants      │   →     │ _____ │
│ _____ │         │                  │         │ _____ │
└─────────────────────┘         └──────────────────┘         └─────────────────────┘
```

2 The organizer in step 1 provides a way of taking notes for part of "Fast Food," but not for all of it. Therefore, do one of the following:

- Add to the graphic organizer in any way you think is appropriate so that it includes all the important information in the text.
  OR
- Create a different organizer that you think works better for the text "Fast Food." Make sure you include all the important information from the text.

Task 2 BUILDING VOCABULARY: USING GRAMMAR AND CONTEXT TO GUESS UNKNOWN WORDS

> When you use both grammatical knowledge and context, you can often guess the meaning of a new word. The first step is to figure out the part of speech of the new word.

1 Look at the words from the text in the left column of the chart at the top of the next page. Find them in the paragraphs in which they appear in the text. Then fill in the part of speech of each word based on your own knowledge and the grammar clues in the right column.

Word	Part of speech	Grammar clues
1. options (pars. 3 and 7)		(1) *-tion* ending (2) *-s* ending
2. convenient (par. 6)		(1) (*be*) *convenient* (2) *convenient and* (<u>adjective</u>)
3. consumption (par. 6)		(1) *the* (<u>adjective</u>) *consumption* (2) *-tion* ending
4. obese (par. 6)		(*be*) *obese*
5. obesity (par. 7)		(1) (<u>preposition</u>) *obesity* (2) *-ity* ending
6. insufficient (par. 6)		(1) *insufficient* (<u>noun</u>) (2) *-ent* ending

2 Now use both the context and the part of speech to help you guess the meaning of the words. Complete the sentences below based on your own knowledge and the clues provided.

1 options: Many Hindus do not eat meat. Therefore there are vegetarian *options* on the menu. People prefer one *option* rather than another.

Options are _____.

2 convenient: It describes food for people with very little time or energy to prepare meals.

Convenient food is _____.

3 consumption: This word describes what people do with food.
Fast-food *consumption* is not the only reason for the national weight problem.

Restate the sentence without using the word *consumption*: _____

_____

4 obese/obesity: Paragraphs 6 and 7 are about health. The text states that *obesity* is a problem. *Obese* is linked with *overweight*.

An *obese* person is _____.
Obesity is _____.

5 insufficient: Two reasons are given for obesity. One is related to the amount of food (too much of it) and the second is related to the amount of exercise.

Americans get *insufficient* exercise. This means Americans _____

_____

Task 3 EXAMINING GRAPHIC MATERIAL

1| The U.S. Department of Agriculture suggests that the normal daily nutritional needs of an average American adult are 2,000 calories, 50–60 grams of fat, and no more than 2,300 milligrams of sodium (salt). Keeping this information in mind, study the two charts below:

1 Nutritional information for some common foods

	Calories	Fat (grams)	Sodium (Salt) (milligrams)
1/2 chicken breast (300 grams)	165	24	213
1 serving of rice (300 grams)	420	0.84	3
1 apple (200 grams)	84	0.34	2
2 eggs (100 grams)	147	10	140
2 carrots (100 grams)	41	0.24	69
2 slices of white bread (50 grams)	132	1.64	340

Source: U.S. Department of Agriculture Nutrient Data Laboratory.

2 Nutritional information for some fast-food choices

	Calories	Fat (grams)	Sodium (Salt) (milligrams)
double cheeseburger	730	40	1,330
milk shake	1,160	27	510
crispy chicken strips	400	24	1,250
French fries	600	30	1,070
eggs and pancakes	730	46	1,460

Source: Fast Food Nutrition Fact Explorer.

2| Discuss the differences between the information in the two charts with a partner or in a small group. What is important about these differences?

Task 4 THINKING CRITICALLY ABOUT THE TOPIC

Recently several people have started legal cases against fast-food companies. They claim that the companies are responsible for their obesity and related health problems. They argue that fast-food restaurants serve food that is dangerous to health. One person also claims that fast food is addictive, like a drug. With your partner or group, discuss the following questions:

1 Are fast-food companies responsible for the health problems of people who eat in their restaurants?

2 Should they have to change their menus or post warnings in their restaurants?

3 Should people be allowed to bring legal cases against fast-food companies?

4 Do you think fast food is like a drug? Why or why not?

Preparing to read

THINKING ABOUT THE TOPIC BEFORE YOU READ

Look at the photographs below, and discuss these questions in a small group or as a class:

1 What do you know about the culture of hip-hop?
2 Do you like rap music? Why or why not?
3 If you like rap music, which rappers do you especially like? Why?
4 Where do you hear rap music? What languages do you hear rap music in?
5 Do you like other aspects of hip-hop culture, such as its dancing, art, and fashion? Why or why not?

Now read

Now read the text "Hip-Hop: The Culture and the Music." When you finish, turn to the tasks on page 224.

3 HIP-HOP: THE CULTURE AND THE MUSIC

African-American music has been extremely influential in the United States throughout its history. The latest example is *rap music,* which is an important part of hip-hop culture. Other aspects of hip-hop culture include special styles of dance, art, and fashion. The impact of hip-hop has been enormous. Today one out of every five CDs sold in the United States is rap, which is now a $4-billion-a-year industry. Although the origins of rap are in the African-American community, today a growing number of listeners in the United States are white. Recently the National Museum of American History, in Washington, D.C., established a collection of hip-hop music and objects.

Hip-hop culture originated in the United States as the voice of young African Americans who struggled with economic and social discrimination. Hip-hop has offered both a way for them to express themselves and an escape from the difficulties they face. In addition, hip-hop music is relatively easy to produce. Even people who cannot pay for music lessons or expensive instruments and equipment can make rap music. Rap is spoken words with music. Usually the words describe the lives of the musicians and their struggles. It often also involves samples of many different artists that are put together into different combinations. Putting the music and words together in new ways is part of the art of hip-hop.

Today hip-hop is part of global culture and is enjoyed by young people all over the world. It has spread far beyond the United States to other countries, where it has been adapted to reflect the ideas of each particular community. Now the rap music made in those countries is finding its way back to the United States. A recent recording, *The Best of International Hip Hop,* included musicians from Algeria, Argentina, Croatia, Greenland, Israel, Japan, Portugal, and Romania.

Some scholars believe that because hip-hop is the expression of a people's history and community, it appeals to all people who have struggled with discrimination and injustice. They argue that it is not just a form of music, dance, art, or fashion and should not be considered simply entertainment. Rather, it is an expression of a shared experience. However, different countries and cultures experience hip-hop in their own ways.

France is the second-largest market for rap music in the world. This may be because France is also home to a large number of minorities who have experienced discrimination. They rap about many of the same social problems as rappers do in the United States: poverty, violence, and hopelessness. The third-largest market for rap music is Japan, which has a history of welcoming new American trends. However, the social and economic conditions there are quite different from those in the United States or France. For the Japanese, hip-hop is more of an expression of youth culture than an expression of protest against social problems. Finally, some cultures have blended elements of hip-hop music with elements of their own music to create something new. The musicians of Puerto Rico, the Dominican Republic, and other communities in the Caribbean have combined hip-hop with local musical styles, such as bomba from Puerto Rico and reggae from Jamaica to create an entirely new kind of dance music – *reggaetón* – which is now very popular in many American cities. A recent concert in New York had an audience of over 20,000 people. In South Africa, a new musical form called *kwaito* has become popular. Like hip-hop in the United States and many other countries, kwaito is not just about music. It is a statement about the experiences and struggles of young blacks in South Africa. Most people outside of South Africa first heard kwaito rhythms in the award-winning film *Tsotsi* in 2005.

The impact of hip-hop across the world extends beyond these few examples. Hip-hop artists and influence can be found everywhere from Iceland to Senegal, in numerous languages, from Arabic and Portuguese to Bulgarian and Chinese, and even in sign language.

6

Below:

Top: Cho, a Korean rapper

Middle: Tigarah, a Japanese rapper

Bottom: Don Miguelo, a Dominican rapper

Matisyahu, a Hasidic rapper (American)

Jin, a Chinese-American rapper

DAM, Palestinian rappers

Gaspar, G.L. Jay, Cae MC: Brazilian rappers

After you read

Task 1 READING FOR MAIN IDEAS AND DETAILS

For each statement listed below, decide which of the following descriptions is most appropriate. Put the correct letter in the blank before each statement.

M = a main idea in the text
D = a detail in the text
NI = no information about this in the text

_____ **1** Rap music is a $4-billion-a-year industry.

_____ **2** Different cultures experience hip-hop in their own ways.

_____ **3** Hip-hop culture is a global trend.

_____ **4** Rap singers are often involved in violence.

_____ **5** Rap music does not require special equipment or instruments.

_____ **6** African-American music has been very influential throughout U.S. history.

_____ **7** Japan has different social conditions than do France and the United States.

_____ **8** Reggaetón is a new form of music that combines rap with other musical styles.

_____ **9** Some artists rap in sign language.

_____ **10** Hip-hop artists earn a lot of money.

Task 2 LANGUAGE FOCUS: USING *EVEN* AS AN ADVERB

The word *even* can be used as either an adjective (for example, an *even* number) or an adverb. When *even* is used as an adverb, it is generally used with one of two meanings:

- **to emphasize a comparison**

  The storm began in the afternoon, and the water in the river started to rise. The situation became **even** more dangerous in the evening.

  The second song was **even** worse than the first one.

- **to express something unexpected or unusual**

  The instructions are very easy to understand; **even** a child could follow them.

  She gets angry at her husband because he always forgets things. Last year he **even** forgot her birthday!

1 Read the examples below that are based on information in this book.

1 *Even* expresses a comparison:

  a Drive-in theaters were **even** more popular than drive-in restaurants.

  b Some Americans like their games **even** faster and with more risk.

2 *Even* expresses something unexpected or unusual:

  a **Even** people who cannot pay for music lessons or expensive instruments and equipment can make rap music.

  b Hip-hop artists and influence can be found everywhere from Iceland to Senegal, in numerous languages, from Arabic and Portuguese to Bulgarian and Chinese, and **even** in sign language.

2 With a partner, take turns explaining the examples in step 1.

1 What are the comparisons that are emphasized in 1a and 1b?

2 What is unexpected or unusual about the information that follows *even* in 2a and 2b?

3 Read the examples below that are based on information in this book. Put *C* before each example in which *even* expresses a comparison. Put *U* before each example in which *even* expresses something unexpected or unusual.

_____ **1** There are elements of the blues and jazz in soul, rock, rap, and **even** some classical music.

_____ **2** Soon the price of cars was so low that **even** the people who worked in Ford's factories could buy cars.

_____ **3** He knew that if he reduced his competition, he would make **even** more money, and so he bought other steel companies.

_____ **4** Sam Walton's success story is different. Walton did not **even** have a specific product or service to sell. He had a concept.

_____ **5** The Latino population will grow **even** faster in the next 50 years.

4 Explain the reasons for your answers to step 3 to your partner.

5 Write two sentences of your own for each use of *even* as an adverb. Compare your sentences with your partner.

Preparing to read

THINKING ABOUT THE TOPIC BEFORE YOU READ

English is an international language used by millions of people. The text you are going to read discusses some of the causes of the dominance of English and some of the results of this dominance.

Read the statements below. Based on your own knowledge, decide if each statement is a cause of the dominance of English (*C*), a result of the dominance of English (*R*), or false (*F*). Write the appropriate letter in the blank before each statement.

_____ 1 Many former British colonies adopted English as one of their official languages.

_____ 2 Most scientific publications are in English.

_____ 3 English is simpler to learn than many other languages.

_____ 4 English is used by many international organizations.

_____ 5 The British spread English throughout their colonies.

_____ 6 English is the language of air and sea transportation.

_____ 7 English is widely used in international relations.

_____ 8 The United States has great political and economic power.

INCREASING YOUR READING SPEED

1 | Review the strategies for increasing your reading speed on page 74.

2 | Enter your starting time. Then read "English as a Global Language."

Starting time: _____

3 | Fill in the time you finished.

Finishing time: _____

Then calculate your reading speed:
Number of words in the text (820) ÷
Number of minutes it took you to
read the text = your Reading Speed

Reading speed: _____

Your goal should be about 150–180 words per minute.

4 | Check your reading comprehension by reviewing your answers to the task above and correcting them if necessary. Then check your answers at the bottom of this page.

Now read

Now read the text "English as a Global Language" again. When you finish, turn to the tasks on page 229.

➡ Remember to review and update your vocabulary notebook.

4 ENGLISH AS A GLOBAL LANGUAGE

English is spoken by more people in more places than any other language in history. Some estimates put the number of people who speak at least some English as high as one billion. There are more nonnative speakers of English than native speakers; it is truly a global language. 1

The different roles of English

English plays different roles in different countries. In some countries, it is the population's first language. According to estimates, there are almost 400 million people who have English as their mother tongue, or first language, with the largest numbers in the United States and the United Kingdom. It is an official language in more than 50 countries. 2

In other countries, English is a second language, but this category is more complicated. In some of these countries, such as India and Singapore, people use English to communicate among themselves, in school, in business, and in government. In other countries, such as Sweden or The Netherlands, most people continue to use their mother tongue among themselves, but they use English so frequently that it is truly their second language. They read English newspapers and books, watch English language television, visit English language Internet sites, and switch into English easily and regularly with members of the international community. It is estimated that the number of speakers who have English as a second language may be as high as 300 million. 3

Children study English in many schools in Latin America.

Finally, throughout Asia and Latin America as well as many other places, English is widely studied as a foreign language but is not used by most of the population in everyday communication. In almost every country in the world, English is the foreign language that most people study in school. 4

Why English has become a global language

Why English and why now? The reasons for the dominance of English are political and economic. The process began as a result of British colonial power, which took English around the globe. As British power began to decrease in the twentieth century, American influence grew until the United States became the world's dominant political and economic power. This increased the importance of English even further. 5

Countries or companies that want to do business with Americans have an advantage if they can do it in English. A large number of scientific and technical publications are written in English because the United States has been a leader in science and technology. As more 6

Scientific and technical publications are often written in English.

and more communication occurs in English, the need to learn English has increased. Today more than half of all academic publications are in English, 85 percent of all Web pages are in English, and 80 percent of all electronic information is stored in English. It is the language of tourism, international business, and air and sea transportation. Increasingly, members of international organizations use English to communicate among themselves. For example, a German, a Greek, and a Thai can all communicate through English more easily than through multiple translations.

Varieties of English

What happens when so many people around the world start speaking the same language? One consequence is that speakers in countries where English is a second language have begun to use it in their own way. English is no longer just the language of the United States, Canada, the United Kingdom, the Republic of Ireland, and Australia; it is a language of countries such as Barbados, Belize, Fiji, Ghana, India, Kenya, Nigeria, Papua New Guinea, the Philippines, Pakistan, Singapore, Sri Lanka, South Africa, and Uganda. In these countries and in many others, local varieties of English have developed to meet local needs. English has become *their* language, a part of the community's identity. Each of these varieties of English has its own accent, special vocabulary, and grammatical features.

Even in places with no local variety of English, such as continental Europe, an international variety of English has developed, one that is somewhat different from the English spoken by native speakers. Although this international English has no native speakers, thousands of fluent speakers use it regularly. English no longer belongs just to its native speakers; it belongs to the world.

English is frequently used as the common language among businesspeople from different countries.

The future of English

The number of people who use English as a second or foreign language is already larger than the number of native speakers, and this gap is expected to grow larger every year. Experts also predict that, in many countries, English will change from a foreign to a second language.

Some people worry that multiple varieties of English will mean a future world where we cannot understand one another's English. However, this is unlikely to happen. First, the written language has stayed relatively unchanged. Second, mass communication and transportation keep the world in constant contact. This prevents language varieties from moving too far away from the original language. Finally, the political and economic cost of losing the ability to understand one another is just too high. We need to be able to understand one another.

After you read

Task 1 LANGUAGE FOCUS: NOUN + INFINITIVE PHRASES

Phrases that include the noun + infinitive form are very common in academic writing. These phrases often express human goals, opportunities, and abilities, for example:

        noun   infinitive

I have a chance to visit California this summer.

          noun   infinitive

She made an effort to finish the job on time.

Nouns that are frequently used with infinitives include:

(in)ability	desire	obligation	refusal
attempt	effort	opportunity	responsibility
chance	need	power	right

1 | In each of the following locations in the text, find one example of a phrase with the noun + infinitive form. Circle the noun and underline the infinitive.

  1 Paragraph 6, line 5
  2 Paragraph 10, line 7

2 | In each sentence below, circle the noun and underline the infinitive.

  1 All people should have an equal chance to succeed.
  2 The Constitution gives Congress the power to create courts.
  3 It seemed to be a land of endless opportunity for someone with a good idea and the willingness to take a risk.
  4 The Nineteenth Amendment gave women the right to vote.
  5 Many settlers believed it was their destiny to populate the land from one coast to the other.
  6 The Japanese are developing a way to pay by using a cell phone.
  7 A car meant the freedom to come and go wherever you wanted.

3 | Using two of the nouns listed below, write two sentences about the United States, Americans, or American culture or history. Use each noun you choose in a noun + infinitive phrase.

ability	duty	responsibility	tendency
chance	effort	right	

1 _____

   _____

2 _____

   _____

Task 2 EXAMINING GRAPHIC MATERIAL

1 Study the graph of predicted trends in the use of world languages by young people from 1995 to 2050, and answer the following questions:

1 Which language shows the largest predicted increase in the number of speakers?

2 What do you think the reason(s) would be for an increase in the use of the language you found in question 1?

3 Which language shows the largest predicted decrease in the number of speakers?

4 What do you think the reason(s) would be for a decrease in the use of the language you found in question 3?

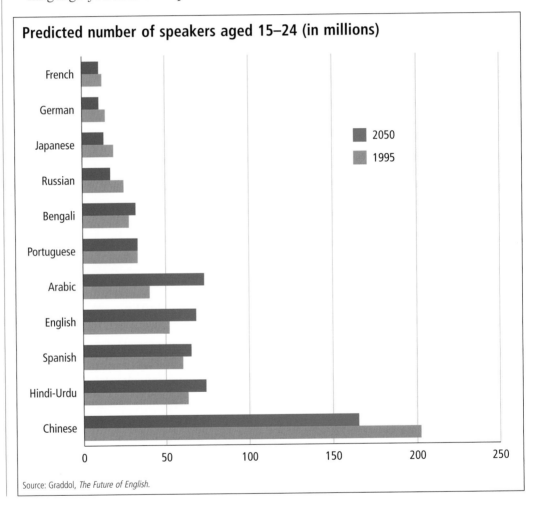

Predicted number of speakers aged 15–24 (in millions)

Source: Graddol, *The Future of English.*

2 Discuss the following questions with a partner:

1 Do any of the figures in the graph surprise you? Why or why not?

2 Do you think these trends will continue? Why or why not?

3 What role do you think young people play in changing the patterns of language use?

Task 3 THINKING CRITICALLY ABOUT THE TOPIC

1 Some people are afraid that the spread of English will cause it to break apart and develop into many different languages, the way Latin did in the Middle Ages. They are afraid that speakers of these languages will not be able to understand each other in the future.

Study the diagram below. It illustrates opposite forces that are affecting English in the twenty-first century.

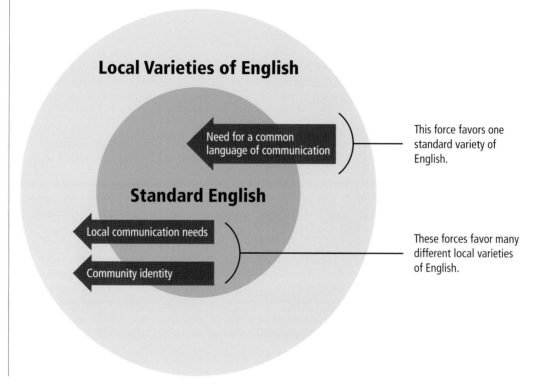

2 In a small group or as a class, discuss which direction you think English will take in the future.

1 Will the number of English speakers continue to grow?

2 Will English break apart and develop into different languages?

3 Now discuss these questions:

1 How much influence does American culture have in other countries that you know? Give some examples.

2 Do you know of any resistance to the English language or to American culture in some countries or communities? If so, what form does this resistance take? For example, some countries don't allow the use of English in certain contexts; some forms of rap music have been prohibited in some countries.

3 Do you think there are good reasons for resistance to the English language or to American culture? Why or why not?

UNIT 5 WRITING ASSIGNMENT B

In this chapter, you have learned about one aspect of globalization: how technology, popular culture, and language are adopted and adapted across national and cultural boundaries. Your assignment is to write a three-paragraph paper that makes a claim about the process of globalization, using an example of a cultural or technological innovation that has spread from one country to another or from one cultural community to another to support your claim.

Preparing to write

1| Think of a technological or cultural innovation that has spread from one country to another or from one cultural community to another and that was not discussed in this unit. What does the spread of this innovation illustrate about the process of globalization?

2| Discuss your innovation in a small group and take notes on your discussion.

3| Think about what claim you can make about how the innovation you chose illustrates globalization. Here are some examples of claims:

- There is cultural globalization in everyday life.
- Every culture changes new ideas and practices that come from somewhere else.
- Some cultures are more dominant than others in the globalization process.

4| Use the Internet or the library to research any details that will make what you say clearer and more interesting to your reader.

Now write

Be sure to include a topic sentence in each paragraph.

Remember that copying more than a few key words or phrases from another author's text without giving proper credit is *plagiarism,* and plagiarism has very serious consequences in American academic institutions.

Paragraph 1
Begin by explaining the concept of globalization. Then present the claim you are making about globalization, and introduce the innovation that you will use to illustrate this claim.

Paragraph 2
Describe the innovation in detail. Explain which country or community it came from and how it is used or practiced in that context.

Paragraph 3

Tell which country or community the innovation has spread to. Explain why you think it spread and how it has changed. End your paragraph with a sentence or two about how the spread of this innovation to a new context illustrates your claim about globalization.

After you write

1 Reread your paper. Make any changes that you think will make your writing clearer.

2 Think about which type of grammar errors your teacher usually finds in your work. Choose one or two of your typical grammar problems, and check your paper for them.

3 Exchange papers with a partner. Read your partner's paper, and answer the following questions:

1 Has your partner made a clear claim in paragraph 1? Highlight it.

2 What innovation has your partner chosen to discuss as an example?

3 Has your partner written appropriate topic sentences for paragraph 2 and paragraph 3? Highlight them.

4 Has your partner clearly explained the original context for the innovation?

5 Has your partner clearly explained why it has moved to another country or community?

6 Has your partner given reasons for why and how the innovation has changed in its new context?

4 Discuss your papers. If the answer to any of the questions in step 3 was "no," how could your partner improve his or her paper? Do you have any other suggestions for improvements?

5 Check each other's papers for grammar and spelling errors.

REFERENCES

2003 Yearbook of Immigration Statistics, Immigrants admitted by selected class of admission and region and country of last permanent residence: *Office of Management, Department of Homeland Security.* http://www.uscis.gov/graphics/shared/aboutus/statistics/IMM03yrbk/IMM2003list.htm

Aaron, H., Mann, T., & Taylor, T. (Eds). (1993). *Values and public policy.* Washington, DC: Brookings Institution.

Adler, C. & Qiandaohu. (2003, March 17). Colonel Sanders' march on China. *Time Asia.*

Alsever, J. (2004, May 9). Quest for a new burrito. *Denver Post.*

Argument and compromise (2003 January). *Cobblestone.*

Avila, O. (2005, July 30). Nostalgia served piping hot. *Chicago Tribune.*

Balio, T. (1993). *The history of American cinema (5) grand design.* New York: Chas. Scribner.

Barlow, W. & Finley, C. (1994). *From swing to soul: An illustrated history of African American popular music from 1930–1960.* Washington, DC: Elliot & Clark.

Baum, S. & Payea, K. (2004). *Education pays: Trends in education 2004: The benefits of education for individuals and society.* The College Board.

Berg, B. (2000). *The women's movement and young women today.* Berkeley Heights, NJ: Enslow Publishers.

Bernstein, N. (2005, December 7). Most Mexican immigrants in a new study gave up jobs to take their chances in the US. *New York Times.*

Bragg, M. *The adventure of English* [DVD]. The Film for the Humanities and Sciences.

Burman, E. (2003). *Shift! The unfolding Internet.* John Wiley.

Carey, K. (2004). *The funding gap 2004.* The Education Trust. Retrieved May 8, 2005, from http://www2.edtrust.org

Chafe, W. (1994). *The road to equality: American women since 1962.* Oxford: Oxford University Press.

Chappel, D. (2005, June). Celebrated, controversial and influential: Thirty years of hip-hop music. *Ebony.*

Collier, J. (1978). *The making of jazz.* Boston: Houghton Mifflin.

Cringely, R., Gau, J., & Segaller, S. *Nerds 2.0.1* [videorecording]: a brief history of the Internet. Series produced and directed by Stephen Segaller. Oregon Public Broadcasting.

Crystal, D. (2003). *English as a global language* (2nd ed.). Cambridge, England: Cambridge University Press.

Crystal, D. (1995). *The Cambridge encyclopedia of the English language.* Cambridge: Cambridge University Press.

Davidson, J., Stoff, M., & Viola, H. *The American nation* (2003). New York: Prentice Hall.

Davis, S. & Meyer, C. (1998). *Blur: The speed of change in the connected economy.* Reading, MA: Perseus.

Delgado, M., & Barton, K. (1998). Murals in Latino communities: Social indicators of community strength. In *Social Work, 43.*

Evans, C. & Herzog, W. (2002). More than a game. In (W. Evans & C. Herzog, Eds.) *The faith of 50 million.* Louisville, KY: Westminster John Knox.

The facts of federalism. (2002, September 20). *Time for Kids, 8.*

Field, R. (2002). *Civil rights in America.* Cambridge: Cambridge University Press.

Fleming, M. (Ed.): (2001). *A place at the table: Struggles for equality in America.* Oxford: Oxford University Press.

Gailbraith, J. K. (1998). (40th anniversary ed.). *The affluent society.* Boston: Houghton Mifflin.

Glazer, N. (1997): *We are all multiculturalists now.* Cambridge, MA: Harvard University Press.

Graddol, D. (1997, 2000). *The future of English.* The British Council.

Grossman, J. (Ed.) (1994). *The frontier in American culture.* Berkeley: University of California Press.

Guernsey, J. (1997). *Affirmative action: A problem or a remedy.* Minneapolis, MN: Lerner Publications.

Hickman, M., & Reaves, B. (2003, January). Local Police Department. Department of Justice Programs, Law Enforcement Management and Administrative Statistics.

Horner, L. (Ed.). (2002). *Hispanic Americans: A statistical sourcebook* 2002 Edition. Palo Alto, CA: Information Publications.

Horton, C. & Smith, J. (Eds). (1990). *Statistical record of black America.* Detroit: Gale Research.

Johnson, L. (1992). *Our Constitution.* Brookfield, CT: Millbrook Press.

King, D. (2005). *The liberty of strangers.* Oxford: Oxford University Press.

Kitwani, B. (2002). *The hip-hop generation. Young blacks and the crisis in African-American culture.* New York: Perseus.

Krakowka, L. (1998, July). Bowling throws a strike. *American Demographics.*

Krull, K. (1999). *A kids' guide to America's Bill of Rights.* New York: Avon.

Magazine Publishers of America Hispanic Latino Profile. (2004).

Mandelbaum, M. (2004). *The meaning of sports.* New York: Public Affairs.

Martin, A. (August 8, 2005). More immigrants find roots in U.S. soil. *Chicago Tribune.*

Murphy, D. (2003, February 23). Managing America without illegal immigrants. *New York Times Upfront.*

Murphy, J. *A young patriot.* New York: Clarion.

Meek, M. (2003, November). Life and death on the Southwest border. *National Geographic Online.* Retrieved July 17, 2005, from http://magma. nationalgeographic.com/ngm/0311/ feature1/online_extra.html

New York Times Poll Class Project (2005, March 3–14).

Nixon, H. (1984). *Sport and the American dream.* New York: Leisure Press.

Onishi, N. (2006, April 2). In a wired South Korea, robots will feel right at home. *New York Times.*

Peart, K. (1996, November 15). English spoken here. *Scholastic Update.*

Pew Hispanic Center Fact Sheet. (January 2002).

Richardson, T. (Ed). (2001). *Global noise.* Middletown, CT: Wesleyan University Press.

Rodriguez, G. (2002, April 7). English likely top tongue at home, abroad. *New York Times.*

Rother, L. (2005, April 7). Brazilians streaming into U.S. through Mexican border, *New York Times.*

Sachs, S. (2001, September 3). The changing face of America. *New York Times Upfront.*

Schatz, T. (1997). *Boom and Bust: The history of American cinema (6).* New York: Chas. Scribner.

Schilling, D. (2001). *The living Constitution.* New York: McGraw-Hill.

Schlissel, L. (1992). *Women's diaries of the westward journey.* New York: Shocken Books.

Schlosser, E. (2001). *Fast-food nation.* Boston: Houghton Mifflin.

Schmeltzer, J. (2006, May 8). Wooing Hispanic shoppers. *Chicago Tribune.*

Scott, J. & Leonhardt, D. (2005, May15). Class in America: Shadowy lines that still divide. *New York Times.*

Sklar, R. (1994). *Movie-made America: A cultural history of American movies.* New York: Vintage Books.

The state of black America, 2005. Prescriptions for change. New York: National Urban League.

Stuckey, S. & Salvucci, L. (2000). *Call to freedom.* Austin, TX: Holt, Rinehart and Winston.

Tavani, H. (2004). *Ethics and technology.* John Wiley.

U.S. Census Bureau. (2002, March). Annual Demographic Supplement.

U.S. Dept. of Commerce. (2000). *Falling through the net: Toward digital inclusion,* National Telecommunications Economic and Statistics Administration and Information Administration. Table I-2 Percentage of households with Internet access.

Unruh, J. (1993). *The plains across: The overland emigrants and the trans-Mississippi west, 1840–60.* Urbana, IL, and Chicago: University of Illinois Press.

Verba, S. & Orren, G. (1985). *Equality in America.* Cambridge, MA: Harvard University Press.

Vilbig, P. (2002, December 13). The new shape of civil liberties. *New York Times Upfront.*

Warner, M. (2006, April 19). Salads or no, cheap burgers revive McDonald's. *New York Times.*

U.S. Census Bureau. (2006). *We the People: American Indians and Alaska Natives in the United States.* Census 2000 Special Reports.

U.S. Census Bureau. (1993). *We the Americans: Blacks.*

U.S. Census Bureau. (1993). *We the Americans: Hispanics.*

U.S. Census Bureau. *We the People. Blacks in the United States,* Census 2000 Special Reports.

U.S. Census Bureau. *We the People. Hispanics in the United States,* Census 2000 Special Reports.

Weber, H. (2005, February 21). More retailers seeking bilingual employees. *Honolulu Advertiser.*

Welles, E. (2004, Winter/Spring). Foreign language enrollments in United States institutions of higher education, fall 2002. *ADFL Bulletin, 35,* Nos. 2–3.

Wodatch, J. (1990). The ADA: What it says. In *Worklife, 3,* 3.

CREDITS

Text credits

Chapter 2

40   Erika Reif, "Hampton man allegedly killed in self-defense ID'd." Adapted from *The Virginian-Pilot* © 2002. Used by permission.

43   Peter Vilbig, "The New Shape of Civil Liberties." Adapted from *The New York Times Upfront*, December 13, 2002. © 2002. Used by permission.

Chapter 3

59   Excerpted from Hughes, Fountain: 'Texts', in *The Emergence of Black English*, edited by Guy Bailey et al. 1991. Pages 29–37. With kind permission by John Benjamins Publishing Company, Amsterdam/ Philadelphia. www.benjamins.com

63   Excerpted from The WORLD BOOK ENCYCLOPEDIA © 2006 World Book, Inc. By permission of the publisher www.worldbook.com

Chapter 4

75   Susan Sachs, "The Changing Face of America." Excerpted from *The New York Times Upfront*, September 3, 2001. © 2001. Used by permission.

86   Excerpted from THE DEVIL'S HIGHWAY by Luis Urrea. Copyright © 2004 by Luis Urrea. By permission of Little, Brown and Co., Inc.

Chapter 5

107   "A Dream Deferred – Harlem [2]", from THE COLLECTED POEMS OF LANGSTON HUGHES by Langston Hughes, copyright © 1994 by The Estate of Langston Hughes. Used by permission of Alfred A. Knopf, a division of Random House, Inc. Reprinted by permission of Harold Ober Associates Incorporated.

109   Excerpted from Martin Luther King, Jr., "I Have a Dream." Reprinted by arrangement with the Estate of Martin Luther King Jr., c/o Writers House as agent for the proprietor New York, NY. Copyright 1963 Martin Luther King Jr., copyright renewed 1991 Coretta Scott King.

Chapter 7

151   Excerpted from Amelia Stewart Knight diary entries from WOMEN'S DIARIES OF THE WESTWARD JOURNEY by Lillian Schlissel © 1992.

Chapter 8

190   *Does Jazz Put the Sin in Syncopation?* by Anne Shaw Faulkner © August 1921, Excerpted with the permission of LADIES' HOME JOURNAL, Meredith Corporation.

Photographic and illustration credits

1   © Howard Chandler Christy, 1940/The Granger Collection

3   © Howard Chandler Christy, 1940/The Granger Collection

4   Currier & Ives/Library of Congress

Irene Williams

Cover: Gee's Bend Quilt by Irene Williams, image courtesy of Tinwood Media

Photo of Irene Williams by William Arnett, courtesy of Tinwood Media

The art on the cover of this book is a quilt by Irene Williams of Gee's Bend, Alabama. Gee's Bend is an African-American community whose women are famous for their original, hand-stitched quilts made of swatches of clothing and other textiles from everyday life. Gee's Bend quilts have been exhibited in museums around the United States; *The New York Times* said they are "some of the most miraculous works of modern art America has produced." For more information about the women of Gee's Bend and their quilts, go to http://www.quiltsofgeesbend.com

TASK INDEX

The skills taught and practiced in *Academic Encounters: American Studies* and all *Academic Encounters* books help prepare students for the TOEFL® iBT test.

Page numbers in boldface indicate tasks that are headed by commentary boxes.